HOW POLICIES MAKE CITIZENS

PRINCETON STUDIES IN AMERICAN POLITICS

HISTORICAL, INTERNATIONAL, AND COMPARATIVE PERSPECTIVES

SERIES EDITORS

IRA KATZNELSON, MARTIN SHEFTER, THEDA SKOCPOL

A list of titles in this series appears at the back of the book.

HOW POLICIES
MAKE CITIZENS

SENIOR POLITICAL ACTIVISM AND
THE AMERICAN WELFARE STATE

ANDREA LOUISE CAMPBELL

PRINCETON UNIVERSITY PRESS

PRINCETON AND OXFORD

Copyright © 2003 by Princeton University Press
Published by Princeton University Press, 41 William Street,
Princeton, New Jersey 08540
In the United Kingdom: Princeton University Press,
3 Market Place, Woodstock, Oxfordshire OX20 1SY
All Rights Reserved.

ISBN 0-691-09189-7

British Library Cataloging-in-Publication Data is available.

This book has been composed in Sabon

Printed on acid-free paper. ∞

www.pupress.princeton.edu

Printed in the United States of America

10 9 8 7 6 5 4 3 2 1

For Allen

CONTENTS

LIST OF FIGURES

LIST OF TABLES

ACKNOWLEDGMENTS

I AM INDEBTED to a great many people who helped this book come to fruition. Many friends and colleagues commented during my years of coursework and dissertation writing that I was the happiest graduate student they knew, and I have the Political Science Department at the University of California, Berkeley, and especially my dissertation committee, to thank. Henry Brady was an ideal chair. From providing countless insights, to alerting me to appropriate data, to challenging and cheering me along, Henry propelled this project forward. I am deeply indebted to him for his enthusiasm and support. Ray Wolfinger was my closest reader and an invaluable professional guide. I learned a great deal about analysis working for and writing with Jack Citrin. Thanks to all those who taught me so much: Dorie Apollonio, Jon Bernstein, Jake Bowers, Bruce Cain, Laurel Elms, Ben Highton, Ann Keller, Samantha Luks, Jane Mauldon, Chris Muste, Eric Oliver, Nate Persily, Nelson Polsby, Ron Schmidt, Laura Stoker, and Cara Wong.

Henry Brady, Kay Lehman Schlozman, and Sidney Verba provided access to their Citizen Participation Study. I am indebted to Henry Brady for suggesting that I look into using the Roper surveys for my study. Funding for the purchase and assembly of the data—now the Roper Social and Political Trends Archive—came from a National Science Foundation dissertation improvement grant awarded to me and a grant from the Pew Charitable Trusts awarded to Henry Brady and Jack Citrin. Henry Brady, Bob Putnam, and I agreed to work together in a joint UC Berkeley/Harvard project to create the time-series dataset. Graduate students Dorie Apollonio and Laurel Elms of UC Berkeley and Steve Yonish of Wisconsin (working with Putnam) took on the enormous task of cleaning and concatenating the 200-plus surveys. I am especially thankful to the Berkeley crew for their painstaking attention to detail and commitment to this huge project.

Harvard was a fertile place to turn the dissertation into a book. And as a Robert Wood Johnson Health Policy Scholar at Yale University, I appreciated the input of Kim DaCosta, Darrick Hamilton, Brad Herring, Vince Hutchings, Jennifer Klein, Evan Lieberman, Ted Marmor, Kimberly Morgan, Abby Saguy, and Mark Schlesinger.

Christine Day, Jennifer Hochschild, Suzanne Mettler, Eric Oliver, and Eric Patashnik read the entire manuscript. The two Erics in particular pushed me hard at critical junctures to improve it. Thanks also to those who read early chapter drafts or papers that were incorporated into the manuscript: Frank Baumgartner, Ted Brader, Barry Burden, Dave Campbell, Claudine Gay, Jim Glaser, Paul Pierson, Laurie Rhodebeck, Laura Olson, Kent Weaver, Steve Yonish, Steve Ansolabehere and the participants in the MIT Conference on New Research on Public Opinion, Theda Skocpol and the participants in the Harvard American Politics Research Workshop, and Kristin Goss and the participants in the Harvard Political Psychology and Behavior Workshop. I am grateful to the students in my Political Participation and Public Policy course at Harvard who helped me hone a number of ideas, and to Erika Abrahamsson, Dan Bress, Alex Mears, Chris Pappas, Alex Patterson, David Powell, and Lisa Schwartz for their invaluable research assistance. Thanks go also to the individuals from a variety of backgrounds, both seniors and nonseniors, who agreed to be interviewed for the book. Some of their stories appear in chapter 3. Names and some identifying details have been changed. I am grateful to Chuck Myers of Princeton University Press for his enthusiastic support of the project and invaluable guidance. Elizabeth Gilbert, Sarah Harrington, and Anne Reifsnyder were enormously helpful during the publication process. A portion of the material in chapter 3 appeared previously in my article "Self-Interest, Social Security, and the Distinctive Participation Patterns of Senior Citizens" in the *American Political Science Review,* vol. 97, no. 3 (September 2002): 565–74, and is reprinted with permission of Cambridge University Press.

I owe a tremendous debt to my parents for instilling in me a love of learning. And finishing a dissertation with one son and completing a book with a second would have been impossible without the assistance of Mary Ann Campbell and Miriam Feinstein, who dropped everything and came great distances to help. Those sons, Henry and Daniel, were incredibly patient with my stealing away to write. The book is dedicated to my husband Allen Feinstein, who took so much time from his conducting and composing to support and even embrace my career in political science. Just ask him what heteroskedasticity is.

HOW POLICIES MAKE CITIZENS

Chapter One

INTRODUCTION: THE RECIPROCAL
PARTICIPATION-POLICY RELATIONSHIP

SOME GROUPS participate more than others—the affluent more than the poor; the educated more than the uneducated; whites more than blacks and Latinos; the elderly more than the young. Does it matter? Do high-participation groups get more of what they want from the government? Do participatory inputs shape policy outputs? Critics allege that the American system of government inadequately represents the interests of the underprivileged, to their detriment.[1] Indeed, one motivation driving researchers to measure participatory differences across groups is an assumption that they lead to unequal policy outcomes. Do they?

And why are some groups more politically active than others? We know part of the story—some individuals possess more politically relevant resources, like income and education, than others, some are more interested in public affairs, and some are more likely to be recruited to participate. And these factors arise from early socialization at home and in school and from affiliations with voluntary associations, workplaces, and religious institutions.[2] But what about the role of public policy? Might government policy also be a source of political resources, a sense of stake in the system, even a mobilizing factor?

This book focuses on the reciprocal relationship between political participation and public policy. I show that mass participation influences policy outcomes—the politically active are more likely to achieve their policy goals, often at the expense of the politically quiescent. And the ability of the politically active to do so is in part a legacy of existing public policy—policy influences the amount and nature of groups' political activity, often exacerbating rather than ameliorating existing participatory inequalities. Public policies can confer resources, motivate interest in government affairs by tying well-being to government action, define groups for mobilization, and even shape the content and meaning of democratic citizenship. These effects are positive for some groups, like senior citizens, raising their participation levels. For other groups, government policy can have negative effects. Because of the difficult and demeaning experience of obtaining welfare, for example, its recipients participate at rates even lower than their modest socioeconomic situations would predict.[3] These effects feed back into the political system, producing spirals in which groups' participatory and policy advantages (or disadvantages) accrue. Citizens' relationships with government, and their experiences at the hand of government policy, help determine their participation levels and, in turn, subsequent policy outcomes.

With its influences on participation, public policy affects the basic mechanisms of democratic government. An important function of government is the allocation of societal goods. In a democracy, the people are supposed to voice their preferences through their political participation. Indeed, democratic theory is predicated on the equal ability of citizens to take part in this way.[4] But policy design—who gets benefits, how generous they are, and how they are administered—affects groups' participatory capacities and interests. The distributional consequences are profound. Policy begets participation begets policy in a cycle that results not in equal protection of interests, but in outcomes biased toward the politically active. Thus the very quality of democratic government is shaped by the kinds of policies it pursues.

Senior citizens in the United States and their activity in relation to Social Security form the empirical basis for this study. Social Security and Medicare transfer 40 percent of the federal budget to seniors, with significant effects on their political behavior. They are the Über-citizens of the American polity, voting and making campaign contributions at rates higher than those of any other age group. They also actively defend their programs, warning lawmakers through their participation not to tamper with Social Security and Medicare. The result is continued program growth, even as programs for the poor are cut.

Seniors were not always so politically active. In the 1950s, when Social Security benefits were modest and covered only a fraction of seniors, the elderly participated at lower rates than younger people. The growth of the program in part fueled the increase in senior participation over time. Social Security provided the once-marginalized senior population with politically relevant resources like income and free time. The program increased seniors' engagement with politics by connecting their fortunes tangibly and immediately to government action. It fashioned for an otherwise disparate group of people a new political identity as program recipients, which provided a basis for mobilization by political parties, interest groups, and policy entrepreneurs. And Social Security incorporated seniors into the highest level of democratic citizenship, their relationship with the state marked by full social and political rights and privileges, including the right to fend off proposals for program change that they find objectionable. Indeed, Social Security (and Medicare) have provided two stimuli: the growth of the programs, which has enhanced seniors' participatory capacity over time, and threats to the programs, which have inspired participatory surges that lawmakers heed and that protect the programs from retrenchment efforts. The combination of these stimuli produces a loop in which senior welfare state programs expand: the programs enhance seniors' participatory capacity so that when their programs are threatened they are able to defend them; thus protected, the programs continue to augment seniors' participatory capacity (figure 1.1). In short, Social Security helped create a constituency to be reckoned with, a group willing, able, and primed to participate at high rates, capable of defeating objectionable policy change.

Welfare recipients are not so fortunate. In contrast to Social Security, welfare has negative effects on its clients. Welfare recipients do have an interest in public affairs arising from their dependence on government action, but this level of interest is lower than that of Social Security recipients and cannot by itself enhance participation levels—adequate political resources and mobilization are needed too, and here welfare recipients are severely disadvantaged. Indeed, the design of welfare, which requires recipients to meet with caseworkers who ask probing personal questions and who appear to have great discretion over benefits, undermines recipients' feelings of efficacy toward the welfare system and the government in general, reducing their rates of political participation.[5] The lack of positive policy feedbacks helps make welfare an easier fiscal target and contributes to greater retrenchment in that policy area.

THE INFLUENCE OF PARTICIPATION ON POLICY

The participation literature has made impressive empirical and theoretical gains in explaining who is politically active, but has largely neglected the crucial question of differential policy outcomes. As the dean of participation scholars, Sidney Verba, notes, there has been much emphasis on equal capacity and equal voice across demographic groups, but understanding the real result of participation requires consideration of equal outcomes. The literature assesses what individuals do rather than what effect their activity has, which is a far more difficult and complex task.[6]

Anecdotally we can think of high-participation groups prevailing in the policy arena and low-participation groups suffering: during the 1990s the wealthy saw capital gains tax rates reduced while welfare lost its entitlement status. But linking participatory inputs to policy outcomes is difficult, and has rarely been done systematically.

There have been some attempts to connect participation and policy. Frances Fox Piven and Richard Cloward argue that low turnout rates among the poor result in public policy that favors higher-status voters.[7] Kim Quaile Hill and Jan Leighley find a correlation between turnout

4

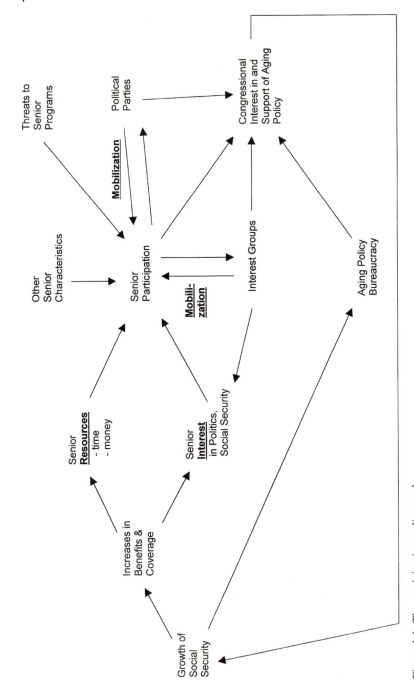

Figure 1.1 The participation-policy cycle

among the poor and levels of welfare spending among the fifty states.[8] But these studies use voter turnout, a "blunt" instrument of participation for which issue content must be assumed.[9] That the poor participate less is compatible with the notion that the highly participatory prevail in the policy arena, but does not itself make the link. No single study has yet connected the dots and shown conclusively that differential participation rates across groups influence policy outcomes.

PROGRAM DESIGN AND THE INFLUENCE OF
POLICY ON PARTICIPATION

Thanks to advances in polling technology over the past half century, we know a great deal about *who* participates in terms of education, income, race, ethnicity, and gender. And increasingly sophisticated models tell us *why* some individuals and groups participate more than others. One factor past work leaves out is the effect of government policy.

In their seminal 1972 work, *Participation in America*, Sidney Verba and Norman Nie showed that participation of all forms, from voting to protesting, is more common among individuals of higher socioeconomic status (SES), which they measured with an index combining education, income, and occupation. In *Who Votes?* (1980) Raymond Wolfinger and Steven Rosenstone took the SES model one step further, disaggregating SES into its three components. They found that education has the most profound effect on voting.

In the most recent major work on political participation, *Voice and Equality* (1995), Verba, Kay Lehman Schlozman, and Henry Brady develop a Civic Voluntarism Model to explain the mechanisms by which SES influences participation. Political activity is fueled by three "participatory factors": *resources*, like income and politically relevant skills; *engagement* with politics, including political interest and knowledge; and *mobilization*. These factors arise from personal characteristics, preadult experiences at home and school, and affiliations with the workplace, religious institutions, and voluntary organizations.

Although these developments in the participation literature have considerably enhanced our understanding of participatory differences, they have largely ignored policy influences on would-be participators—how government policies might influence these participatory factors. The policy feedbacks literature in American and comparative politics suggests that policy effects are central. The work of historical institutionalist scholars such as Theda Skocpol, Paul Pierson, Sven Steinmo, and Peter Hall shows, at the macro level, how existing policy structures constrain subsequent policymaking. Current policies foreclose some possibilities, preordain others.[10] For example, Skocpol argues that the extensive system of pensions for Civil War veterans delayed the broader implementation of old-age pensions for decades, because of their association with corrupt patronage politics.

Like Skocpol's work, most research in this area examines policy influences on states and elites. But Pierson suggests that policy influences on mass publics, while understudied, are among the most important.[11] He further asserts that they take two forms, material and cognitive. Indeed, the development of Social Security fulfills Pierson's predictions about the influences policies might have on client groups. By conferring politically relevant resources, Social Security has had tremendous material effects, fundamentally enhancing seniors' participatory capacity above what they could have achieved in the absence of the program. The program's cognitive effects may be even more significant. Cognitive feedback effects provide otherwise scarce and costly information to individuals. According to Pierson, these cues "may influence individuals' perceptions about what their interests are, whether their representatives are protecting those interests, who their allies might be, and what political strategies are promising."[12] Social Security's cognitive effects have fostered senior interest in public affairs and enhanced their feelings of political efficacy as they achieved the notice of elected officials.

The political learning literature suggests an additional mechanism by which the cognitive effects operate—that the manner in which government policies treat clients instills lessons about groups' privileges and rights as citizens. Policy design sends messages to clients about their worth as citizens, which in turn affects their orientations toward government and their political participation. Policy experiences convey to target populations self-images and outgroup images (who is "deserving" and who is not). Program recipients learn what actions are appropriate for their group. "Advantaged" groups like Social Security recipients consistently hear messages that they are "good, intelligent people" who have legitimate claims with the government.[13] Social Security fosters seniors' participation not only by enhancing their participatory capacity and giving them a compelling reason to pay attention to public affairs but also by affirming their rights as citizens to defend their benefits.

The profound effect of policy design on democratic citizenship is perhaps most evident with low-income seniors. Decades of participation research have shown that high-income individuals are more politically active. The income-participation gradient is particularly steep in the United States, which lacks lower-class mobilizing agents like leftist parties or strong unions. As we will see in chapter 3, however, low-income seniors are more likely than high-income seniors to participate with regard to Social Security. They are, for example, more likely to write a letter to a government official about the program, so that the usually positive relationship between income and participation is reversed. The difference in this policy area is that low-income seniors are more dependent on the program: Social Security makes up a larger share of their income, and so they are rationally more active. Furthermore, as a universal, non-means-tested program, Social Security includes low-income seniors in its "advantaged" recipient group. Unlike other low-income groups, poor seniors absorb from their policy experiences the same positive citizenship lessons their more affluent counterparts learn, including the message that defending their self-interests through political activity is legitimate.

Thus Social Security has implications for self-interest as a political motivation. The program ties seniors as citizens to state functions in an immediate way. Their engagement with public affairs is enhanced because their self-interest is so significantly and obviously implicated. Self-interest is seldom a guide to behavior, since people often do not recognize their interests or may choose to act in an altruistic manner.[14] But seniors' interest in Social Security is so immediate, quantifiable, and tangible that it influences their activities. The political gerontologist Neal Cutler predicted twenty-five years ago that the life changes associated with aging and retirement—reduced income, dependence on Social Security, and need for medical care—would produce a new set of self-interests that are important and immediate enough to shape behavior.[15] Social Security's design empowers both high- and low-income seniors to defend these new interests.

And Social Security fundamentally alters the nature of citizenship for seniors, shaping the manner and extent to which they are included as members of the political community.[16] According to T. H. Marshall, citizenship has three components: civil, social, and political.[17] As American citizens, seniors enjoy the civil rights of liberty, property, freedom of speech, and equality before the law. As *senior* citizens receiving Social Security, they enjoy, more than most other groups, the social rights of security and welfare that are crucial aspects of twentieth-century notions of citizenship.[18] And in part because of their full enjoyment of social rights, seniors have realized political rights—access to democratic decision making via participation—to a greater degree than many other groups, and more completely than they would have in Social Security's absence.

The Senior Citizen Case Study

According to the comparative politics literature, social movements and interest groups shape welfare state outcomes.[19] Welfare state programs supposedly spawn large, active constituencies that exert political pressure to maintain or expand their programs, even in an era of retrenchment.

Nowhere does this seem as likely as with Social Security and Medicare, the two largest social welfare programs in the United States.

This theoretical claim is plausible enough that political commentators and pundits have seized upon it. Journalistic accounts of "greedy geezers," "golf-cart grannies," and "the pampered elderly" abound.[20] Media coverage of election outcomes often refers to a powerful senior voting bloc.[21] Such accounts correctly note that senior citizens vote at high rates, but writers often make unsubstantiated claims about seniors' policy preferences and cohesiveness.

Political scientists have left these assumptions largely unexamined, and even make such assumptions themselves. American government textbooks, for example, often cite seniors as a powerful voting bloc or as an example of an effective interest group, with little evidence: "The political risks associated with Social Security cutbacks are too great for most politicians to bear. As a group, older Americans exercise enormous political power" asserts one prominent textbook, a plausible but undocumented statement.[22] Even scholarly treatments make assumptions about seniors' political power.[23] Basic questions about senior participation have been left unanswered: the level of senior participation beyond voting; changes in senior participation over time; the meaning of that participation; and the effect of senior participation on the policymaking process.[24]

Demographic and fiscal trends suggest the normative importance of a study of senior participation and its effects. Seniors[25] are a large and growing portion of the U.S. population. The senior segment has grown from 8.1 percent of the U.S. population in 1950 to 12.7 percent in 1999, and is projected to reach 20 percent in 2030.[26] There are now more than 34 million Americans aged 65 and over, nearly three times as many as there were in 1950. Seniors form an even larger proportion of the electorate. In 1996, when seniors were 12.7 percent of the total population, they made up 17.2 percent of the voting-age population and 24 percent of all voters in the presidential election.[27] As the senior population has grown, so have welfare state programs conferred on the basis of age. Social Security and Medicare together totaled $555 billion in 1997, almost 35 percent of federal budget outlays and 40 percent of outlays excluding interest on the national debt.[28] This is twice the size of the defense budget and twenty-seven times federal and state spending on welfare.

Fortunately, given its theoretical and normative importance, the senior citizen case study offers analytical tractability as well. To link participation and policy in a given issue area it is necessary to know the participation rate of the "issue public," that is, the participation rate among people interested in the issue.[29] This is calculated by dividing the number of issue public members who participate by the total number of issue public members. These data usually come from surveys of the mass public. The difficulty in many issue areas is that we do not know the denominator, the size of the issue public. Without the appropriate identifying questions in surveys, the researcher cannot determine who is interested in the environment or gun rights or abortion. Longitudinal research is even more difficult, since chances are slim that identifying questions were repeated consistently over time.

Issue publics must also be large enough for statistical analysis. There are so many issues in the public realm that even with the appropriate identifying questions, few would yield publics large enough for analysis in a typical survey of 1,500 or 2,000 respondents.

In addition, we often know from surveys whether respondents participated but not the content of their participation. We might know that a survey respondent wrote a letter to an elected official but we do not know the issue mentioned or the position the respondent took. It is difficult in these circumstances to determine the meaning of respondents' participation.

The senior citizen case study avoids these problems. Well over 90 percent of senior citizens receive Social Security and Medicare, and senior citizens are identifiable in virtually all relevant surveys, including longitudinal datasets. Constituting such a large proportion of the voting-age population, the elderly provide plenty of cases for statistical analysis in typical national survey samples.[30]

Further facilitating analysis is the fact that the vast majority of seniors are on the same side of the Social Security issue. Opinion data show that senior citizens are virtually unanimous on Social Security: they don't want their programs cut. When asked in the 2000 National Election Study (NES) whether they wanted federal spending on Social Security increased, decreased, or kept the same, only 2 percent said decreased; when asked about Social Security benefit levels in the 1992 NES, just 2 percent said benefits were too high. Seniors want either to preserve the status quo or to increase spending on their programs. That seniors are on one side of the issue greatly aids interpretation of two key data sources. The 1990 Citizen Participation Study includes program-specific participation questions, asking respondents whether they have voted, made a campaign contribution, or written a letter about Social Security. Seniors' near unanimity on this issue means we can be assured of the pro–Social Security direction of that participation. A new dataset assembled for this study—the Roper Social and Political Trends Archive—consists of surveys administered ten times per year over a twenty-year period and includes questions on participatory activities such as writing letters to Congress. These data can reveal participatory reactions to specific policy events, and so the timing of the letters makes evident the issue content. This overcomes the problem that plagued earlier attempts to link participation and policy—having to assume the issue content of the vote. And near unanimity in support of Social Security means we can interpret a surge in senior letter writing in response to proposed cuts as a defensive move.

From this study a complex picture of senior participation and policy emerges. One aspect is that, as with many stereotypes, there is a grain of truth in the "greedy geezer" image. To an extent, seniors defend their own programs at the expense of policies benefiting others. Economists have shown, for example, that the proportion of elderly residents in a location is associated with a significant reduction in per child education spending.[31] By contrast, there was a positive association between elderly population share and school spending in the early 1900s, before Social Security's enactment.[32] Government policy seems to have shifted seniors' self-interests away from supporting the education of younger people upon whom they were once directly dependent, toward defending the government benefits upon which their livelihoods now depend.

But if this crowding-out effect is not desirable from the standpoint of democratic governance, other age-related policy effects are. Social Security has democratized senior participation, reducing participatory inequality within the senior constituency. Hence seniors' welfare state programs have exacerbated political inequality between age groups, but have moderated it within the senior population. Social Security has both deleterious and laudable effects on American democracy. The reality of "senior power" is therefore more ambiguous—and the development of the senior constituency considerably more complicated—than previous accounts suggest.

ORGANIZATION OF THE BOOK

Chapter 2 describes two historical trends: the rise of senior participation since the 1950s and the development of Social Security and Medicare during the same period. Over time seniors eclipsed nonseniors in the participatory arena, and now are disproportionately active. At the same time, Social Security and Medicare coverage expanded and benefits grew, with profound effects on seniors' empirical and attitudinal well-being. This chapter hints at the causal connections between these two phenomena, which are explored systematically in chapter 3.

Chapter 3 shows the individual-level mechanisms behind senior participation in cross-sectional data. Like younger people, seniors with higher levels of participatory resources, political engagement, and mobilization opportunities are more likely to participate in politics. We also see that Social Security has some unusual participatory effects. Although general engagement with politics increases with income among seniors (as among nonseniors), interest in Social Security is greater among lower-income seniors, who are more dependent on the program. This boosts the participation of low-income seniors above what we would expect for persons of such low socioeconomic status and helps explain the high level of senior participation overall. This effect is reinforced by the pattern of mobilization by political parties, which are more likely to mobilize low- than high-income seniors.

Chapter 4 elaborates on the participation-policy cycle depicted in figure 1.1, showing how the factors identified as important in senior participation grew over time and, in particular, examining the role of senior welfare state programs in enhancing those factors. Among the trends the chapter explores are: the rise in senior resources, the rise in senior dependence on Social Security as coverage and benefits levels increased, the politicization of senior programs and senior interest groups, and changes in party strategies.

Chapters 2 through 4 show how senior participation increased over time and how Social Security contributed to that increase—in short, how policy influences participation. Establishing the other half of the reciprocal relationship—the influence of participation on policy—is the subject of chapters 5 and 6. Making the link between participation and policy requires three steps: showing that the group in question participates at high rates; determining that the high participation sends a distinctive message to the government; and demonstrating that lawmakers hear and react to that distinctive message. That a group participates at disproportionately high rates is of no consequence if the participation does not send a unique message to the government. That unique message is in turn meaningless if lawmakers fail to take it into account in their policymaking.

The earlier part of the book shows that seniors participate at high rates; chapter 5 demonstrates the distinctive message behind that participation. Seniors are not just interested in Social Security, but also react to Social Security policy events. Using the new Roper data, I show that seniors respond to threats to their programs with surges in letter writing to Congress, their contacting rates rising by as much as 50 percent. Senior participation is high and sends a message to lawmakers: do not tamper with Social Security and Medicare. Social Security has been called the "third rail of American politics"—touch it and you die—not because seniors are interested in politics generally, or even because they are vigilant about Social Security, but because they act when their programs are threatened. Politicians see these surges in senior participation in reaction to policy events and come to interpret high participation by seniors in general as focused on their welfare state programs, an indication that to propose program changes or cuts is to invite electoral retribution.

Chapter 6 shows how members of Congress react to senior participation. Senators and representatives who hear more from their senior constituents are more protective of senior programs. In some dramatic cases, lawmakers even switch their votes on age-related policy in the face of protests by their senior constituents. Participation shapes policy outcomes.

Chapter 7 looks briefly at the participation of others who receive government benefits—veterans and welfare clients—to begin to explore the conditions under which government programs contribute to upward or downward participation-policy spirals. Like Social Security, veterans' benefits confer resources that enhance participation, foster interest in public affairs, endow recipients with a political relevance that invites mobilization by interest groups and parties, and enhance recipient feelings of government responsiveness. These program recipients participate at higher levels than they would in the absence of the programs. Welfare recipients, by contrast, participate at even lower levels than their already modest participatory capacities would predict, largely because of the disengaging aspects of program design that relegate them to a lower tier of democratic citizenship.[33]

Chapter 8 summarizes the study's findings about the reciprocal relationship between policy and participation. I consider the political implications of proposed changes in Social Security's design, such as the introduction of individual accounts (Social Security "privatization"), and discuss the degree to which Social Security is likely to retain its "third rail" reputation in the future. Privatization threatens to demobilize the poor elderly in particular, by breaking the tie between their well-being and government action. Their resource levels may also be reduced if administrative costs or the vagaries of the market produce lower returns than Social Security's current defined benefit structure. Whether through diminished engagement or reduced benefits, privatization could exacerbate political inequality among seniors, erasing Social Security's democratizing effect. Indeed, proposals to change the program's structure could expose differential class interests among the elderly, heretofore hidden by Social Security's universal, if somewhat redistributive, design. Cleavages could open in this population that until now has successfully maintained cohesion around its welfare state programs. In short, privatization could break the back of the senior lobby.

DATA SOURCES

This study uses mass survey data to evaluate the participation and attitudes of seniors and nonseniors. These data come from a variety of cross-sectional and time-series sources.

The National Election Study time series is crucial for determining the participation rates of seniors and other age groups since the early 1950s (chapters 2 and 4). Although the NES participation time series does not begin before the implementation of Social Security in 1940 (which would be ideal), it does extend back to 1952, when only 16 percent of seniors received benefits and when the real value of the average benefit was just over one-third of today's benefit. I also use some of the recent NES cross-sectional surveys to perform multivariate analyses of the influences behind senior participation (chapter 3).

The American Citizen Participation Study is the most comprehensive survey of participatory activity currently available.[34] It contains detailed questions about political engagement and mobilization unavailable in other datasets, and also includes Social Security–specific participation items that are crucial to this study. The survey was conducted in two stages. First, 15,053 Americans were interviewed by phone about their political and voluntary activities and demographic characteristics. A longer, in-person follow-up interview was conducted with 2,517 of the original respondents. I chiefly use data from the follow-up interview, along with select variables from the initial screener interview (chapter 3).

The heart of the book's argument is based on a time series–cross sectional dataset assembled for this project: the Roper Social and Political Trends Archive, a series of approximately 200 national cross-sectional surveys conducted ten times per year from September 1973 through October 1994. The Roper surveys contain a battery of twelve participation questions as well as basic demographic information. Each of the 200-plus surveys has approximately 2,000 respondents, so that the concatenated dataset contains over 400,000 cases.[35] One limitation of the NES data is that the participation battery consists mostly of electoral items, and the survey itself is administered biennially in tandem with the election cycle. The Roper surveys contain nonelectoral participation items like letter writing to Congress, and because the surveys were conducted approximately monthly, the concatenated dataset can be used to assess participatory reaction to specific policy events (chapter 5). Occasionally the Roper Organization also asked questions about interest in Social Security and other matters relevant to the study of age-related policy, and I use several of the individual surveys for cross-sectional analysis as well (chapter 3).

Finally, in chapter 6 I combine the Roper surveys with congressional roll-call data to assess lawmaker responsiveness to senior constituents.

Chapter Two

OVERVIEW: RISING SENIOR PARTICIPATION AND THE GROWTH OF THE AMERICAN WELFARE STATE

In MANY observers' eyes, the United States is facing a crisis of democracy. Participation in a variety of political activities has declined—fewer people attend political meetings, work for political parties, attend political rallies, or sign petitions.[1] There is even more hand wringing among pundits and scholars over the decline of voter turnout—now barely half of eligible Americans vote in presidential elections, only a third in off-year elections.[2] Observers fret over the "disappearance" of the American voter, and ask "What if we held an election and no one showed up?"[3]

But one group does show up, and in force: senior citizens. They vote and make campaign contributions at higher rates than any other age group. Their campaign work and letter-writing rates are comparable to those of younger people (and their letter-writing spikes during critical policy junctures, as we will see in chapter 5). Seniors are the super-participators of American democracy.

This wasn't always the case. In the 1950s the elderly participated at lower rates than younger people. But over time seniors have bucked the downward trends that cause so much consternation. As participation by nonseniors has declined, senior voting and contribution rates have increased in absolute terms, and their campaign work and letter-writing rates have increased relative to those of younger people.

This chapter describes these trends and begins to make the argument, pursued further in the next two chapters, that the increase in senior participation has been fueled by the development of seniors' welfare state programs. At the same time that seniors' participation has risen, their programs have grown, with large and positive effects on their retirement rates, income, poverty, health, and subjective financial status. This chapter details the profound changes in seniors' empirical and attitudinal well-being over the last fifty years. It then describes the age trends in participation, and closes by suggesting that the changes wrought by seniors' welfare state programs are in part responsible for the increases in their political activity. The programs have enhanced both seniors' ability to participate (by improving their physical and financial health and providing mobilization opportunities)[4] and their interest in participating (by giving them a stake in the system).

Thus the crucial feature of mass politics in the United States is not the decline in participation, but the participatory divergence of young and old. And the real crisis in American democracy is not the diminution of public life, but the unequal effect of policy on participation. Seniors respond rationally to the huge role of government in their lives. Younger people have no equivalent. Participatory divergence by age is in part a product of the differential relevance of government policy across groups.

EMPIRICAL EFFECTS OF SENIOR CITIZENS' WELFARE STATE PROGRAMS

April Jefferson was born in Alabama in 1917. She left school in her early teens to help support her widowed grandmother. Later she married an abusive husband, who eventually abandoned her and their six sons. To support her family, April worked as a domestic for over forty-five years. In retirement, April's modest income is derived solely from Social Security. But she feels positive about her situation, especially compared with the hardships her parents and grandparents endured, trying to survive in an era before Social Security: "Like I told 'em, it's [Social Security] a blessin' . . . I remember when my parents were comin' on, they didn't have anything. They didn't get no check of no kind, so we just had to live the best we could."[5]

The elderly were once the most impoverished age group. Indeed, early advocates of old-age pensions peppered their rhetoric with heart-rending tales of destitute elders committing suicide and dying alone. In one poignant account, a desperate 76-year-old offered his eye for sale in the want ads.[6] Since Social Security's enactment in 1935 there has been a sea change in conditions for seniors. Social Security has increased senior incomes and reduced poverty; retirement with some measure of financial stability has become a reality, indeed a societal expectation. With the enactment of Medicare and Medicaid, seniors went from the lowest rate of health insurance coverage to near universal access to health care. These programs are the most effective pieces of social legislation in American history. Contemporary critiques of "the pampered elderly" are a testimony to their tremendous success. Even low-income seniors like April Jefferson are better off today than were their grandparents.

Older people were valued in an agrarian society as repositories of farming knowledge and moral sensibility, but found themselves increasingly marginalized by the emerging urban, industrial order of the early twentieth century.[7] The few who were able to find and perform work did so, because most people lacked personal savings or private pensions with which to support themselves in old age. Others faced the uncertainty of dependency, the lucky few living with family, the more desperate relegated to a series of almshouses, asylums, and occasional church or settlement aid.[8] The severe economic conditions of the Depression, which affected the elderly more than any other age group, exposed the inadequacy of existing provisions for old age and provided the impetus for the passage of the Social Security Act in 1935.

The Social Security Act established two programs for the nation's aged population.[9] Title I provided grants to the states to pay half the cost of Old Age Assistance (OAA, replaced by Supplemental Security Income, or SSI, in 1971), a means-tested program in which the states determined benefit levels.[10] Title II created Old Age Insurance (OAI), the contributory, self-financed pension program we think of today as "Social Security." The retirement age was set at 65, the first payments were to be made in 1942 (changed to 1940 by the 1939 amendments), and total cessation of paid, covered employment was made a condition for receipt of a pension (a requirement much liberalized over the following decades).[11]

Initially only 20 percent of workers were in occupations covered by Social Security.[12] Coverage was extended to additional categories of workers and dependents in 1939, 1950, 1954, 1956, and 1965.[13] The first payments, in 1940, went to just 112,000 retirees, but the percentage of persons 65 and over receiving Social Security soon increased, particularly after the coverage extensions of the 1950s; in 1950, 16 percent of persons 65 and over received Social Security, increasing to 60 percent in 1960, 82 percent in 1970, and 90 percent by 1980. In 1996 over 26 million retired workers received Social Security payments.[14]

The real value of Social Security benefits has also increased substantially over the years. The average monthly Social Security payment to retired workers in 1950 was $278 (in 1996 dollars), rising to $745 by 1996, an increase in real dollars of 268 percent, as shown in figure 2.1.[15] By comparison, the average monthly AFDC (Aid to Families with Dependent Children) payment increased less than 2 percent in real terms, from $132 in 1950 to $134 in 1996.[16] Social Security benefits even increased more than the wages and salaries of covered workers. Between 1965 and 1997, the Consumer Price Index rose 397 percent, average wages 476 percent, and Social Security benefits 502 percent.[17] Benefits increased so much for two reasons. Until 1975, benefit levels were set by legislation, and large increases were passed in the early 1970s for political reasons, explored in chapter 4. Benefits were then indexed to inflation starting in 1975, but the measure chosen for the cost-of-living adjustments is a

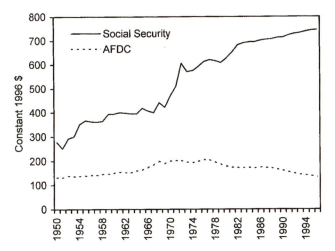

Figure 2.1 Average monthly Social Security and AFDC benefits, 1950–96. (*Social Security Bulletin Annual Statistical Supplement 1997*, p. 146.)

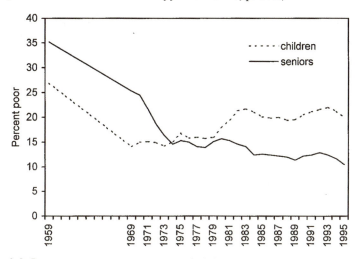

Figure 2.2 Poverty rate among seniors and children, 1959–95. (*Social Security Bulletin Annual Statistical Supplement*, various years.)

particularly generous one, causing the value of the payments to rise in "real" terms, as shown in figure 2.1.

The coverage expansions of the 1950s and the large benefit increases of the 1970s created a truly enormous program with tangible effects on seniors' well-being. Social Security has been instrumental in allowing seniors to retire. The labor force participation rate of men aged 65 and over fell from 46 percent in 1950 to 17 percent in 1996.[18] The actions of private firms as well as technological change contributed to the increase in retirement over the past forty years, but changes in welfare state policy have been of fundamental importance.[19] Social Security affected retirement rates both directly, by increasing the affordability of leisure through higher benefits, and indirectly, through the private pensions that sprang up in the wake of the federal program.[20] The advent of Social Security fostered interest among union members and other workers in supplementary (private) retirement benefits. Corporations also had incentives to offer private pensions. The new benefits did not cost much—since retirees would also receive Social Security, the private pensions could be relatively modest—but they reduced corporate taxes as a result of favorable laws and allowed companies to justify wage freezes.[21] Because of these direct and indirect effects of Social Security, aging brings not dependency or a desperate search for work but retirement.[22]

Although the great majority of seniors are retired, they are not poor, as they once would have been upon leaving the work force. The poverty rate among the aged during the Depression is believed to have been at least 50 percent.[23] Today it is 10.5 percent. Social Security is largely responsible for this vast decrease; minus the value of government cash transfers like Social Security, the senior poverty rate today would still be 50 percent.[24] Children serve as a compelling counterexample. At 20.8 percent, the child poverty rate is nearly double that of senior citizens and has generally risen over the last thirty years while senior poverty has fallen steadily, as shown in figure 2.2.[25]

Social Security has also figured prominently in the rise of senior incomes over time. In the 1950s and 1960s the real median income of all families grew dramatically, but the rate of increase for families headed by persons 65 and over was slower than that of younger households. In the 1970s and 1980s, the pattern reversed, and the income of senior families grew at a faster rate than that of any other age group, as shown in figure 2.3. Changes in the real median income of men only (not families) show even more dramatic differences between seniors and nonseniors, since the increasing proportion of two-income families over this period masks decreases in real wages. During the 1980s the real median income of men in every age group below 65 fell or remained flat while that of senior men increased 20 percent. A portion of the income increase for seniors comes from personal savings and private pensions, but Social Security also played a crucial role. Because of rising benefit levels, Social Security's share of seniors' incomes has increased from 22 percent in 1958 to 42 percent in 1994.[26]

Falling poverty rates and increasing incomes due largely to Social Security have had a tremendous impact on seniors' subjective evaluations of their financial situation. Settlement workers interviewing elderly New

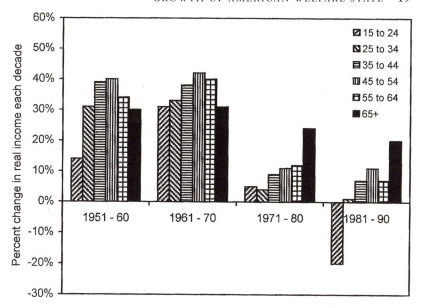

Figure 2.3 Change in real family income by age of householder, 1951–90. (U.S. Bureau of the Census, *Money Income of Households, Families, and Persons in the U.S., 1991.*)

Yorkers around 1915 found them "consumed by fear—fear of poverty, fear of illness, fear of becoming a burden to their children, fear of being left alone, fear of having to go on relief, most of all fear of being sent to an institution on Blackwell's Island."[27] By contrast, contemporary seniors are less worried about personal finances than any other age group.[28]

Responses to questions in the 1984, 1992, and 2000 National Election Studies and the 1990 Citizen Participation Study show that seniors are far less likely than younger respondents to have cut back on expenses in order to make ends meet.[29] Seniors are less likely to have put off medical and dental care, borrowed money, dipped into savings, delayed rent or mortgage payments, cut back on amount or quality of food, or cut back on entertainment (table 2.1). In the Citizen Participation Study, two-thirds of senior respondents made no lifestyle changes compared with just one-third of nonseniors. Not until family incomes reach $125,000 and above are nonsenior respondents as likely as seniors as a group to have taken no action to make ends meet.

Empirical improvements in seniors' economic situations are also reflected in their subjective social class designations. When respondents were first asked in the 1956 NES whether they thought of themselves as belonging to the middle or working class, there were no significant

TABLE 2.1
Measures of Financial Stability by Age

	18–64	65+	Difference of Means Test
2000 NES: *Over the past year . . .*			
Put off medical/dental care	30%	16%	***
1992 NES			
Been able to buy what you needed	44	57	***
Put off medical/dental care	34	19	***
Borrowed money	41	12	***
Dipped into savings	48	42	*
Got second job/worked more hours	51	7	***
Fell behind on rent/mortgage	14	3	***
Saved money	43	34	***
1990 Citizen Participation Study			
Put off medical/dental care	28	13	***
Worked extra hours	33	2	***
Delayed rent/mortgage payments	13	1	***
Cut back on amount/quality of food	20	10	***
Cut back on entertainment	54	25	***
No action needed to make ends meet	35	67	***
No action needed to make ends meet, by income, aged 18–64:			
Under $15,000	20		
$15,000–$34,999	27		
$35,000–$49,999	31		
$50,000–$74,999	52		
$75,000–$124,999	50		
$125,000 and over	73		

Difference of means tests: $*p < .05$; $**p < .01$; $***p < .001$.

TABLE 2.2
Subjective Social Class by Age, 1956 and 1994

% Middle Class		18–34	35–64	65+	Chi-square Test
1956	All respondents	35%	39%	34%	
1994	All respondents	46	52	62	***
	By occupation[a]				
	Executives and professionals	65	75	84	*
	Pink collar	51	51	71	*
	Blue collar	29	28	46	*

Chi-square tests: *p < .05; **p < .01; ***p < .001.
Source: National Election Studies.
[a] Current occupation among working nonseniors and former occupation among retired seniors.

differences by age: just over one-third of respondents in each age group said they were in the middle class (table 2.2).[30] By 1994 there were marked differences among the age groups, and seniors were most likely to say they are middle class: 62 percent compared with 52 percent of 35- to 64-year-olds and 46 percent of 18- to 34-year-olds. The difference is not due solely to "working-class" seniors who choose the middle-class designation because they no longer work. The NES records the former occupation of retired respondents so we can compare the subjective class designations of, say, current blue-collar workers with those of retired blue-collar workers. Retired seniors of all types—former executives and professionals, pink-collar workers, and blue-collar workers—are more likely than their working counterparts to say they are members of the middle class.[31] The meaning of this middle-class self-identification is not entirely clear, but it seems to be yet another indication of seniors' positive economic situation.

Although the Social Security Act of 1935 contributed to seniors' financial security, not until thirty years later were their medical needs met. Because of the infirmities caused by aging, senior citizens have always been greater consumers of health care than younger people. But before the enactment of Medicare and Medicaid in 1965, seniors were the age group least likely to have health insurance and consequently were most likely to go without medical care when symptoms indicated a need.[32]

With the advent of Medicare (and Medicaid), senior citizens overnight became the group most likely to have health coverage.[33] On the eve of Medicare/Medicaid enactment half of seniors had no private health insurance, but now virtually all are covered by these government programs.[34] By 1970 seniors became the group other than infants most likely to receive medical care appropriate to their symptoms.[35] Physician visits per older individual did not change between 1964 and 1980, but Medicare dramatically increased hospital services received. Various analysts conclude that Medicare greatly improved seniors' quality of life. Of course advances in medical technology account for some of the improvement, and the effects of these advances must be controlled for to isolate the effects of government programs. One useful exercise is to compare the health of American seniors with that of seniors in other Western industrialized nations where medical technology is similarly advanced, but where access to health care is limited by queues and quotas.[36] Since 1965 mortality has declined more sharply for seniors in the United States than in Canada and Europe.[37]

POLITICAL ATTITUDE EFFECTS OF SENIOR CITIZENS' WELFARE STATE PROGRAMS

The empirical evidence shows the tremendous influence of Social Security and Medicare on the economic and physical well-being of senior citizens. The importance of these programs is reflected in seniors' attitudes about public affairs: Social Security and Medicare are highly salient issues for older Americans. The Roper surveys occasionally include questions about current events, asking whether respondents are following a given news story closely, casually, or not paying much attention.[38] On the three occasions when questions about Social Security appeared in the surveys, seniors were more likely than younger respondents to follow news about the program closely. In June 1977, respondents were asked about "government proposals to change the way Social Security is financed." As shown in table 2.3, 56 percent of respondents aged 60 and over said they were following this news story "closely," compared with 38 percent of 30- to 44-year-olds.[39] Similarly, in February 1978, 72 percent of seniors said they were following news of "Social Security costs and benefits" closely, and in August 1981, 82 percent were closely following news of "legislation to deal with changes in Social Security," percentages in both cases higher than those for any other age group. Indeed, in each of the three surveys, Social Security was the news topic seniors were watching most closely, next to the direction of prices and the weather.[40]

Seniors also expect presidential candidates to pay attention to issues of aging policy. In 1984, 1988, and 1992, Roper polled respondents about the considerations they take into account in deciding their presidential vote.[41] Each year, those aged 60 and over were more likely than any other age group to cite social issues as a major consideration, as opposed to

TABLE 2.3
News Stories Followed Closely

News Story	Percentage "Following Closely"				Chi-square Test	% Difference between 60+ and 30–44
	18–29	30–44	45–59	60+		
June 1977						
Which prices are going up or down, and how much	58	66	78	73	***	7
Govt. proposals to change way Social Security financed	**26**	**38**	**51**	**56**	***	**18**
President Carter and his administration	28	35	52	55	***	20
Govt. proposals for dealing with the energy crisis	56	62	65	57	***	−5
Govt. proposals for getting the economy moving again	42	48	58	50	***	2
Govt. proposals to change the welfare system	27	35	46	44	***	9
Relations between U.S. and oil-producing Arab nations	30	36	49	42	***	6
Our relations with Russia	25	25	35	39	***	14
The David Frost–Richard Nixon interviews on TV	13	13	19	27	***	14
Relations between Israel and the Arab countries	21	22	29	28	***	6
February 1978						
This winter's weather reports and forecasts	80	83	89	87	***	4
Which prices are going up or down, and how much	61	70	75	80	***	10
Social Security costs and benefits	**33**	**50**	**63**	**72**	***	**22**
Talk about the state of the economy	42	51	59	61	***	10
President Carter and his administration	22	37	48	57	***	20
The controversy over the Panama Canal	28	41	50	56	***	15
Legislation to deal with the energy problem	41	48	56	52	***	4
Proposed changes in income taxes	40	52	56	50	***	−2
Relations between Israel and the Arab countries	31	40	42	45	***	5
Proposed arms control agreement between the U.S. and USSR	19	25	29	39	***	14
The threats that man-made satellites in orbit pose	17	20	26	25	***	5
Reports about UFOs	26	24	24	21		−3

Chi-square tests: $*p < .05$; $**p < .01$; $***p < .001$.
Source: Roper Surveys 7706, 7803, 8108.

TABLE 2.3
News Stories Followed Closely (*cont'd*)

News Story	Percentage "Following Closely"				Chi-square Test	% Difference between 60+ and 30–44
	18–29	30–44	45–59	60+		
August 1981						
The legislation to deal with changes in Social Security	35	53	71	82	***	29
Which prices are going up or down, and how much	50	67	69	70	***	3
Legislation to reduce income taxes	33	52	60	58	***	6
Interest rates charged by banks	51	65	64	57	***	−8
Air traffic controllers' strike	45	46	50	49		3
Marriage of Charles and Diana	32	32	32	44	**	12
Relations between Israel and the Arab countries	28	41	42	42	***	1
The situation in Poland	22	36	38	42	***	6
Riots in England	22	28	30	35	***	7
Hunger strikes by Irish prisoners	30	34	32	35		1
Attempts to buy Conoco	12	21	24	21	***	0

Chi-square tests: $*p < .05$; $**p < .01$; $***p < .001$.
Source: Roper Surveys 7706, 7803, 8108.

other issues like the economy, foreign policy, and law and order, and were most likely to select Social Security as the social issue of greatest importance. In 1984, for example, 29 percent of respondents aged 60 and over chose social issues as the number one consideration in their presidential vote, compared with only 19 percent of 30- to 44-year-old respondents. And among social issues like education, health, women's rights, civil rights, and poverty, Social Security was chosen as the most important issue by 41 percent of seniors compared with just 18 percent of 30- to 44-year-olds. The most important social issue for nonseniors was not Social Security but education. Thus for senior citizens, Social Security is a highly salient issue, much more so than for nonseniors. From 1984 to 1992 the proportion of respondents of all ages choosing Social Security as the most important consideration among the social issues decreased, probably because threats to the program peaked in the early 1980s (see chapter 5). But while nonsenior interest in Social Security fell by almost half from 1984 to 1992 (from 30 percent to 16 percent for 30- to 44-year-old respondents), senior interest remained strong, decreasing by only one-sixth (from 41 percent to 34 percent).

A similar question from early 1984 shows the high salience of Medicare for senior citizens. Respondents were asked on which three or four subjects they would most like to see the presidential candidates focus (Medicare was substituted in the survey for Social Security). Among non-seniors, unemployment was the issue most often cited, but among seniors Medicare benefits and financing were the top concern. Sixty percent of seniors cited Medicare as a subject they wanted candidates to address, compared with 40 percent of 45- to 59-year-olds and 22 percent of 30- to 44-year-olds.

Senior interest in Social Security remains strong today. In the 1998 midterm election exit poll administered by the Voter News Service, seniors were most likely to cite Social Security as the issue of greatest importance in deciding their vote for the House of Representatives. Thirty-one percent chose Social Security, followed by "moral and ethical standards" (20 percent), education (14 percent), taxes (11 percent), the economy/jobs (10 percent), health care (8 percent), and the Clinton/Lewinsky matter (6 percent).[42] Similarly, when asked by the 2000 National Election Study to name the most important problem facing the nation, seniors most often cited Social Security; for those under 65, the most important problem was education.

Thus the enactment and development of Social Security and Medicare have had enormously beneficial effects on senior well-being. By every indicator—income, poverty, health, leisure—seniors are better off. Even those with modest resources, like April Jefferson, are in better shape than their predecessors. And the crucial importance of the programs is evidenced in seniors' attentiveness to age-related policy news and their expectation that elected officials will concentrate on these issues as well.

TRENDS IN PARTICIPATION

Over the same period that senior welfare state programs developed and spread, senior political participation increased. To illustrate the changing patterns of participation by age since the early 1950s, I show trends for four participatory activities—voting, contributing, working on campaigns, and contacting elected officials.

I focus on these four activities for several reasons. First, they represent several different types of political acts. Voting is the most fundamental electoral act, and the one political activity in which the most citizens take part. Contributing money and working on campaigns are campaign activities, and contacting is a nonelectoral act.[43] Taken together, they show that the rise in seniors' participation over time is not limited to just one type of activity.

Second, these participatory acts are perhaps the most important in the contemporary political system. Votes are a politician's most fundamental need. Money is crucial in today's increasingly expensive and media-driven campaigns. Campaign work enables a single person to influence many others. Contacting is a citizen-initiated act that is information rich: letter writers reveal their specific issue concern, their stand, and often their politically relevant demographic identity. Letters inform Congress about constituent concerns and prompt casework (where members try to solve constituent problems), both of which contribute to members' reelection efforts.

Third, these acts have different underlying mechanisms, and yet seniors' programs have affected them all over time.[44] This illustrates the breadth of the welfare state program effects and the way in which they influence the entire array of factors underlying participation.

Today the political participation of senior citizens equals or exceeds that of younger Americans. Seniors are more likely to vote than younger people; 84 percent of National Election Study respondents aged 65 and over said they voted in the 1996 election compared with 77 percent of 35- to 64-year-olds (the "middle group") and 57 percent of 18- to 34-year-olds (the "youth group"). In the 1998 midterm election, 73 percent of seniors voted versus 59 percent of the middle group and just 30 percent of the youth group. In 1996, seniors were more likely to make campaign contributions; 12.2 percent of seniors contributed money to a political campaign compared with 8.6 percent of the middle group and 2.9 percent of the youth group. At 2.3 percent, seniors were about as likely as the middle (2.5 percent) and youth groups (2.0 percent) to work on campaigns. And data from the Roper Social and Political Trends Archive show that seniors wrote letters to their congressmen or senators at about the same rate as the middle group in 1993 (13 percent versus 14 percent) and at twice the rate of the youth group (6 percent).[45] In the 2000 election, the gap between seniors and nonseniors in voting and campaign work narrowed slightly, as the political parties aggressively mobilized groups like union members and African Americans.[46] But seniors were even more active as contributors in 2000, with 13.7 percent making contributions, compared with 10.5 percent of the middle group and less than 3 percent of the youth group.

In 1972 Sidney Verba and Norman Nie showed that with differences in education and income controlled for, seniors were more participatory than younger people; now seniors have reached and surpassed parity without need for statistical adjustments.[47] As figure 2.4 shows, contemporary participation differences by age are as great or nearly as great as those that have received more attention from scholars—differences by education, income, race and ethnicity, and gender. For example, seniors

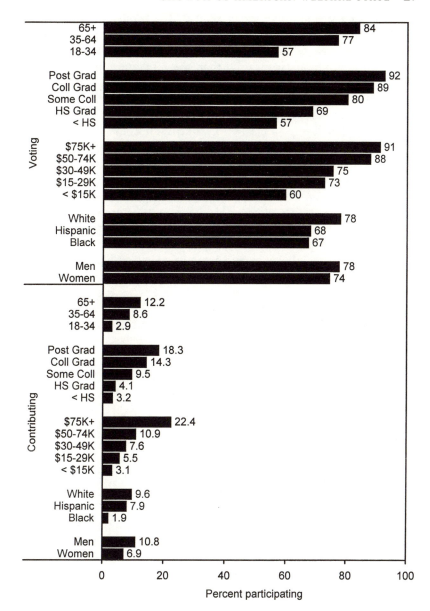

Figure 2.4 Voting and contributing by demographic subgroup, 1996. (National Election Study, 1996.)

were 27 percent more likely than 18- to 34-year-olds to vote in 1996. Although this difference is not as large as the 35 percent gulf in turnout between those with postgraduate educations and those who did not graduate from high school, it is larger than the 20-point gap between high school- and college-educated respondents. Turnout differences by age are larger than those by race—where 11 points separate whites and blacks—and by gender—where the difference between men and women is not statistically significant. Similarly, for contributing, the 9-point gap between seniors and young people is not as great as the 19 points separating those earning over $75,000 per year from those earning less than $15,000. But it is larger than the gap between the lowest-income group and the $50,000–$75,000 group. And again the age difference in contributing is larger than that of race (8 points) and gender (4 points). The "young old" (those aged 65–74) are even more active than the senior population as a whole.

Seniors have not always participated at equal or higher rates than younger people. NES and Roper data reveal that senior participation was generally lower than that of the middle 35- to 64-year-old group and for some activities even lower than that of the under-35 youth group until the 1980s, when seniors became the most active segment of the population.

Voting

Since 1952, seniors alone have increased their turnout in presidential elections. Seniors have always voted at higher rates than the youth group, but from the 1950s through the 1970s they voted at lower rates than the middle group of 35- to 64-year-olds. Beginning in the 1980s seniors reached parity with and then overtook the middle group. Senior voting participation in presidential election years rose from 73 percent in 1952 to 84 percent in 1996, while middle-group turnout remained flat at 77 to 78 percent and the youth group declined from 68 to 57 percent (figure 2.5).[48] Through 1996, turnout for both under-65 groups declined from the 1960 peak, while that of seniors rose from a low point in 1972. Seniors were the only age group whose turnout increased in 1996, when overall voter turnout reached its lowest level in modern history. Senior voting dipped slightly in 2000 while that of the younger groups increased 1 percent, but seniors remained the group most likely to cast a ballot. Thus citizens under 65 now vote near their lowest rates since the advent of the NES in 1952, while seniors are at their highest.[49] And studies of confirmed versus reported voting show that it is the young who are more likely to lie about having voted, so the differences between young and old shown here are, if anything, understated.[50]

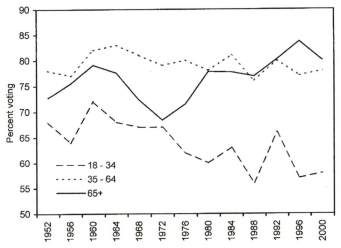

Figure 2.5 Turnout in presidential elections by age, 1952–2000. (National Election Studies.)

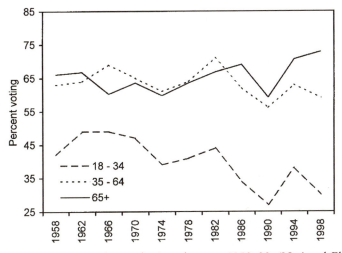

Figure 2.6 Turnout in midterm elections by age, 1958–98. (National Election Studies.)

Contemporary turnout differences among age groups are even greater for midterm elections (figure 2.6). From 1958 to 1998, midterm turnout declined from 42 percent to 30 percent for the youth group and from 63 percent to 59 percent for the middle group, but rose from 66 percent to 73 percent among seniors. Seniors are now more than twice as likely to vote in midterm elections as those under 35. And seniors are the only group whose turnout increased from 1994 to 1998. As with presidential year voting, senior turnout today is at a historical high while nonsenior turnout is at a low.

Contributing

The rise of senior participation is even more dramatic for campaign contributions. Seniors have more than quadrupled the rate at which they make contributions in presidential election years, increasing from 3 percent in 1952 to nearly 14 percent in 2000.[51] As with voting, the rise in senior contribution rates dates from the early 1970s, with seniors reaching parity with and then overtaking 35- to 64-year-olds in the 1980s, as shown in figure 2.7. Also like voting, senior contribution rates are rising while nonsenior rates are for the most part declining. The contribution rate among the middle group peaked in 1976 at 13.9 percent, falling to 8.6 percent in 1996 with a small up-tick in 2000. The trend in youth contributing is virtually the opposite of the senior trend, falling from 11 percent in 1960 to 3 percent in 2000. Once again, the contemporary political landscape shows seniors at a historical peak in their participation rate, while nonseniors are near historical lows.

Midterm contribution rates among all age groups peak in 1978, with declines since then as seen in figure 2.8. However, seniors increased their contribution rates in 1994 and 1998 as the youth slide continued.

Campaign Work

The rate at which seniors work on campaigns has not risen in absolute terms as with voting and contributing, but seniors have made gains relative to younger people. From the 1950s through the 1970s, seniors were the age group least likely to work on campaigns. In the 1980s and 1990s seniors surpassed the youth group and reached parity with the middle 35- to 64-year-old group (figure 2.9).[52] Among all age groups campaign work has decreased, probably because today's campaigns are increasingly executed through media buys rather than through grassroots campaign work. But seniors have gained on younger people, just as they have with voting and contributing, which is particularly remarkable since campaign work is a more physically taxing activity than getting to the voting booth once a year or putting a contribution in the mail.

Contacting

Yearly aggregations of the Roper data reveal trends in contacting comparable to those for voting, contributing, and campaign work. Unlike those activities, however, contacting is not tied to the electoral cycle, and can

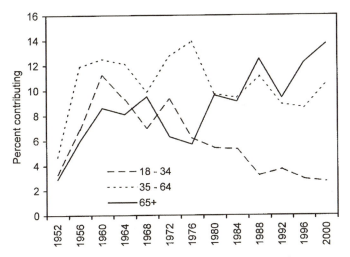

Figure 2.7 Contributors in presidential elections by age, 1952–2000. (National Election Studies.)

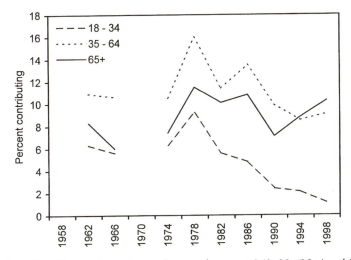

Figure 2.8 Contributors in midterm elections by age, 1962–98. (National Election Studies.)

be done at any time. It is therefore more responsive to specific events. Until 1983, seniors were less likely than nonseniors to write their congressman or senator. In response to a series of policy events surrounding Social Security and Medicare that will be detailed in chapter 5, senior contacting peaked at 20 percent in 1983 and then decreased to 11 percent by 1994, when the policy threats subsided.[53] By contrast, nonseniors expe-

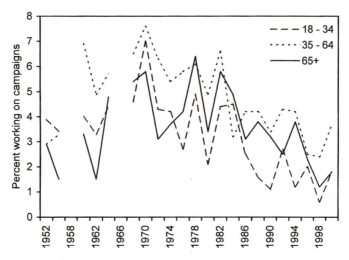

Figure 2.9 Campaign workers in presidential and midterm elections by age, 1952–2000. (National Election Studies.)

rienced a steady decrease in contacting from 1973 to 1994, from 19 percent to 12 percent for the middle group and from 12 percent to 6 percent for the youth group, as shown in figure 2.10.

The impact of seniors' relative increase in participation is especially noticeable in the changing composition of participators. In 1952, seniors made up 13 percent of the NES sample, 13 percent of voters, 12 percent of campaign workers, and just 9 percent of contributors. By 2000, seniors made up 17 percent of the NES sample, reflecting the aging of the population, but were 12 percent of workers (17 percent in 1996), 20 percent of voters, and 28 percent of contributors (figure 2.11). For midterm elections the story is the same, with seniors constituting an increasing share of participators. In the Roper data seniors were 20 percent of the sample and only 17 percent of the contactors in 1974. In 1989, seniors had grown to 24 percent of the sample and over 30 percent of all contactors.

LINKING SENIOR PROGRAMS AND PARTICIPATION

Over the last five decades senior political participation has increased so that seniors now participate at the same or higher rates than nonseniors across a variety of activities. During the same period, senior welfare state programs grew and developed—Social Security coverage expanded and benefit levels increased, Medicare was introduced—vastly improving se-

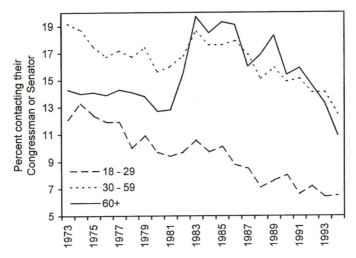

Figure 2.10 Contacting by age, 1973–94. (Roper Social and Political Trends Archive, yearly aggregates.)

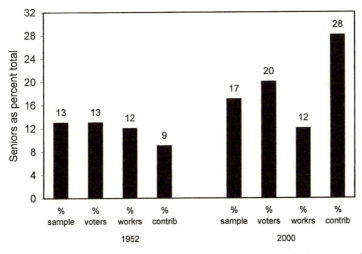

Figure 2.11 Seniors as participators, 1952 and 2000. (National Election Studies.)

niors' financial status and health. Figures 2.12 through 2.15 suggest ways in which these two phenomena may be causally linked.

Figure 2.12 shows one path by which Social Security might influence senior participation: it provides senior citizens with money. As average Social Security benefits have risen over time, so has the rate at which seniors make campaign contributions relative to nonseniors. In 1952, when the

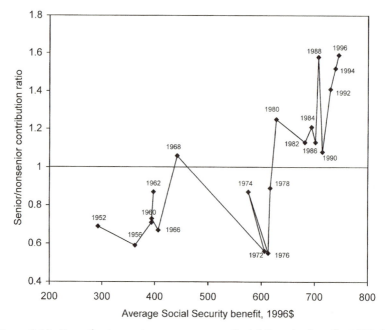

Figure 2.12 Contribution ratio versus average Social Security benefit, 1952–96. Contribution ratio equals senior contribution rate each year divided by the nonsenior contribution rate. (Contribution ratio calculated from National Election Studies; average Social Security benefit from *Social Security Bulletin Annual Statistical Supplement*, various years.)

average monthly Social Security benefit for retired workers was $293 in 1996 dollars (and the senior poverty rate was over 35 percent), seniors were only 60 percent as likely as nonseniors to make campaign contributions. In 1996, when average Social Security benefits had grown to $745 (and the senior poverty rate was just 10.5 percent), seniors were 1.6 times as likely to make campaign contributions. Social Security vastly improved seniors' financial well-being, providing a steady, predictable income that has freed seniors to think beyond subsistence to other topics, like politics, and to participate in political activities that require disposable income.

Social Security also allows seniors to retire, which enables them to pursue time-intensive activities like campaign work. Figure 2.13 shows that as the retirement rate increased (measured by the percentage of senior men no longer in the workforce), seniors became more active campaign workers than nonseniors.[54] In 1956, when 55 percent of senior men were retired, seniors were just 45 percent as likely as nonseniors to work on campaigns. In 1994, when the retirement rate among senior men had risen to 83 percent, seniors were 1.2 times as likely to work on campaigns.

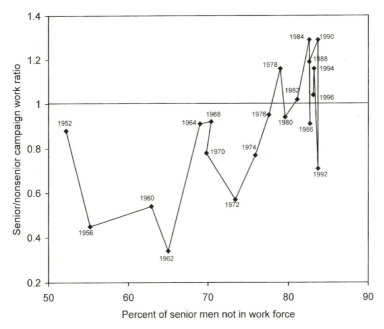

Figure 2.13 Campaign work ratio versus retirement rate, 1952–96. Campaign work ratio equals senior campaign work rate each year divided by the nonsenior campaign work rate. (Campaign work ratio calculated from National Election Studies; percentage of senior men not in workforce from *Social Security Bulletin Annual Statistical Supplement*, various years.)

Social Security may have contributed to senior participation by allowing seniors to retire and increasing their free time, which facilitates participation in time-based activities.

We might also expect that Social Security would affect seniors' engagement with public affairs. Here Social Security matters not so much in the absolute amount of income it provides—as was the case with contributing—but in the relative share of income it makes up. As seniors' well-being is ever more closely tied to government action, we might expect them to be more engaged with politics and more likely to participate. Figure 2.14 shows that as Social Security benefits constituted an increasing percentage of senior incomes over time, senior turnout levels increased compared with those of nonseniors.[55] In 1968, when Social Security made up 28 percent of total senior income, seniors were 94 percent as likely as nonseniors to vote; in 1994, when Social Security had risen to 42 percent of total senior income, seniors were 1.28 times as likely to vote as nonseniors (to use another presidential election year for comparison with 1968, seniors were 1.12 times as likely as nonseniors to vote in 1996). Thus

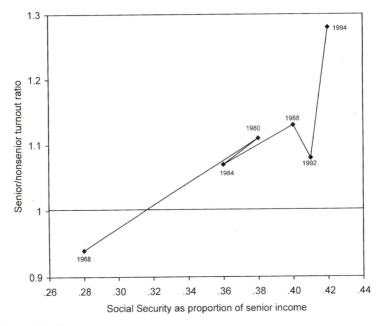

Figure 2.14 Turnout ratio versus proportion senior income from Social Security, 1968–94. Turnout ratio equals senior turnout rate each year divided by the nonsenior turnout rate. (Turnout ratio calculated from National Election Studies; Social Security as proportion of senior income from *Social Security Bulletin Annual Statistical Supplement 1997*, p. 21.)

seniors' increasing stake in government activity drives their participation rates up as they have more interest in and want more say about the policies that affect their lives so fundamentally.

Finally, Social Security may have influenced senior participation over time by politicizing the group. Absent Social Security, senior citizens are a disparate group of people whose common characteristic, age, has little political meaning. Once governmental benefits are conferred on the basis of age, however, the group has political relevance and is ripe for mobilization by policy entrepreneurs, interest groups, and political parties. Appeals are made on the basis of the program; senior program recipients are asked to participate in politics—to make contributions, to write letters—in defense of their programs. They are directly recruited to political activity at rates far higher than would be the case in the absence of these programs, especially given their relatively low socioeconomic status. Figure 2.15 shows that as the proportion of seniors on Social Security increased, the rate at which they were mobilized by the political parties during election campaigns rose relative to younger people. In 1956 only 16 percent

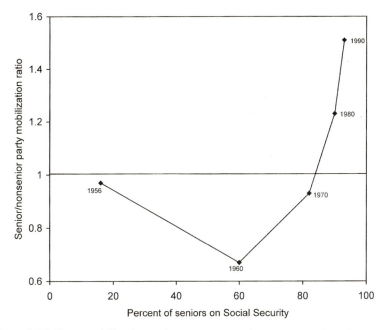

Figure 2.15 Party mobilization ratio versus proportion seniors on Social Security, 1956–90. Mobilization ratio equals senior rate of mobilization by the political parties each year divided by the nonsenior mobilization rate. (Mobilization ratio calculated from National Election Studies; proportion seniors on Social Security from Robert M. Ball, "The Original Understanding on Social Security: Implications for Later Developments," in *Social Security: Beyond the Rhetoric of Crisis*, ed. Theodore R. Marmor and Jerry L. Mashaw, Princeton: Princeton University Press, 1988.)

of seniors were on Social Security, and they were slightly less likely than nonseniors to be mobilized by the parties. By 1990, 93 percent of seniors received Social Security, and they were 1.5 times as likely to be mobilized. Hence politicization and subsequent mobilization is a third path by which Social Security may influence senior participation.

As seniors' welfare state programs have developed over time, seniors have become disproportionately active political participators. I have hinted at the ways in which senior programs and senior participation may be causally connected. Chapter 3 develops a model linking senior welfare state programs and seniors' political participation through these paths and begins to test them empirically, in cross-sectional data.

Chapter Three

A MODEL OF SENIOR CITIZEN
POLITICAL PARTICIPATION

At age 75, Martha Malone is extremely active in politics. She has chaired the environmental committee in her Pennsylvania town, served on the local planning board, has long been a poll worker, and of course votes in every election—"a privilege of citizens," she says. Her high rate of activity in civic affairs is to be expected: she is college educated—only 9 percent of women her age are[1]—and affluent. As for current debates, she fears Social Security and Medicare "could be taken away." That would be devastating for her and especially for other, less affluent seniors, because "we can't remake our lives at this point."[2]

Harry Smith, 70, also lives in Pennsylvania. He does not share Martha's privileged background. More closely resembling the average senior, he has a high school education and worked in a supermarket all his life. And yet he is politically active too. A regular voter, he ran for city council upon retirement and served eight years. He remembers the days before Social Security was widespread. "You joined the Junior Mechanics. Paid dues each month. They weren't much—I only made $17 a week—but [the organization] helped out a little when there was a death in the family. Of course it wasn't much money. Thank goodness for Social Security. It's a godsend."[3]

Harry's son Charles, 29, is a college-educated high school teacher. But unlike his father, he neither votes nor engages in other political activities. "I don't follow politics that closely," he says. "It's a nuisance. I'm happy with the country but I'm not getting involved in running it. It seems to be working fine."[4]

Why is the less privileged Harry nearly as active as Martha? And why is Charles less active than his father, despite his greater resource levels? Participation research tells us that politically relevant resources like education and income are extremely important in predicting individuals' political participation. Indeed, variations in participation rates among groups can often be explained by differential resource levels. Activity differences between women and men and between blacks and whites, for example, disappear when disparities in education and income are taken into account.

But if education and income are such important predictors of political activity, how is it that Harry—modest education, modest income—participates on a par with Martha (and outstrips the more privileged Charles)? This chapter seeks to explain the puzzle of senior participation—how it is that on average seniors participate at high rates without having high levels of formal education and income. It explores the major factors behind senior participation—resources, political engagement, and mobilization—and demonstrates how the usual relationships differ for this population. Martha and Harry's comments about the importance of Social Security hint at a major part of the explanation—Social Security alters how each of those participatory factors operates for seniors.

I begin by discussing the traditional significance of education and income for participation—why it is that more affluent and educated individuals are typically more active in politics. I then explore how resources, engagement, and mobilization influence seniors' participatory activity. This analysis reveals a number of unique effects.

For example, seniors' low levels of politically relevant resources like income and education are mitigated in several ways. They have fewer expenses, holding less debt and paying lower taxes than nonseniors, which helps stretch their incomes. Despite having less formal education, seniors have benefited from a lifetime of experience with government and other bureaucracies that helps them meet the hurdles of registering to vote or locating a congressman's address. Thus what appear to be low levels of income and education are not as detrimental to senior participation as they are to nonsenior participation.

Seniors' engagement with politics takes an unusual form too, because of Social Security. Typically interest in public affairs—and participatory activity—is greatest among high-income citizens. But participation specifically regarding the issue of Social Security is more prevalent among low-income seniors, because they are the most dependent on the program. This effect is strongest for letter writing concerning Social Security, the act lower-income seniors are most likely to engage in if they have a problem with their benefits or a concern about policy. Voting and contributing with Social Security in mind are also less common among high-income seniors. Seniors' participation on issues other than Social Security is like that of younger people—the affluent are more active. But with regard to Social Security affluent seniors are less active, which makes the relationship between income and participation overall flatter for seniors than for nonseniors.

And seniors are mobilized to participate at high rates, especially by the political parties. Although such efforts are usually focused on higher-status groups, again there is a different pattern among seniors, with parties reaching out to low- and moderate-income seniors in particular. Unlike other low-income groups, lower-income seniors are promising prospects because of their great stake and heightened interest in government activity and political affairs.

Thus we begin to see the effect of public policy on participation. Social Security both changes the level of resources, engagement, and mobilization seniors bring to the participatory arena and alters the basic participatory equation. These effects combine to make senior participation both high and more democratic.

Social Security is therefore distinctive in what it means for politics in the United States. It mobilizes a low-income group around an economic issue; Social Security has participatory effects on all seniors, boosting their activity levels, but these are greatest for low-income seniors. This is quite unusual in the United States, where, to the extent economic self-interest influences behavior, it often simply augments the high participation rates of the most active portions of the population. For example, in 1978 affluent homeowners were more likely than other Californians to support Proposition 13, the property tax rollback initiative, because of the large tax savings the measure promised them. But of course such individuals were "the most politicized and vocal" segment of the population to begin with.[5] Social Security is unusual both because it inspires self-interested behavior, which is rare, and because it inspires it in a low-income group, which is rarer still. When interests are so large and tangible, they can shape behavior. And the keen interest in Social Security helps seniors—especially the less affluent—overcome the typical resource-based obstacles to participation.

The Traditional Significance of Education and Income for Participation

Decades of participation research show that education and income are positively related to participation.[6] These relationships hold for voter turnout,[7] campaign contributions, contacting, group activism, and even unconventional forms of participation like protest and violence. Education and income affect political activity as resources that facilitate participation, as enhancers of political engagement, and as determinants of social network position, which influences exposure to participatory norms and recruitment efforts.

Education increases individuals' willingness to take part in political activity. Citizenship education in school instills a sense of civic duty; indeed, this was an early purpose of and justification for public schooling in the United States.[8] Better-educated people are more likely to absorb prevailing social norms, including expectations about civic participation.[9]

Education also fosters political interest. Individuals who are more interested in politics are more likely to turn from other pressing commitments—work, family, church—and participate in the political arena. More educated people are both more knowledgeable about public affairs and better equipped to learn new information. In addition, education confers politically relevant skills, such as the ability to write a letter to an elected official, to make a speech, or to overcome the bureaucratic hurdle of voter registration.[10]

Finally, education is important for participation in partly determining social network position.[11] The higher one's position, the more likely one is to develop even more skills (in a high-status job or in positions of responsibility in voluntary organizations or religious institutions), to get recruited to political activity, and to absorb the participatory social norms of the surrounding high-status, high-participation individuals.

In general, people participate in politics "when they get valuable benefits that are worth the costs of taking part."[12] Education both reduces the perceived costs and enhances the perceived benefits of participation. Skills, recruitment, and political knowledge make participation easier; interest in politics, a sense of civic duty, and immersion in participatory norms make it more rewarding.

Like education, income matters to participation by reducing the costs and increasing the benefits of participation. Below a certain income people are preoccupied with simple survival and have no time for luxuries like politics.[13] Higher-income individuals have the discretionary income to make campaign contributions, to hire baby-sitters and gardeners to free their time for political work, and so on. People with higher incomes "can simply afford to do more—of everything—than citizens with little money."[14] The greater availability of political participation to the affluent is a version of what economists call an "income effect": the wealthy have more leisure because they are able to purchase it.[15]

High-income individuals are also more likely than poorer citizens to occupy high-status social network positions. Practicing politically relevant skills like letter writing and speech making increases with job level and income, as does political recruitment.[16] High-income people are more likely to belong to nonpolitical voluntary organizations, where they also develop skills and get recruited.

Finally, income enhances participation by increasing individuals' sense of political engagement and stake in the system. Higher-income people have a greater stake in a variety of policy areas. Perhaps the best example is tax policy; the wealthy have higher incomes and therefore more to lose in taxes. High-income individuals are also more likely to perceive their stake; their political interest is stimulated by their high-level jobs, in which they learn how government activity affects their business and personal lives.[17]

For these reasons education and income are positively related to political interest and participation. And yet seniors participate at high rates without having high average levels of education and income. Their activity levels are due to the unusual operation of resources, engagement, and mobilization for the Social Security–receiving senior population.

RESOURCES

At first glance, seniors hardly seem likely super-participators. They have the lowest formal education and household income levels of any age group. One-third lack a high school diploma, compared with 9 percent of Citizen Participation Study respondents aged 35 to 49. Less than one-fifth of seniors have graduated from college compared with one-third of 35- to 49-year-olds. Average family income for seniors in 1990 was just over $24,000 compared with almost $46,000 for respondents aged 35 to 49. Over 40 percent of seniors have incomes under $15,000 per year, and 80 percent have incomes under $35,000.

But while seniors have less education and income than do younger citizens on average, these low levels are mitigated in a number of ways. With retirement individuals effectively trade one politically relevant resource, income, for another, free time. The Citizen Participation Study asked respondents how much time they spend working, doing housework, studying, and sleeping. Free time can be calculated as the number of hours per day not consumed by those activities. Respondents aged 35 to 49, 85 percent of whom work, report just five hours of free time per day. Seniors, 10 percent of whom work, report over twelve hours.[18] Retired senior men have even more free time, fourteen hours per day.

Seniors' incomes also "go further" because of their life circumstances. Senior homeowners have lower mortgage payments on average than non-seniors; three-quarters of them own their houses free and clear.[19] They also hold less nonmortgage consumer debt.[20] Seniors benefit from a variety of financial breaks that are conferred to all on the basis of age rather than a means test: they are exempt from the Social Security and Medicare taxes on earnings; get an extra deduction on their federal income taxes; pay taxes on a smaller share of their incomes; and receive discounts at many retail stores, restaurants, hotels, and so on. The economist Marilyn Moon calculates that the median senior couple with an income of $25,000 would owe $294 in federal taxes, or 1.15 percent, while the median non-senior couple with income of $45,000 would owe $5,164, or 11.5 percent. On an income of $40,000, seniors would pay $2,664 or 6.6 percent in federal taxes, compared with $4,414 or 11 percent for nonseniors.[21] Seniors do spend a greater share of their income on health care—12 per-

TABLE 3.1
Average Annual Expenditures of All Consumer Units and Senior Units, 1997

	Expenditures		Expenditures as % of Total		Senior Expenditures as % of All Consumers' Expenditures
	All Consumers	Seniors	All Consumers	Seniors	
Total	$34,819	$24,413	100%	100%	70%
Selected categories:					
Food	4,801	3,486	14	14	73
Mortgage	2,225	547	6	2	25
Property taxes	971	1,060	3	4	109
Utilities	2,412	2,157	7	9	89
Home furnishings	1,512	1,059	4	4	70
Apparel	1,729	1,045	5	4	60
Transportation	6,457	3,812	19	16	59
Health care	1,841	2,855	5	12	155
Entertainment	1,813	1,103	5	5	61
Personal taxes	3,241	1,325	9	5	41

Source: U.S. Bureau of the Census, *Statistical Abstract of the United States 1999* (Washington, D.C.: U.S. Government Printing Office, 1999), p. 471.

cent before taxes compared with 5 percent among all households (table 3.1). A higher share of senior incomes goes to property taxes, in part because seniors are more likely than nonseniors to own their homes (82 percent versus 70 percent according to the 1992 Current Population Survey). They also spend somewhat more of their incomes on food and utilities. Across other areas, however, senior spending is less than that of nonseniors, both in absolute terms and as a percentage of income. Overall senior spending comes to 70 percent that of all households, but in some areas totals less, as in entertainment (61 percent), apparel (60 percent), and transportation (59 percent). Most notably, seniors' personal taxes total just 41 percent those of all households, and their mortgage costs come to just 25 percent.

One way to account for seniors' advantage is to divide family income by household size. Senior households are smaller on average than nonsenior households—1.6 persons versus 3.1 for respondents aged 35 to 49 in the

Citizen Participation Study. Per capita adjustments probably overadjust in seniors' favor, since they fail to take into account economies of scale in rent and the differential needs of adults and children,[22] but the calculation is of interest nonetheless. While seniors' mean family income is half that of 35- to 49-year-olds, seniors' per capita income is nearly the same. Senior incomes may not be as low as they seem on the surface.[23]

Seniors' low levels of formal education are mitigated in several ways as well. There appears to be an age effect in which life experience is a substitute for formal education.[24] Over a lifetime one may absorb participatory norms and values, learn to process political information, and become accustomed to voting through sheer habit.[25] The "school of hard knocks" may impart the same experience with bureaucratic relationships that helps educated people overcome the procedural hurdles necessary to register and vote.[26] In addition there may be cohort effects, particularly in education content and quality. Earlier cohorts may have been more steeped in democratic, "American" values in school.[27] Differences in education quality might also mitigate seniors' lower levels of formal schooling; when administered a ten-item vocabulary test in the Citizen Participation Study, seniors score nearly as high as 35- to 49-year-olds, getting 6.3 definitions correct on average compared with 6.6 for the younger, more educated group.[28] Perhaps one picks up vocabulary through life experience as well.

One of the most important ways education affects participation is by imparting politically relevant skills like the ability to write a letter to an elected official.[29] But such skills can be learned elsewhere—on the job, in voluntary organizations, and in religious institutions—where letter writing, speech making, meeting planning, and decision making may be practiced. Seniors report high rates of exercising such skills in these nonschool settings.[30] We do not know how many skills seniors practiced on the job before retiring, a set of questions the Citizen Participation Study did not ask. The 10 percent of seniors still working practice just 1.6 skills (out of four) compared with 2.2 among 35- to 49-year-olds, as shown in table 3.2.[31] But in other institutional settings seniors practice as many skills as younger people—1.3 on average in nonpolitical organizations and 1.6 in religious institutions—and belong to those institutions at the same or higher rates. Three-quarters of seniors belong to nonpolitical groups, about the same as 35- to 49-year-olds. And more seniors are members of a religious institution or attend religious services two or more times per month: 79 percent versus 67 percent of 35- to 49-year-olds. Thus seniors practice a large number of current skills, and possess an unknown but presumably nontrivial number of skills from their preretirement years.

With seniors' lower income and education levels mitigated in these ways, when we see in table 3.3 that seniors with incomes under $15,000 are twice as likely to make contributions as comparable 35- to 49-year-

TABLE 3.2
Institutional Affiliations and Skills Practiced by Age

	18–34	35–49	50–64	65+	Difference of Means Test 35–49 vs. 65+
% Affiliated					
Job	76%	85%	59%	10%	***
Nonpolitical organization	61	72	68	74	
Church or synagogue	63	67	67	79	***
No. of Skills Practiced (among those affiliated)					
On the job	1.8	2.2	2.1	1.6	**
In nonpolitical organization	1.2	1.3	1.3	1.3	
In church or synagogue	1.4	1.7	1.4	1.6	

*p < .05; **p < .01; ***p < .001.
Source: Citizen Participation Study.

olds (10 percent versus 5 percent) or that seniors without high school diplomas are more than twice as likely to vote as their younger counterparts (63 percent compared with 28 percent), we understand that having an income or education level that is that low is different, less desperate, for seniors than for younger people. Nonetheless, seniors' high political participation rates are extraordinary given such low absolute levels of income and education. If at each education level senior citizens voted at the same rate as nonseniors, seniors' overall 1996 turnout would have been 66 percent rather than the 84 percent reported in the 1996 NES. If at each income level seniors made campaign contributions at the same rate as nonseniors, their 1996 contribution rate would have been under 5 percent, less than half their actual contribution rate of 12 percent.

The varieties of ways senior education and income levels are mitigated help explain why they are so active in public affairs. Some of the unusual effects are due to characteristics of seniors themselves—living in empty nests helps stretch their incomes, for example. But the role of policy is crucial. The income provided by Social Security lifts most seniors above poverty and facilitates retirement, both of which enhance seniors' ability to participate. The importance of Social Security for seniors' political engagement is even greater.

TABLE 3.3
Participation by Resource Level

	18–34	35–49	50–64	65+	Difference of Means Test 35–49 vs. 65+
Giving money by family income by age					
Under $15,000	5%	5%	4%	10%	
$15,000–$34,999	16	19	16	29	*
$35,000–$49,999	20	32	26	34	
$50,000 and over	22	47	54	67	#
Turnout by education by age					
< HS	7%	28%	64%	63%	***
HS grad.	49	70	76	87	***
Some college	60	77	90	95	**
College grad.	77	85	95	100	*
Post grad.	76	93	96	100	

#*p* < .10; **p* < .05; ***p* < .01; ****p* < .001.
Source: Citizen Participation Study.

POLITICAL ENGAGEMENT

Political engagement is a psychological impetus or desire to follow the political world. Political scientists have identified four aspects of engagement: political interest, knowledge or information, efficacy, and partisanship. These are major factors in predicting political activity. People who care about politics, who keep abreast of public affairs, who feel their participation is effective in some way, and who are strongly attached to a political party are more likely to participate.[32]

Compared with the special resource effects operating for seniors, the pattern of political engagement among the elderly is even more unusual from the perspective of existing theory and empirical evidence. Customarily political engagement is highest among affluent individuals, who have the most at stake. But on the issue of Social Security it is poorer citizens whose interests are most implicated. Figure 3.1 divides seniors into quintiles by total income and shows the percentage of income each quintile derives from Social Security. Seniors in the lowest two quintiles get over 80 percent of their income from the program, compared with

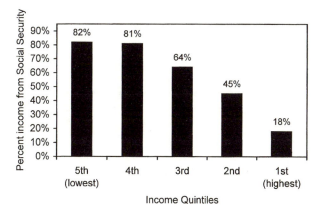

Figure 3.1 Percentage of senior income from Social Security by total income quintile, 1998. (Federal Interagency Forum on Aging-Related Statistics, *Older Americans 2000: Key Indicators of Well-Being*, Washington, D.C.: Government Printing Office, 2000, p. 66.)

just 18 percent for the top quintile. With this great dependence on Social Security, we would expect low-income seniors to be more interested in and active vis-à-vis the program, and the gradients between income and interest in and participation regarding Social Security to be negative rather than positive as is traditionally the case.

A comparison of seniors' general engagement levels with their engagement with Social Security begins to illustrate these differences. Seniors' general engagement with politics is unexceptional, in part because of their lower education levels. Average scores by age for the four measures of engagement—partisanship, interest, information, and efficacy—are shown in table 3.4. Seniors do exhibit greater partisanship than nonseniors. On a scale in which strong partisans of either party received 3 points, weak identifiers received 2 points, independent leaners, 1, and true independents, 0,[33] seniors have a mean score of 2.2 compared with 1.8 for 35- to 49-year-olds.[34] Nearly half of all seniors are strong partisans compared with a quarter to a third of respondents under 50. Political socialization during the New Deal era left the cohorts making up the current senior population with stronger partisanship[35] (and with more Democratic Party identification—according to the 1996 NES, the same proportion of seniors and nonseniors are Republican (38 percent), but seniors are slightly more likely to be Democrats (55 to 52 percent) and much more likely to be strong Democrats (27 to 17 percent)—more on this in chapter 4).

Although seniors have stronger party affiliations than nonseniors, their scores on the other measures of political engagement are comparable to

TABLE 3.4
Mean Political Engagement Scores by Age

	18–34	35–49	50–64	65+	Difference of Means Test 35–49 vs. 65+
Partisanship (3-point scale)	1.9	1.8	2.1	2.2	***
Political interest (8-point scale)	5.4	5.9	6.0	5.9	
Political information (8-point scale)	3.9	4.5	4.3	4.2	*
Political efficacy (16-point scale)	9.1	9.5	9.2	8.9	**

*p < .05; **p < .01; ***p < .001.
Source: Citizen Participation Study.

or lower than those of younger people. Seniors exhibit the same level of interest in local and national affairs as 35- to 49-year-olds: 5.9 on an 8-point scale.[36] Seniors scored lower than other respondents except the youngest on a scale of political information asking respondents basic factual questions about American government, getting 4.2 out of 8 answers correct.[37] And when asked about political efficacy—how responsive government is and how much influence someone like them has in government—seniors scored the lowest of any age group.[38] Lower formal education levels among seniors can explain some, though not all, of their middling engagement responses—when mean engagement scores are calculated by age and education, seniors have the highest scores about two-thirds of the time.[39]

Thus seniors' general political engagement is not higher than that of nonseniors. But their issue-specific interest in Social Security is. Roper Survey 8108 asked respondents how closely they follow news of various topics.[40] Seniors follow Social Security more than younger people do—scoring 2.76 versus 2.41 on a 3-point scale as shown in table 3.5, the largest gap among all the issue areas.[41] And seniors follow Social Security more closely than any other topic. Hence the highest level of interest shown by any age group in any issue is seniors' interest in Social Security. Moreover, senior interest in Social Security is tightly distributed around that high average; the standard deviation in the salience of Social Security to seniors, .53, is the smallest among all the news topics for both age groups.

Senior interest in Social Security not only is great but also takes an unusual form. The structure of political interest by education and income

TABLE 3.5   SENIOR CITIZEN POLITICAL PARTICIPATION   49

TABLE 3.5
News Salience Scores by Age

News Story	Nonseniors		Seniors		Difference of Means Test
	Mean	Std. dev.	Mean	Std. dev.	
Social Security					
Social Security legislation	2.41	0.71	2.76	0.53	***
Domestic					
Which prices are going up or down	2.56	0.61	2.64	0.58	*
Legislation to reduce income taxes	2.36	0.69	2.43	0.71	
Interest rates charged by banks	2.45	0.73	2.38	0.74	
Air traffic controllers' strike	2.23	0.80	2.27	0.81	
Attempts to buy Conoco	1.72	0.75	1.79	0.80	
International					
Marriage of Charles and Diana	2.04	0.77	2.24	0.80	***
The situation in Poland	2.06	0.76	2.17	0.80	*
Riots in England	1.97	0.74	2.16	0.81	*
Israeli–Arab relations	2.15	0.75	2.20	0.77	
Hunger strikes by Irish prisoners	2.10	0.73	2.10	0.74	

Source: Roper Survey 8108, August 1981.
Note: Salience scored from 1 (not paying much attention) to 3 (following fairly closely).

is different for Social Security compared with other issue areas. I combined the news topics appearing in table 3.5 into three scales—domestic, international, and Social Security.[42] Each of the scales is scored from 1 to 3, with higher scores indicating more attention to news. Figure 3.2 shows seniors' mean interest levels by education. The gradient is steeply positive for domestic and international topics; as is usually the case, highly educated respondents display much more interest than the less educated. The difference in interest between seniors with postgraduate educations and those with grade school educations is .5 for domestic issues and .7 for international issues on the 3-point scale.[43]

With Social Security there is a different pattern. Social Security is highly salient to seniors overall—interest in Social Security for the *least* educated seniors is greater than interest in domestic or international issues for the

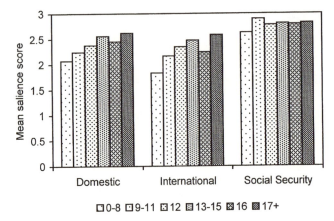

Figure 3.2 News salience scores for seniors by education. Salience scored from 1 (not paying much attention) to 3 (following fairly closely); education in years. (Roper Survey 8108, August 1981.)

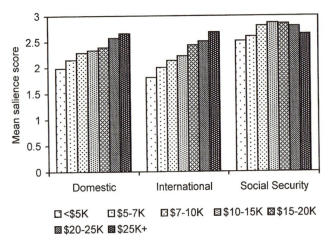

Figure 3.3 News salience scores for seniors by income. Salience scored from 1 (not paying much attention) to 3 (following fairly closely). (Roper Survey 8108, August 1981.)

most educated. And the education gradient is nearly flat. Seniors of all education levels have very similar levels of interest in Social Security. The difference in interest between the most and least educated seniors is only .2 for Social Security, not statistically different from zero.

The pattern of interest by income is also different. High-income seniors are much more attentive than low-income seniors to news of domestic and international issues, as shown in figure 3.3; the difference in the mean salience scores between the highest- and lowest-income seniors is .7 for domestic issues and .9 for international issues.[44] By contrast, the relationship between income and Social Security interest is curvilinear; the salience of Social Security news is lower for low-income seniors (although high compared with other domestic and international issues), rises as income (and education) increase, and then falls again for the highest-income seniors.

Thus even at the bivariate level it is evident that interest in Social Security bears a different relationship to education and especially to income than does interest in traditional issues. It is particularly this income effect that we want to focus on, given the steep gradient in Social Security dependence by income shown in figure 3.1. We would expect interest in Social Security to fall as income rises. The bivariate results in figure 3.3 do not show this, because of the interrelationship between education and income. In truth these two factors are inversely related to interest in Social Security: the true effect of education on Social Security interest is positive, and the true effect of income negative. But these effects are masked in bivariate analysis, which does not control for the effects of other variables. Highly educated seniors are more interested in Social Security than the less educated, being more interested in public affairs generally, but the fact that the more educated also tend to have higher incomes drives down their interest in Social Security. Similarly low-income seniors are more interested in Social Security, but the fact they also are less educated decreases their political interest. Therefore multivariate analysis is necessary to hone in on the true effect of each variable while controlling for others.

In addition to performing multivariate analysis, a move to political participation, rather than political interest, is in order. The pattern of political participation, and Social Security's role in seniors' political activity, is what we are really interested in. We want to know how the Social Security dependence gradient affects senior participation regarding Social Security, particularly seniors' propensity to participate by income, controlling for other factors.

Fortunately the data necessary to examine these relationships exist. The 1990 Citizen Participation Study both asked respondents about their participation in traditional activities and asked Social Security recipients about their program-specific participation—whether they had written a letter to complain about Social Security, voted with regard to Social Security, or made a campaign contribution with regard to the program.[45] Figures 3.4 and 3.5 show the likelihood of performing traditional and Social Security–oriented political acts by income, after controlling for the demographic characteristics of education, gender, age, race, marital status, and work status as well as general political interest (see appendix tables A.1 and A.2 for the logistic regression results).

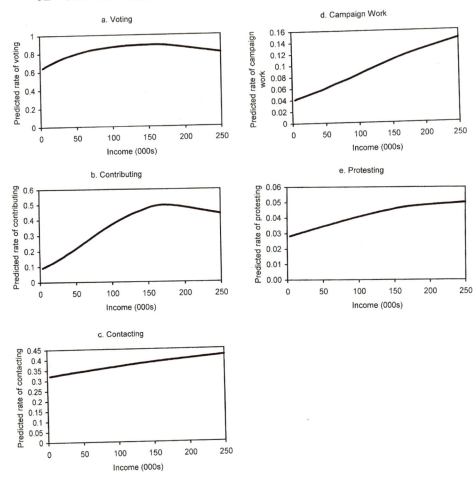

Figure 3.4 Predicted rate of traditional participatory activity by income, all respondents. (1990 Citizen Participation Study; full equations in appendix table A.1.)

For one activity—Social Security voting—I estimated a different model. The Social Security voting item is probably "contaminated" with other concerns; people make voting decisions on the basis of many issues, even when they say they voted with regard to Social Security. To "purge" Social Security voting of non–Social Security considerations, I estimated a model in which Social Security voting is a function of income with a control for the propensity to participate on non–Social Security topics (figure 3.5b; see appendix B for a description of this specification). This control for other issues allows us to focus on the portion of reported Social Security

a. Social Security Contacting

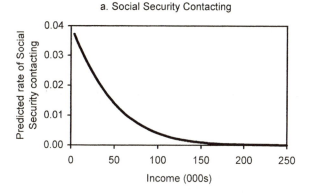

b. Social Security Voting "Purged" Results

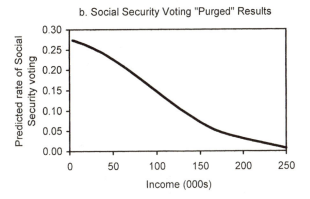

c. Social Security Contributing

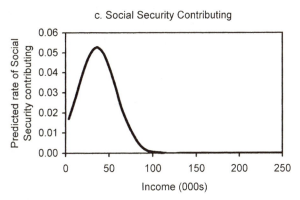

Figure 3.5 Predicted rate of Social Security–related participatory activity by income, seniors. (1990 Citizen Participation Study; full equations for Social Security contacting and contributing in appendix table A.2, for Social Security voting in appendix table B.1.)

voting that truly concerns Social Security. The purging procedure is not necessary for Social Security contacting: letters, unlike vote decisions, generally concern one topic, so contacting is a "purer" act. As for Social Security contributing, I did not have an expectation a priori about the level of non–Social Security contamination. It is conceivable that people make contributions with a single issue in mind. Or perhaps not. Empirically the regular and purged models yield similar results—by "regular," I mean Social Security contributing as a function of demographics and political interest, as in the Social Security contacting analysis. I show the regular results in figure 3.5.

For traditional political activities, participation among all respondents increases as income rises. Figures 3.4a–e show the likelihood by income, with controls for demographic characteristics and political interest, that respondents vote, contribute, work on campaigns, contact, and protest.[46] The income coefficients are positive, and in several cases are statistically significant. These figures reflect what decades of participation research has reported: participation in political activities is greater among higher-income individuals.

By contrast, participation concerning Social Security is greater among low-income individuals. Figure 3.5 shows the likelihood that senior citizens will participate specifically with regard to Social Security, again controlling for demographics and political interest. As expected, the negative income-participation relationship is most pronounced for Social Security contacting, the probability of which drops precipitously as income rises (figure 3.5a). The coefficient for income is negative, and the income and income-squared coefficients are jointly significant ($p < .001$).

Social Security voting also falls monotonically with income (figure 3.5b). In the purged model, the income coefficient is negative, and Social Security voting falls with income just as Social Security contacting does.[47]

We would not expect the relationship between income and Social Security contributing to be monotonically negative as with Social Security contacting. One needs disposable income to make a contribution—so low-income seniors are less likely to do so. But so are high-income seniors, who have less at stake with the program (figure 3.5c).

One more analysis demonstrates affluent seniors' smaller likelihood of participating with regard to Social Security. In the preceding analyses, the income and income-squared coefficients were jointly significant, but the income coefficients were not themselves significant given the relatively small number of Social Security recipients in the Citizen Participation Study. The Roper Social and Political Trends dataset contains many more respondents. No questions about Social Security–oriented participation were asked, but I can perform a purging analysis on the regular congressional-contacting item to isolate the Social Security portion of letter writing (see appendix B).

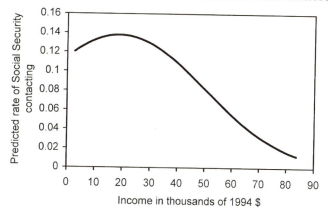

Figure 3.6 Predicted rate of Social Security contacting among seniors, "purged" Roper results. (Roper Social and Political Trends Archive, pooled 1973–94 data; full equation in appendix table B.2.)

Just as in the Social Security voting analysis, I estimate senior contacting as a function of income and of the propensity to participate in general; this approximates seniors' propensity to contact regarding Social Security (since I control for the tendency to participate on other issues). Although the resulting income coefficient is positive, the income-squared coefficient is large and negative, and so Social Security–oriented contacting among senior citizens falls at higher income levels (figure 3.6). With the large number of cases afforded by the Roper dataset, both the income and the income-squared coefficients are individually statistically significant.

Issue-specific engagement begins to address the puzzle of high senior participation. Although seniors do not have exceptionally high levels of general political engagement, they are quite attentive to news of Social Security. This issue interest heightens the participation of all seniors above what it would be if the program did not exist. And low-income seniors, who are more dependent on Social Security, participate at higher rates vis-à-vis the program than affluent seniors, the opposite of the usual income-participation relationship. That the more dependent are more politically active is significant in two regards. First, researchers looking for self-interest effects are usually disappointed,[48] but here is an instance that fits the particular conditions under which self-interest—the pursuit of immediate material benefits—is more likely to be a potent influence: the stakes are high and clear, and self-interest is manifested in political behavior rather than in attitudes. Second, Social Security both raises and democratizes senior participation; compared with that of the rest of the population, senior citizens' political participation is less unequal because of low-income seniors' great activity with regard to Social Security.

TABLE 3.6
Activity Mobilization by Age

	18–34	35–49	50–64	65+	Difference of Means Test 35–49 vs. 65+
% Asked to					
Work/contribute	23%	37%	41%	38%	
Contact	22	37	28	29	*
Protest	13	13	9	5	* * *
Community activity	18	23	17	13	* * *

$*p < .05; **p < .01; ***p < .001.$
Source: Citizen Participation Study.

MOBILIZATION

In addition to resources and political engagement, mobilization is an important factor in participation; one is more likely to perform political activities if asked to do so.[49] And another reason behind political inequality is that recruitment and contact with others in politically relevant settings are unevenly distributed across the citizenry.[50] Mobilization techniques like direct mail and door-to-door canvassing tend to be focused toward high-status individuals or neighborhoods.[51] Membership in voluntary organizations, in which much mobilization takes place, is also concentrated among the affluent.[52] But again, seniors are an exception: despite their low education and income levels, they too enjoy a high level of mobilization.

Questions in the Citizen Participation Study ask whether respondents personally received any request to perform campaign work and/or make contributions, contact, protest, or engage in community activity (serve on a board, attend board meetings, or engage in informal activity).[53] Seniors were recruited to work and/or contribute at a high rate—38 percent—exceeded only by 50- to 64-year-olds at 41 percent (table 3.6). Somewhat fewer seniors were asked to contact elected officials—29 percent—but at 37 percent only 35- to 49-year-olds were asked more often. Seniors were less likely to be asked to take an active role in their community: 13 percent versus 23 percent of 35- to 49-year-olds. In recruitment to protest seniors fell significantly behind younger age groups. While 13 percent of 35- to 49-year-olds were asked to participate in a protest, only 5 percent of seniors were asked. This is not surprising to the extent that protest is a physically taxing political activity more available to the

TABLE 3.7
Mobilization in Institutions by Age

	18–34	35–49	50–64	65+	Difference of Means Test 35–49 vs. 65+
% Asked to vote					
On the job	9%	10%	7%	0%	***
In church/synagogue	15	15	10	6	***
In a nonpolitical organization	13	17	16	9	***
% Asked to take other action					
On the job	16	23	13	8	***
In church/synagogue	30	36	30	19	***
In a nonpolitical organization	26	28	28	18	**

$*p < .05; **p < .01; ***p < .001.$
Source: Citizen Participation Study.

young.[54] Thus relatively few seniors are recruited to community work and protest, but large proportions are mobilized to campaign work, contributing, and contacting.

A separate set of questions in the same study explores where respondents are recruited, asking whether they were asked to vote or to take other political action within the institutional settings of the workplace, voluntary organizations, or religious organizations.[55] The rate at which seniors are mobilized within these institutions is surprisingly low. None of the seniors in the sample who were working was asked to vote on the job (table 3.7). Only 8 percent were asked to take other political action, far fewer than the 23 percent of 35- to 49-year-olds who were asked to do so. Even in church and voluntary organizations senior mobilization rates are fairly low. Only 6 percent of seniors were asked to vote in church and 9 percent in voluntary organizations, compared with 15 percent and 17 percent for 35- to 49-year-olds. Seniors were also asked to take other political action in these settings at lower rates than nonseniors.

Seniors report being recruited to perform various political acts at high rates, but few are recruited on the job, in church, or in voluntary organizations. Just where seniors are being recruited is a puzzle. One possible

TABLE 3.8
Mobilization by Political Parties by Age, 1996

	18–34	35–49	50–64	65+	Difference of Means Test 35–49 vs. 65+
Total	19%	29%	32%	38%	*
By income quartile					
Fourth (lowest)	11%	17%	33%	31%	*
Third	15	23	28	41	*
Second	24	36	28	31	
First (highest)	23	39	39	51	*
Incomes in each quartile by age group					
Fourth (lowest)	< $15K	< $25K	< $20K	< $11K	
Third	$15K– 29.9K	$25K– 44.9K	$20K– 34.9K	$11K– 16.9K	
Second	$30K– 49.9K	$45K– 74.9K	$35K– 59.9K	$17K– 29.9K	
First (highest)	$50K+	$75K+	$60K+	$30K+	

*p < .05; **p < .01; ***p < .001.
Source: National Election Study, 1996.

answer is presented by NES data (table 3.8). In 1996 more seniors were contacted by someone from a political party than any other age group: 38 percent.[56] That the political parties are a chief source of senior recruitment makes sense since the activities seniors are recruited to most heavily are campaign work and contributions, exactly the kind of appeals political parties would make.[57]

The rates of party mobilization by income quartile are particularly striking. I calculated income quartiles within age groups, to take into account differences in income levels. Party mobilization of seniors runs very deep. In the lowest-income quartile, 31 percent of seniors were contacted by someone from a political party, compared with 17 percent of 35- to 49-year-olds, as shown in table 3.8. Similarly, 41 percent of seniors in the next lowest, or third, income quartile were mobilized compared with 23 percent of 35- to 49-year-olds. The political parties make extensive efforts to reach out to seniors even in the bottom-income quartiles, despite the fact that senior incomes are so low—the third quartile, for example, run-

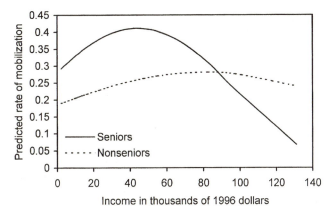

Figure 3.7 Predicted rate of party mobilization by income, seniors versus nonseniors. (1996 National Election Study.)

ning from $11,000 to $17,000 for seniors compared with $25,000 to $45,000 for 35- to 49-year-olds, more than twice as high.

Figure 3.7 further demonstrates how the pattern of party mobilization by age varies. The figure shows the likelihood of being contacted by someone from a political party at each income level, after controls for demographic characteristics and political interest. Nonseniors exhibit the customary pattern; the probability of being mobilized by a political party increases with income. From the party's perspective, this focus on higher-income people makes sense; they are more likely to vote, to make contributions, to work on campaigns, and to try to influence the votes of others. The pattern is different for senior citizens. Just as Social Security–oriented interest and participation decreased at higher-income levels, so does party mobilization. Concentrating party mobilization efforts on lower- and middle-income seniors is a reasonable strategy for two reasons: high-income seniors participate at very high rates already (outside of Social Security), so mobilizing them is an inefficient use of party resources; and low- and moderate-income seniors can reasonably be expected to participate, especially with a little party prodding, so mobilizing them is a productive activity.

The concentration of party mobilization efforts on lower- and middle-income seniors is yet another reason these groups participate at rates higher than one might predict from their socioeconomic status. In their study of participation and mobilization, Rosenstone and Hansen find that, "In the American participatory system, class differences in mobilization typically aggravate rather than mitigate the effects of class differences in political resources."[58] Once again, seniors are different: party mobilization efforts are directed toward low-resource seniors, a strategy that works against the usual gradients we see in participation.

This examination of the unusual operation of resources, engagement, and mobilization for seniors begins to explain the puzzles at the beginning of the chapter. Harry Smith may have lower resource levels than Martha Malone, but he has *enough* education and income to participate at a high rate. And his keen interest in Social Security also helps overcome potential resource limitations. Harry's stake in public affairs is much more immediate and tangible than his son's, for example. When asked how government affects his life, Charles responds, "Well, every government decision affects you one way or another—taxes, security—but it's not enough to get me involved." His comments are echoed by Kelly Lambert, another college-educated but politically inactive twenty-something: "I got some tax breaks for being a college student," she says, but "you never think of things like that, you know. I'm not involved in any income assistance or anything. I just make my salary and pay my taxes and go on my way. Government just doesn't affect me that much."[59] By comparison, the relevance of government policy couldn't be clearer to someone like Harry. That Harry and Martha are regularly contacted by the political parties during elections—while Charles and Kelly are not—reinforces these patterns.

THE FACTORS BEHIND SENIOR CITIZEN PARTICIPATION: MULTIVARIATE MODELS

In seeking to explain the political participation of senior citizens, I have described seniors' levels of three participatory factors—resources, political engagement, and mobilization—and their special characteristics vis-à-vis senior citizens. In preparation for the longitudinal analysis in the next chapter, it is necessary to assess these factors together in multivariate models, examining the individual-level causal mechanisms behind seniors' participation. If we know what factors drive senior participation, we can begin to understand why senior participation rose over time. We would expect Verba, Schlozman, and Brady's Civic Voluntarism Model to work for both nonseniors and seniors. That is, we anticipate that when it comes to general participation, seniors with more resources, engagement, and mobilization are more likely to participate than those with less (the important exception, as previously noted, is that senior participation specifically regarding Social Security decreases with income). If the previous sections helped explain why Harry almost participates on a par with Martha, and why they as senior citizens participate more than young Charles and Kelly, this analysis shows why Martha, with her greater resources, participates more than Harry.

Table 3.9 summarizes the factors significant in explaining senior participation across three datasets, Roper Survey 8108, the 1992 and 1996 NES studies (combined to get a sufficient number of seniors), and the 1990 Citizen Participation Study data. The full logistic regression results are in appendix tables A.3, A.4, and A.5. The results for nonseniors also appear there and form the basis of the senior-nonsenior comparisons that follow.

The Civic Voluntarism Model works for seniors as well as for nonseniors. The Citizen Participation Study results show that as with younger respondents, seniors with more education, income, political interest, and those who are mobilized to participate are more likely to vote than seniors with less of those factors. Income, civic skills, and mobilization requests are important factors influencing whether respondents—of all ages—make campaign contributions.[60] Both seniors and nonseniors with more civic skills, political interest, and mobilization requests are more likely to contact elected officials (as are seniors with *less* income; the income coefficient is negative in the Citizen Participation Study data because much contacting is about Social Security). Finally, campaign work is more likely among seniors and nonseniors with more civic skills, political interest, and mobilization requests.

With the 1992 and 1996 NES, again education, income, political interest, and mobilization (here, mobilization by the political parties) figure importantly in explaining senior and nonsenior participation.

The results from the Roper data show that specific interest in news of Social Security influences senior participation. While general political interest predicts contacting and petition signing by nonseniors, it is specific interest in Social Security that predicts contacting and petition signing by seniors. As in the 1992 and 1996 NES findings, none of the available variables is significant in explaining which seniors work on campaigns.

Hence senior participation is driven by education, income, mobilization, and political interest—both general and Social Security specific. Except for education, Social Security influences each of these factors, as indicated by the boldface type in table 3.9. To preface the next chapter's argument, over time Social Security's development fed levels of these participatory factors and therefore enhanced seniors' participation.[61]

SUMMARY

Senior citizens in the United States participate at very high rates, especially considering their relatively low levels of education and income. Although senior participation seems to present a challenge to traditional models of participation, a closer look at the mechanisms behind participation—

TABLE 3.9
Summary: Factors in Senior Participation

Source/Activity	Resources	Engagement	Mobilization	Other
CitPart 1990				
Voting	Educ. Income Working (−)	**Pol. interest** —	**Mobilization**	
Contributing	Income Retired Skills	—	**Mobilization**	Male (−)
Campaign Work	Skills	**Pol. interest** Pol. info	**Mobilization**	
Contacting	Educ. Income (−) Skills	**Pol. interest** —	**Mobilization**	Male Married
NES 92/96				
Voting	Educ. Retired	**Pol. interest** — Pol. info	**Mobilization**	Married
Contributing	Educ. Income	**Pol. interest** —	**Mobilization**	
Campaign Work	—	—		
Roper 8108				
Contacting	Educ. Income Retired	**Soc. Sec. interest** —	—	
Campaign Work	Educ. Income Retired	—	—	
Petition Signing	Educ. Income Retired	**Soc. Sec. interest** —	—	

Source: Appendix tables A.3, A.4, and A.5.

Note: Cells contain factors statistically significant in explaining each kind of participation. Boldface indicates factors to which Social Security and Medicare have contributed over time. Blank cells indicate variables that are not statistically significant in explaining the participatory act. Minus signs indicate variables negatively related to the participatory act. Cells with dashes indicate variables unavailable in the dataset. CitPart–Citizen Participation Study; NES–National Election Study.

resources, engagement, and mobilization—begins to provide an explanation for high senior participation rates. Seniors' low resource levels are mitigated in several ways. Seniors have low incomes but also lower expenses on average than nonseniors. Because most seniors are no longer working, they have more free time. Even in terms of education seniors are not as disadvantaged as they may appear. To some extent, the civic values, political interest, political knowledge, and politically relevant skills imparted by formal education can be acquired through life experience and in other institutional settings.

When we turn to engagement and mobilization we begin to see in a compelling way why overall senior participation is so high. Levels of both engagement with Social Security and mobilization by political parties are higher for seniors than for nonseniors, and greater for lower-income than for upper-income seniors. Seniors receive almost half their income on average from Social Security.[62] Like some other special societal groups— farmers, government employees—seniors have a large stake in government action that contributes to their political participation.[63] Social Security is especially important to poorer seniors—the 40 percent who depend on Social Security for over four-fifths of their income—boosting their participation and working against the usually positive income-participation gradient. This unusual effect is most evident for Social Security contacting. It is through letter writing that those concerned about Social Security can most specifically communicate their problems and anxieties.

Lower-class mobilization to politics is the exception rather than the rule in the United States. In Europe, socialist parties and labor unions mobilize the working class, in some countries to levels of political activity rivaling those of the middle class.[64] But there is no significant working-class politics in the United States because turn-of-the-century labor unions, unlike their counterparts in Europe, failed to develop ties to a labor-based political party.[65] With weak working-class institutions—weak unions, no significant parties of the Left—low-income Americans are rarely mobilized to political activity.[66] This in part explains the pronounced class inequality in American participation. Churches mobilize lower-income people to some extent, but regarding moral issues—such as temperance in the past, abortion today—not economic issues. Social Security, by contrast, politicizes a low-income segment of the population and therefore helps reduce political inequality. From the perspective of democratic governance, this is the beneficial aspect of Social Security: it is responsible for the successful mobilization of at least one group of low-income people in the U.S.

The goals here are to discover which factors influence senior participation and to see whether welfare state programs for seniors, especially Social Security, have participatory effects. We have seen that senior participation is driven by several factors that Social Security influences: income, retirement, political interest, interest in Social Security, and mobilization. Ideally, we could examine whether Social Security has participatory effects by comparing a test group of senior Social Security recipients with a control group of senior nonrecipients. But such data do not exist, even in a quasi-experimental sense, because virtually all seniors today receive Social Security; there is no variation in the causal variable. There are, however, other sources of variation that help tease out Social Security's participatory effects. As we saw here, some seniors are more dependent on Social Security than others, and they are more likely to participate in relation to the program. The next chapter takes advantage of another source of variation, examining how seniors' participation has risen as their welfare state programs have developed and grown over time.

Chapter Four

SENIOR CITIZEN PARTICIPATION
AND POLICY OVER TIME

The NAMES by which groups are known have a way of changing, with increased tolerance, with political fashion, and with attempts to replace negative stereotypes with positive images. The handicapped become the disabled become the differently abled. Colored people become Negroes become blacks become African Americans. The old become the aged become the elderly become senior citizens. In many ways, this last term is the most accurate, for it captures the most profound aspect of seniors' changing social and political status. They are indeed senior *citizens*, fully incorporated into social and political citizenship. Through their age-related programs they have realized the social citizenship rights of security and welfare to a fuller degree than any other constituency in the United States. They have in turn parlayed their well-being into increased political participation. Their vigorous exercise of the franchise and other forms of political activity further protect their programs. This chapter chronicles the development of the senior constituency since Social Security's enactment, describing how participation and policy have spiraled upward, transforming "the old" into one of the preeminent groups in American politics.

The growth of Social Security over time has affected seniors as individuals and the political institutions surrounding them. As the real value of Social Security benefits increased over time and the program spread to more retirees, the level of both senior resources and senior political engagement increased. Senior interest in politics rose dramatically compared with that of nonseniors. The political parties reached out to seniors at ever higher rates, both because seniors became such a large proportion of the electorate and because the constituency was an important source of votes for both parties. Senior interest groups also grew as wealthier and more leisured seniors flocked to them for selective benefits. These associations in turn provided seniors with relevant policy news that helped spur their participation.

Social Security's direct and indirect effects on American political institutions were also pronounced. A large bureaucracy concerned with age-related policy grew up around seniors' welfare programs, pushing for policy expansions. And perhaps most important, lawmakers realized the political necessity of pleasing this large and electorally crucial group through enhanced benefits.

Over time, trends in these factors and subsequently in policy outputs spiraled up, as we saw in the participation-policy cycle illustrated in figure 1.1. *Cycle* is the most appropriate description, because the developing Social Security program was first a causal influence, enhancing seniors' participatory capacity, and later became an effect, or outcome, as the increased level and pattern of senior participation began to shape policy outputs. I first discuss Social Security's effects on individuals and institutions, and then detail the rise of the senior constituency historically, showing how the two-way relationship between participation and policy operated over time.

SOCIAL SECURITY'S EFFECTS ON INDIVIDUALS

Senior participation is influenced by education, income, political interest, and mobilization to activity. Except for education, each of these factors is affected by seniors' welfare state programs. In some instances the effects on individuals are direct: Social Security provides income, for example. In others, the effects are indirect: Social Security and Medicare created policy niches for interest groups to fill—such as selling medigap insurance to cover shortfalls in Medicare coverage—and as a by-product, the interest groups enhance seniors' interest in public affairs. Program growth has fueled an upward trend in seniors' participatory factors and hence in their political activity.

Resource and Engagement Effects

Cross-sectional data analysis reveals that wealthier seniors are more likely to vote and contribute and that retired seniors are more likely to vote, contribute, work on campaigns, and contact elected officials. Thus over time, as Social Security expansions increased senior incomes and enabled seniors to retire, senior participation grew.

Social Security also enhances senior participation through its effect on seniors' engagement with politics. We saw in chapter 3 that seniors who are more dependent on Social Security are more interested in news of the program and are more likely to take action regarding it. Similarly, we might expect that over time, as Social Security has become more important to seniors as a group—with coverage becoming universal and real benefits almost tripling—that senior interest in Social Security specifically and in politics in general would increase.

As mentioned in chapter 2, Social Security has accounted for an increasing share of senior incomes over time. Another measure of the growing

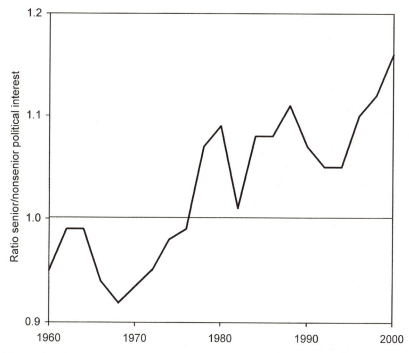

Figure 4.1 Senior/nonsenior political interest ratio, 1960–2000. Political interest ratio equals seniors' mean level of political interest (how closely they follow public affairs on a 1–4 scale) each year divided by the nonsenior level. (National Election Studies.)

importance of Social Security is the trend in replacement rates, in which new retirees' Social Security benefits are expressed as a percentage of their earnings in the year before retirement. Social Security provided one-fifth of the average worker's preretirement earnings in 1950, but over half in 1981.[1] Replacement rates have since fallen back to 43 percent for workers retiring in 1990, but are still more than twice the 1950 level.[2]

With Social Security's role in senior incomes rising over time, we would expect senior interest in the program to increase. Existing longitudinal datasets do not directly measure senior interest in Social Security, but do reveal changes in senior interest in politics generally. Beginning in 1960 the National Election Studies asked respondents how closely they follow public affairs. Figure 4.1 shows the mean level of interest expressed by seniors divided by that of nonseniors.[3] Compared with nonseniors, seniors have grown more interested in politics, overtaking younger people in 1978. With their incomes increasingly dependent on Social Security, elders have good reason to pay attention to public affairs.

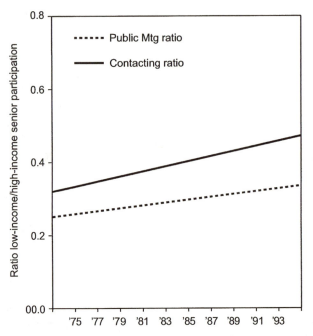

Figure 4.2 Activity ratios: Low- versus high-income seniors, 1973–94. Figure shows OLS regression lines fitted to data points, which are ratios calculated by dividing low-income-senior participation in public meetings and contacting by high-income-senior participation. See text. (Roper Social and Political Trends Archive.)

Variations among Seniors

We see how one part of the participation-policy cycle works: resources and political interest influence senior participation; as levels of those participatory factors have risen over time, fueled in part by the growth of Social Security, senior participation has risen. We would expect these Social Security effects to be most pronounced over time for low-income seniors. These are the individuals Social Security lifted out of poverty; these are the citizens most dependent on the program for income. Because their relative gain in politically relevant resources is greatest, their increases in participation over time should be the largest. Furthermore, this differential effect should be most pronounced for Social Security–related activity, where mobilization and engagement effects operate in addition to the resource effect that influences all senior participation. Thus there should be more convergence between low- and high-income seniors for Social Security–related acts than for other participatory acts.

Figure 4.3 Senior/nonsenior party mobilization ratio, 1956–2000. Party mobilization ratio equals senior mobilization rate each year divided by the nonsenior mobilization rate. (National Election Studies.)

No existing longitudinal surveys include participation items related to Social Security. But we can compare the congressional contacting question from the 1973–94 Roper dataset—which would include contacting regarding Social Security—and a question about attending public meetings on local or town affairs—which should include no Social Security element since it is a federal program. In the Roper data, I divided seniors into low-, medium-, and high-income groups for each year. Figure 4.2 shows the ratio of low-income senior participation to that of high-income seniors.[4] As we would expect, this ratio is below one. For both contacting and local meeting attendance, low-income seniors' participation increases relative to high-income seniors' over time (the two regression lines go up). But there is more convergence for contacting than for public meeting attendance (the contacting line goes up more). The difference is that just one effect—the resource effect—boosts public meeting attendance (and it is fairly mild; the effect would be greater if the Roper data extended back to the early 1950s, before Social Security was universal). For contacting, two or perhaps three effects are operating—resources, engagement, and possibly mobilization—enhancing low-income seniors' participation even more.

Political Parties and Mobilization

The growth of Social Security enhanced senior resources and interest in politics, increasing senior participation rates. Now we turn to another part of the participation-policy cycle, where seniors' growing political relevance is evident in changing party strategies. Although senior citizens are now the age group most likely to be mobilized by political parties, this was not always the case. In 1960 seniors were only two-thirds as likely to be mobilized as nonseniors. Starting in 1976 seniors reached parity, and have been more likely to be mobilized than nonseniors ever since (figure 4.3).[5] Another indication of seniors' increasing electoral importance is that *both* the Democratic and the Republican parties have increasingly mobilized them, exhibiting remarkably similar patterns in which seniors reach parity with and then exceed nonseniors in the 1970s (1976 for the GOP, 1978 for the Democratic Party; see appendix C for this figure). Not only are both parties reaching out to seniors, but in some cases the parties are reaching out to the same individuals. In 1996 individual seniors were on average twice as likely as nonseniors to be contacted by both the Democrats and Republicans. And again, the senior/nonsenior ratio has been increasing (see appendix C). The change in the ratio is caused both by an increase in senior mobilization by both parties and by a decrease in nonsenior mobilization. The parties became more fine tuned, more exacting in their mobilization of younger people (not "wasting" mobilization efforts by contacting partisans of the other party), while doing the opposite for seniors. The parties think seniors are too important a group to cede to the opposition.

Indeed the parties have played tug-of-war with the senior vote. The seniors of the 1950s belonged to a cohort socialized to politics during the Republican era of the early 20th century. Concomitantly they were more likely to be Republicans than were nonseniors (40 versus 33 percent) and less likely to be Democrats (50 versus 58 percent), according to the 1952 NES. Seniors were more likely to vote Republican for president until 1980, when the senior vote became more Democratic than the nonsenior vote (although the Democrats did not actually win seniors' two-party vote for president until 1992; see figure 4.4). Until 1994, congressional voting overall was more Democratic than presidential voting—hence the long period of Democratic control of the House—but here too seniors were less firmly in the Democratic camp than nonseniors before 1976. Then seniors voted Democratic like nonseniors until the 1990s, when younger people started voting Republican and seniors remained Democratic (figure 4.5). And as noted in chapter 2, seniors are now slightly more likely than nonseniors to identify with the Democratic Party.

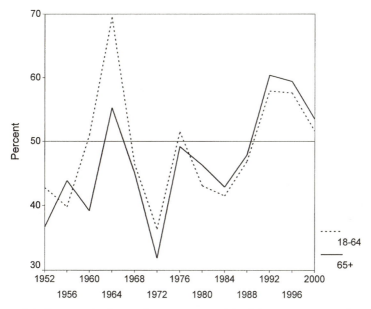

Figure 4.4 Democratic share of two-party presidential vote among seniors and nonseniors, 1952–2000. (National Election Studies.)

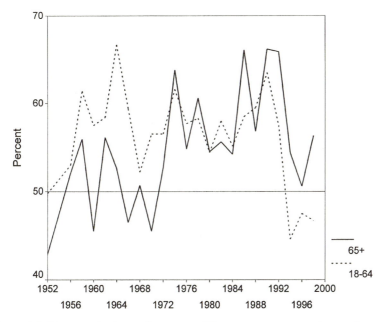

Figure 4.5 Democratic share of two-party House vote among seniors and nonseniors, 1952–2000. (National Election Studies.)

TABLE 4.1
Republican and Democratic Presidential Coalitions, 1952 and 1996

	1952		1996	
	Republican	Democratic	Republican	Democratic
Seniors	14%	11%	23%	26%
White females, aged 18–64	44	39	34	35
White males, aged 18–64	40	41	42	26
Black females, aged 18–64	1	4	0	9
Black males, aged 18–64	1	4	0	5

Source: National Election Studies, 1952 and 1996.
Note: Figures in cells represent the percentage of total presidential votes coming from each demographic group. In 1952 nonsenior voters were aged 21–64.

But the two parties continue to vie for the senior vote. Neither party can afford to dismiss the senior constituency, which now constitutes a quarter of the presidential coalition for both parties. Table 4.1 shows the percentage of total presidential vote each party received in 1952 and 1996 from seniors and four groups under 65: white women, white men, black women, and black men. In 1952 seniors were a smaller share of both parties' coalitions, and were slightly more important to the Republicans—they provided 14 percent of the votes for the Republican presidential candidate that year compared with 11 percent for the Democratic candidate. In 1952 white females provided somewhat more Republican votes than Democratic votes (44 versus 39 percent), white males provided the same proportion of votes to both parties (40 versus 41 percent), and blacks were more important to the Democratic coalition than to the Republican. By 1996 there is a considerable shift—white males maintain their share of Republican votes (42 percent) but fall to 26 percent of Democratic votes, while blacks provide 14 percent of Democratic votes and virtually no Republican votes. But two groups are very competitive, representing nearly equal shares of voters for both parties—white women and seniors. Seniors provide slightly more Democratic votes than Republican ones (26 versus 23 percent), but form a large proportion of the presidential coalitions of both parties. The parties work so hard to mobilize seniors because they are an electorally crucial group for Democrats and Republicans alike.

An analysis of party platforms over time also demonstrates the importance of senior citizens as a constituency. Figure 4.6 shows the percentage of platform space devoted to seniors and their programs by each party over time.[6] In 1932, prior to the passage of the Social Security Act, there was no mention of older Americans in either party's platform. Beginning

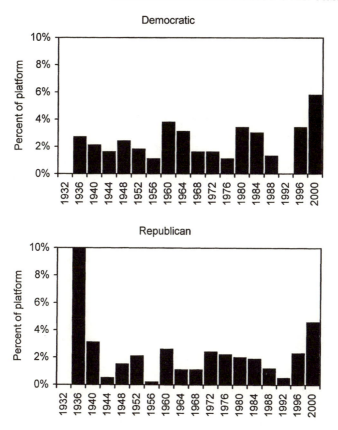

Figure 4.6 Party platform mentions of seniors and their programs, 1932–2000. Bars show the percentage of platform column inches devoted to seniors, Social Security and Medicare. (Author's calculations from Donald Bruce Johnson, *National Party Platforms* [Urbana: University of Illinois Press, 1978] and *CQ Almanac*, various years.)

in 1936 the platforms discuss senior citizens and their programs, the Republicans devoting 10 percent of their platform to Social Security. In the early years (1936–52) references to seniors and their programs were mostly contained in sections on "Social Security" or "Security."[7] In 1956 the Democrats included both a section on Social Security and a new section entitled "Additional Needs of Our Older Citizens." This marked the beginning of separate platform recognition of the senior constituency. From 1960 through 1984 both parties included separate sections on "Older Citizens," "The Elderly," or "Older Americans." Democratic mentions of seniors and their programs rose in the 1960 and 1964 elections and again in 1980 and 1984. Republican mentions picked up in

1960 and 1972. After relative inattention in 1992, both parties' mentions of seniors increased in 1996 and again in 2000, reaching modern peaks.

Another indication of party interest is the advent of constituency clubs for seniors. The first of these was the "Senior Citizens for Kennedy" project in 1960. During the 1950s senior citizens had voted Republican—an average of 55 percent in the 1948, 1952, and 1956 presidential elections—and trying to shift long-term partisan loyalties seemed futile.[8] But the new Medicare proposal and increasing attention to the problems of the elderly from within the Democratic-controlled Congress promised to give the Democrats some inroads with the senior constituency. The Democratic National Committee established the Senior Citizens for Kennedy club with two and a half months to go in the 1960 general election campaign. Chaired by Congressman Aime Forand (D-R.I.), a champion of senior legislation, the organization recruited volunteers, printed campaign material, made radio and television spots directed at senior concerns, publicized Kennedy appearances among elderly voters, and lobbied for senior interests within the party. While the Senior Citizens for Kennedy organization seems to have had limited short-term success—seniors were less supportive of the Democrats in 1960 than any other age group— it had powerful longer-term effects in educating party leaders about the concerns of seniors and their potential as an electoral constituency.[9] Since then both parties have had senior clubs or constituency desks at the national committee headquarters, although such efforts wax and wane over the years (in the early seventies the Republican National Committee had a senior desk and the Democratic National Committee did not; in 1999 the DNC had a senior desk while the RNC did not, and so on).

Political party attention to seniors is one of the elements of the participation-policy cycle that is both an effect and a cause. In making seniors program beneficiaries, Social Security defined them as a political group. Only with the advent of Social Security are there platform mentions of the program and, later, appeals to the senior constituency. Without Social Security, there is no senior constituency to appeal to, just an age group which, like its younger counterparts, is divided by other cleavages and interests. But with government benefits conferred on the basis of age, a political identity is forged.

Party attention to seniors is an outcome variable as well. Parties try to appeal to seniors because they vote at high rates. But one reason they vote at high rates is that they are mobilized by political parties during the election season. As the cross-sectional analysis of chapter 3 showed, seniors who are mobilized are more likely to vote and contribute. This is also true over time. Multivariate analysis of National Election Study data reveals that from 1952 to 1996, seniors who were contacted by someone

TABLE 4.2
Role of Party Mobilization in Senior Participation, Pooled 1952–96 Results

	Voting	*Contributing*	*Campaign Work*
Mobilization	Mobilization	Mobilization	Mobilization
Resources			
Education	Educ.	Educ.	Educ.
Income	Income	Income	
Engagement			
Political interest	Pol. int.	Pol. int.	Pol. int.
Other characteristics			
Male	Male		Male
Black			
Married	Married	Married	
Age			Age (−)

Source: National Election Studies, 1952–96.

Note: Cells show variables statistically significant in explaining participation among seniors; derived from logistic regression results in appendix table A.6. Variables followed by a negative sign (−) are negatively related to participation.

from a political party were more likely to vote, contribute, and work on campaigns (table 4.2).[10]

Senior Citizen Interest Groups

Like political parties, senior citizen interest groups are both effects and causes in the participation-policy cycle. A brief history will introduce the first phenomenon, interest group development as an outcome of Social Security.

The largest contemporary senior interest group, AARP, originated as the National Retired Teachers Association (NRTA), founded in 1947 by the California educator Dr. Ethel Percy Andrus. The NRTA offered its members life insurance, which was often difficult for older people to obtain. In 1958 the American Association of Retired Persons was founded to provide such benefits to older people of all occupations. The two organizations eventually merged and are now known collectively as AARP.[11] AARP is famously the largest voluntary group in the United States. From 50,000 members in 1959, the group has grown to 33 million (figure 4.7). Membership was opened to 50-year-olds in 1983, and as of 1999, 51 percent of AARP members were under 65. The organization has a large Washington-based staff of 1,200 as well as 3,600 state and local groups.

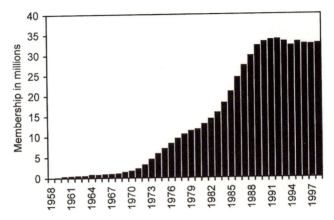

Figure 4.7 AARP membership, 1958–98. (AARP Membership Office.)

The National Council of Senior Citizens (NCSC) arose from the Democrats' Senior Citizens for Kennedy organization and the campaign for Medicare. It was founded in 1961 with the support of the AFL-CIO and the Democratic National Committee and has retained a blue-collar membership and liberal Democratic flavor (in contrast to the nonpartisan, mostly white-collar and professional AARP). The NCSC now has a membership of 500,000 and a staff of 120 in its Washington office.

There are numerous other aging interest groups. One of the largest is the Gray Panthers, founded in 1970 by Maggie Kuhn, which has a more radical orientation and concentrates on grassroots mobilization and protest rather than on lobbying. By 1990, it had 40,000 members, sixty local groups, and a headquarters staff of four. The National Committee to Preserve Social Security and Medicare was founded in 1982 and had its heyday in the 1980s, during the Reagan retrenchment efforts and the Medicare Catastrophic Coverage Act episode (see chapter 5). There are yet other, generally smaller groups as well.

These contemporary mass membership groups did not exist when Social Security was enacted in 1935 and therefore were not forces in its development. There were some early organizations, like the Townsend movement and the Ham and Eggers, that advocated old-age pensions in the years before Social Security's enactment. Dr. Francis Townsend of Long Beach, California, outlined a plan in 1933 to give each American aged 60 and over a pension of $200 per month to be spent within 30 days, a huge amount of money when per capita personal income was $625 per year.[12] The pension was to be funded by a national sales tax, with the mandated spending intended to boost the economy. Similarly, the Ham and Egg movement advocated "Thirty dollars every Thursday" for unemployed people aged 50 and over.[13] Although some assert that these early groups, especially the Townsend movement, contributed to the passage of Social Security by publicizing the conditions of the elderly,[14] most scholars agree that the mass elderly organizations at the time had relatively little influence.[15] Their leaders and plans lacked credibility—the Townsend Plan would have cost $66 billion per year when the gross national product was $90 billion[16]—and the timing of events shows that the Townsend movement was not decisive. The Townsend Clubs were just beginning to form when President Roosevelt established the Committee on Economic Security and delivered his June 1934 speech calling for a social security program.[17] More important were other forces like worsening economic conditions for seniors during the Depression, the apparent inadequacy of private sector efforts to relieve senior misery, the need to reduce the number of individuals looking for work, and the desire of some segments of the business community to replace older workers with healthier, younger ones.[18] And of course the idea of old-age pensions had been in the "policy primeval soup" for some time, encouraged by the example of state pension plans and the already decades-old pension plans of Western Europe.[19]

Senior mass membership groups did not create Social Security policy. Rather, the policy helped create the groups.[20] Social Security's effects on individuals—the increases in income, free time due to retirement, and political interest—enhance the likelihood of group membership. Social Security created a constituency for interest group entrepreneurs to organize, just as it defined a group for political parties to mobilize. And policy gaps that the welfare state programs inevitably left provided a raison d'être for senior interest groups: lobbying for new proposals and offering products and services to address benefit shortfalls. Indeed, contemporary senior interest groups learned from the mistakes of their predecessors. Early social insurance organizations like the American Association for Old Age Security (AAOAS) and the American Association for Labor Legislation (AALL), which campaigned for old-age pensions in the 1920s, were unable to sustain themselves after the passage of the 1935 Social Security Act. This was due in part to the broader political environment that turned to other pressing issues, but also to the groups' failure to reformulate themselves once the goal of Social Security had been attained. Later groups learned to avoid this inflexibility, expanding the list of issues they were interested in as legislative victories were achieved (NCSC) and developing broad arrays of selective incentives to recruit and retain members (AARP).[21] Program shortcomings—like Medicare's lack of prescription drug coverage—gave the interest groups as policy entrepreneurs something for which to lobby. Gaps in Social Security and later Medicare coverage created needs that groups could fill: supplemental medigap insurance (one of AARP's main sources of revenue),[22] mail-order prescription drug programs, and so on. More directly, government agencies created to implement policy can act as interest group patrons, awarding contracts, for example, that provide a stable source of funding. In 1994 AARP received $86 million in federal grants to run job-training programs for seniors—18 percent of its operating revenue.[23]

In these ways senior interest groups are an outcome in the participation-policy cycle; their growth was made possible by senior welfare state programs. They also operate as a cause, influencing their mass memberships and lawmakers. They enhance their members' political knowledge and interest and mobilize them to political activity. They also directly influence the policymaking process through lobbying activities in Washington.

The Citizen Participation Study identifies AARP members, enabling us to see whether membership in the group influences participation, at least in cross-sectional data. When demographic characteristics and political interest are controlled for, AARP members are more likely than nonmembers to contact elected officials and to contact them about Social Security specifically (see appendix table A.7 for logistic regression results). AARP membership approaches traditional levels of statistical significance as an influence on voting, but does not have a significant effect on contributing, working on campaigns, voting with regard to Social Security, or giving money with regard to the program. At the bivariate level, AARP members are more likely to perform these political acts, but when one controls for the fact that AARP members are more affluent, educated, male, and white, AARP membership exerts no independent effect except in contacting and specific Social Security contacting as noted.

That AARP membership is a significant influence on contacting and Social Security contacting allows us to speculate about the mechanism by which membership influences participation. Unfortunately with existing data we cannot test directly whether AARP members are more likely to contact elected officials because they are more interested in politics or because they were mobilized to do so; there are no questions in the Citizen Participation Study asking respondents whether they were mobilized by AARP or how interested they are in Social Security (the Roper survey appearing in table 3.5 asked about Social Security interest but not about AARP membership). We might speculate, however, that AARP membership influences participation more through mobilization than through interest or information effects. Social Security is a dominant, front-page issue in which senior citizen interest and knowledge are high, so AARP membership may add little. But the fact that AARP membership has a significant influence on contacting suggests that mobilization is at work, since contacting elected officials is precisely the type of mobilization in which AARP engages.[24]

We cannot explicitly look at the influence of AARP on individuals over time, because no longitudinal participation dataset contains AARP membership questions. But again we can speculate that these effects grew as the group turned from service to political activism in the late 1970s and 1980s (AARP/Vote, the grassroots political education and outreach arm, was established in 1985, for example).

A second way senior interest groups influence the policy process is through their Washington activities. AARP in particular has a large lobbying division. The organization provides technical information to congressional staffs and committees and lobbies individual members on important bills. AARP is frequently cited in works on lobbying because of its size and perceived effectiveness.[25] The group's size can be a liability; at times internal cleavages have surfaced and hurt the group's claim to represent all seniors (especially with the Medicare Catastrophic Coverage Act, which AARP endorsed but which many members opposed; see chapter 5). But certainly AARP remains an important and influential lobbying group.

SOCIAL SECURITY'S EFFECTS ON INSTITUTIONS

The development of Social Security has had effects on individual recipients, and in turn on political party strategy and on senior interest group growth. Social Security also created a bureaucracy and an age-related policy network that have proved important advocates of senior interests, especially in the early years before seniors had the participatory capacity to act on their own behalf.

The Bureaucracy and the "Aging Enterprise"

The passage of Social Security necessitated the creation of an agency, the Social Security Administration (SSA), to administer the program.[26] The agency has long enjoyed a reputation as efficient and client friendly.[27] Administrative costs totaled just 0.8 percent of Social Security benefits payments in 1996.[28] Among the SSA's 66,000 employees are economists, demographers, sociologists, and gerontologists with an interest in aging policy. As will be discussed later in this chapter, SSA advocacy was crucial to the expansion of Social Security in the 1950s: the agency was largely responsible for making the program universal back when recipients lacked the political clout to secure expansions themselves.

Another important executive branch agency is the Administration on Aging (AoA), which is located within the Department of Health and Human Services. The AoA was established in 1965 as part of the Older

Americans Act, largely through congressional initiative. Although its funding has always been modest, the AoA has served as a valuable coordinator of federal-state efforts and, perhaps more important, as a focal point for senior interest groups, professionals, providers, and others with an interest in age-related policy. The AoA must be reauthorized periodically, and these hearings provide regular opportunities to direct public and lawmaker attention to age-related policy issues.[29]

The AoA not only serves this important policy function, but also has direct effects on individual senior citizens. It started as a tiny agency, with $6 million in funding. At the 1971 White House Conference on Aging, the AoA's small budget was criticized, and Congress took steps to enlarge its role. The next year Congress expanded senior nutrition programs and placed them under AoA control, which greatly increased the agency's size and visibility to policymakers and the public. In 1973 Congress established the Area Administrations on Aging (later Area Agencies on Aging), local units under the AoA that administer the nutrition programs and other projects.[30] Across the nation these senior centers serve as places for otherwise isolated elderly to congregate. And while the programs administered by the AoA are not means tested, they tend to attract lower-income seniors. There they hear political discussion and policy news, with significant effects on their attitudes and political behaviors. One study from the 1960s found that while seniors active in old-age social welfare clubs in Minneapolis–St. Paul were demographically similar to nonmembers, the club members were more likely to talk about health and medical care (25 percent versus 2 percent) and other problems of old age (16 versus 5 percent), were more likely to believe that "older people ought to organize to demand their rights" (68 versus 39 percent), and were more likely to believe that older people ought to be more active in politics (74 versus 48 percent).[31] Seniors are unusual in that unlike younger age groups, both high- and low-income members of the group have sources of information and mobilization. This helps explain why differences in participation by income are smaller for seniors than for nonseniors.

Beyond the Social Security Administration and the Administration on Aging, there are other extensive networks of policy professionals in the age-related field. Government programs besides Social Security and Medicare, such as Medicaid, Supplemental Security Income (SSI), food stamps, and veterans' benefits, have large numbers of senior citizen beneficiaries, adding to the community of professionals and providers with an interest in aging policy. In addition to the senior mass membership groups there are professional groups like the National Council on the Aging (NCOA, founded 1950), National Association of State Units on Aging (NASUA, founded 1964), and the National Association of Area Agencies on Aging

(NAAAA, founded 1975), which also lobby Congress and provide technical information to lawmakers.

Congress

In the participation-policy cycle the mass public, aging interest groups, and age-related bureaucracy all influence congressional activity and decision making on age-related policy.

The vote is a legislator's most basic need. One does not have to believe that members of Congress are single-minded seekers of reelection to accept that reelection is their dominant goal, without which other goals like achieving institutional power and making good policy would be impossible.[32] Increasingly, seniors are the constituents lawmakers want to please. They are a large presence in most congressional districts and states. Because their distinguishing characteristics are physical, they are easily identifiable, and of course age is a variable recorded by the U.S. Census. Indeed, the percentage of the population aged 65 and over is one of the characteristics of congressional districts noted in the *Almanac of American Politics*. In an average congressional district there are 445,000 people of voting age. During midterm elections, turnout runs around 35 percent; a 55 percent winner therefore receives 85,660 votes. The average number of seniors per congressional district is 78,000. Of course not all of those seniors vote. But because senior turnout is higher than nonsenior turnout, and because the gap is particularly large in midterm elections, members of Congress have great incentive to appeal to their senior constituents. Members have to consider both their geographic and their reelection constituencies; seniors are particularly important in the latter.[33]

Members who wish to maximize their reelection chances will attempt to please these constituents, to vote in ways congruent with their wishes. R. Douglas Arnold says that members "choose among policy proposals by estimating citizens' potential policy preferences."[34] Knowledge of senior preferences on Social Security and Medicare is easy to acquire. Common sense tells one that seniors are dependent on and wish to defend these programs.[35] Casework requests also help members figure out which issues are important to seniors and where their preferences lie. Data from both members of Congress and the public reveal that seniors make a large contribution to the congressional mailbag. In interviews, House members say that the most common subject of casework requests is Social Security and pension claims.[36] Similarly, analysis of 1978 and 1980 NES data shows that age is the only statistically significant factor in generating casework requests.[37]

Interest groups are also a source of the political considerations that lawmakers take into account. Group officials profess to speak for their members when they lobby Congress. These organizations influence congressmen's political calculus in other ways as well. The National Council of Senior Citizens lists proponents and foes of major age-related policy proposals in its newsletter, issues legislative scorecards, and endorses candidates for office. AARP, which tries to maintain a nonpartisan stance, does not rate members or endorse candidates, but like the NCSC and other mass membership groups, writes about legislative action in its publications. Members of Congress crave favorable mentions—*Modern Maturity*, the bimonthly AARP magazine, is the largest circulation magazine in the country. On average there are just over 75,000 AARP members in each congressional district, half of whom are 65 and over.

Congressional attention to senior issues is generated through contacts with the mass public and interest groups. Concern for aging policy may rise from within Congress as well. Over the years important individual champions of aging policy have included Senators Patrick McNamara (D-Mich.), Frank Church (D-Idaho), and David Pryor (D-Ark.) and Representatives Aime Forand (D-R.I.) and Claude Pepper (D-Fla.). Although age-related policy forums were institutionalized with the establishment of special committees on aging in the Senate in 1961 and in the House in 1974, many other members are also directly involved in senior legislation. Aging policy is fragmented across many programs; in 1978, forty-nine committees and subcommittees had jurisdiction.[38] Personal experience also matters. An advantage seniors have over many constituencies is that each of us is a current or future member of the group. One reason that both political parties put forward proposals to help with the cost of long-term care for the elderly and disabled in 1999 is that members of Congress themselves are trying to figure out what to do about aging parents.[39]

As the participation-policy cycle shifts to Congress, we see the influence of senior participation and interest group lobbying on policy outputs. Seniors constitute an "attentive public"; they know when a specific issue is on the congressional agenda, and they have strong preferences about what Congress should do.[40] Members of Congress are keenly aware of this and try to capitalize on it: of all casework requests, those from seniors are most likely to generate legislative proposals.[41]

THE PARTICIPATION-POLICY CYCLE OVER TIME

I have discussed the function of each part of the participation-policy cycle—Social Security, senior participation, political parties, senior interest groups, the age-related policy bureaucracy, and Congress. Now I turn to the operation of the cycle over time, showing its upward spiral since the first benefits were paid in 1940.

Early Political Struggles, 1935–1949

In its early years, Social Security was not a broad-based program with significant effects on recipient political participation.[42] Indeed, the program struggled politically at first until controversies over its basic principles and "financial philosophy" were resolved.[43] The initial story is one of elite politics—the mass politics of Social Security emerges later and is a consequence of the program expansions set in place during the 1935–49 period.

The 1939 amendments to the Social Security Act accelerated the first payments from 1942 to 1940 and added a benefit for widows and children of covered workers who died before retirement age; the program was renamed Old-Age and Survivors' Insurance (OASI). But the 1939 amendments also jeopardized two characteristics of Social Security that differentiated it from public assistance. Franklin D. Roosevelt and Secretary of the Treasury Henry Morgenthau had originally insisted on a "self-supporting" system that would build a large reserve fund in its early years to supplement later tax revenues (in 1980, for example, the founders projected that a combined tax rate of 6 percent for employer and worker would fund 60 percent of benefits, the reserve the other 40 percent).[44] But Keynesian economists warned that accumulating a surplus could diminish consumer spending power, and fiscal conservatives feared Congress would be unable to resist the temptation to spend the surplus on other projects. Thus in the 1939 legislation Congress both abandoned the accumulation of large reserves and authorized the use of general revenues to pay for a portion of benefits, diminishing the insurance design of the program. That design was further undermined during the 1940s, when the House Ways and Means Committee and the Senate Finance Committee— the tax-writing committees with jurisdiction over Social Security—repeatedly chose to freeze the payroll tax rate at the initial 2 percent, further reducing the surplus and increasing the likelihood that general revenues would be needed.

Not only did Social Security's basic principles and financing remain unsettled. As of the late 1940s, many categories of workers were still excluded from Old Age Insurance and had to apply for Old Age Assistance instead, and benefits for those who did qualify for insurance were quite low. In 1949 the federal government spent three times as much on welfare as on insurance, and the average OAA payment was 70 percent greater than the average insurance benefit.[45]

The Social Security Administration joined forces with fiscal conservatives in Congress, led by Wilbur Mills of the House Ways and Means Committee, to stabilize the tax system and establish the primacy of insurance over public assistance. The resulting 1950 Social Security amendments built up OASI by broadening coverage and raising benefits. The amendments also barred the use of general revenues. Bringing more people into the insurance program reduced the welfare portion. And the new benefits were paid out immediately to beneficiaries who had not yet contributed fully, reducing the trust fund surplus, which pleased the fiscal conservatives. On the one hand, "The 1950 Amendments really saved the concept of contributory social insurance," as former Social Security commissioner Robert Ball noted.[46] On the other hand, the legislation put Social Security on a pay-as-you-go rather than a fully funded basis, with current taxes funding current benefits, a structural change that would have significant fiscal and political implications down the road.

Program Expansion, 1950–1959

The 1950 amendments mark the real beginning of the participation-policy cycle. Although the policy controversies leading up to their enactment were fought out in an elite arena, the program expansions of 1950—and those that followed in 1952, 1954, and 1956—set the stage for a mass politics of Social Security in subsequent decades.

During the 1950s senior citizens themselves participated in politics at relatively low rates. In the presidential elections of 1952, seniors were about as likely to vote as nonseniors and just two-thirds as likely to make campaign contributions. Because the Social Security program was still so limited in coverage and benefit levels, it did not have the kind of influence on senior participation that it did later. Nor were there large senior membership groups with access to the policymaking process. Indeed, Henry Pratt in his study of the "gray lobby" termed the 1940s and 1950s "the dismal years," when the membership organizations of the 1930s were no longer active and the organizations important in later periods had not yet been founded.[47]

The relative inattention to senior members of the mass public is evident in party platform and congressional hearings data. The party platforms of this period typically contained a paragraph on Social Security but no special section on senior citizens. Little space was devoted to senior issues compared with later periods. Similarly a relatively small number of congressional hearings on age-related policy issues were held during this period (see figure 4.8 below); the Senate and House select committees on aging had not yet been founded.

Despite the fact that neither seniors themselves nor senior interest groups were much of a political force during this period, Social Security developed in crucial ways. Social Security Administration advocacy continued even after the 1950 amendments. Many supporters feared that

Social Security increases would be halted under a Republican administration. But the political appointees at the top of the SSA, who were supposed to constrain the career program executives, were instead dependent upon them for information and proposals and gave them great latitude in communicating with members of Congress. The "technical assistance" the program executives gave was not neutral but expansionist, and Congress willingly increased Social Security coverage and benefits.[48] There was a sense that seniors were still a needy group deserving of government help. And a strong economy meant that gradual coverage expansions were possible without sharply increasing payroll taxes; OASDI tax rates were 1 percent of the first $3,000 earnings in 1937, 3 percent of the first $3,000 in 1950, and 3 percent of the first $4,800 in 1960.[49] That Social Security is financed through trust funds, not out of general revenue, also reduced the visibility of expenditures and eased program growth.[50]

These expansions constituted the largest one-decade growth in Social Security coverage in program history. In 1950 only 16 percent of persons aged 65 and over received Social Security benefits. That increased to 60 percent by the end of the decade as the nonfarm self-employed were added in 1950; farmers, self-employed members of some professions, and farm and domestic employees in 1954; and self-employed persons except physicians, additional farm owners and operators, and certain state and local government employees in 1956. The retirement test was also liberalized, and the retirement age for widows and female parents was lowered to age 62 in 1956. Average monthly benefits increased from $278 in 1950 to $394 in 1960 (in 1996 dollars, as are all the benefit figures in this chapter), after increases of 12.5 percent, 13 percent, and 7 percent in 1952, 1954, and 1959. These early expansions of Social Security through SSA advocacy set the participation-policy cycle of figure 1.1 going.

Increasing Interest in Aging Issues, 1960–1970

During the 1960s senior citizens' economic and political gains continued. From 1960 to 1970 Social Security coverage increased from 60 percent to 82 percent, average benefits increased from $394 to $471, and the senior poverty rate fell from 35 percent to 25 percent. Seniors were about as likely as nonseniors to vote, but went from being two-thirds as likely as nonseniors to contribute to a campaign to being more likely to contribute by 1968.

After two decades of relative inattention, interest in senior citizens and age-related policy increased during the 1960s. The political parties began to recognize seniors as an important constituency, with the Senior Citizens for Kennedy group inaugurating a new attempt to reach out to the group.

The Democratic Party platform in particular greatly increased the amount of space devoted to senior concerns, from 155 words in 1952 to 632 words in 1964, and both parties began to refer to seniors as a constituency group.

During the 1960s, stable senior mass membership groups were established and, according to some scholars, began to exercise influence on policymaking. AARP largely stayed out of politics, focusing instead on increasing its membership through an array of selective incentives. The more partisan National Council of Senior Citizens helped fight for Medicare, although other actors like organized labor were more important in securing health care for seniors.[51] In contrast to the 1950s, when policy change was achieved on behalf of seniors, now seniors began to bring about change themselves. In 1958, when the Older Americans Act hearings first began, no senior interest groups testified. By 1963 the senior interest groups were present in force.[52]

Congress became increasingly aware of senior interests. Age-related policy not only appeared on the agenda more frequently and in more institutionalized forums, but also made some historic gains. In 1961 the Senate Special Committee on Aging was established, arising from hearings on nursing homes chaired by Patrick McNamara. In November 1961 a White House Conference on Aging was held, an idea that also originated in Congress, with Representative Forand.[53] In 1965 Congress passed Medicare, which vastly increased senior access to health care, and the Older Americans Act, which established the Administration on Aging.

The 1960s also witnessed growth in the age-related policy bureaucracy and professional interest groups. The National Association of State Units on Aging was established in the 1960s. By the late 1950s, about half the states had age-related policy commissions.[54] In an important shift, the National Council on the Aging, which in 1960 had pledged to stay out of politics, changed its mind in 1966 and began taking policy stances.

In the 1960s seniors became a more notable electoral presence. For the first time stable mass membership groups formed and began to have some influence in the policy process. The growth of senior welfare state programs brought an increase in aging policy professional groups, adding to senior presence in the interest group world. Although the major legislative battles of the decade—Medicare and Social Security benefit improvements—were still secured largely through the efforts of seniors' allies like organized labor and consumer groups rather than by seniors themselves,[55] the decade witnessed a growth in senior membership groups and a new institutionalization of policy forums like the Senate Special Committee on Aging and the Administration on Aging. Now senior policy would be reviewed regularly, not just when championed by individual members of Congress.

Seniors as a Political Force, 1971–1980

During the 1970s senior citizens truly emerged as a political force. Initially launched by Social Security expansion in the 1950s, the participation-policy cycle was in full swing. Social Security was expanded again in the 1970s, but this time the impetus was seniors' new political relevance and influence.

By 1970, 82 percent of seniors received Social Security and average monthly benefits were $471, increasing to 93 percent and $627 by 1980. In 1975 the average new retiree's Social Security benefit equaled 42 percent of his preretirement income, compared with just 20 percent in 1950, and the replacement rate continued to rise throughout the decade, to 54 percent in 1981.[56] The senior poverty rate, which was 35 percent in 1959, had fallen to 15 percent by 1975. The importance of Social Security to seniors' new prosperity is seen in their growing interest in public affairs; in 1978 seniors overtook nonseniors in their level of political interest.

During the 1970s the participatory effects of earlier Social Security expansions were felt. Seniors overtook nonseniors in working on campaigns in 1978, and in voting and contributing in 1980. With the participatory resources and interest in government activity that Social Security fosters, seniors became disproportionately active in politics.

The two major parties recognized seniors' political importance. During the 1970s seniors overtook nonseniors in the rate at which they were mobilized by the political parties. From 1976 through 1984, senior citizens received more attention in the party platforms than any other constituency group.

Senior interest groups became important political players. The 1971 White House Conference on Aging legitimized interest group participation in the policy process.[57] In congressional hearings leading up to the conference, which investigated criticisms of the Administration on Aging, twelve of the fifteen witnesses were from national senior interest groups (in contrast to the hearings prior to the 1961 White House conference at which no representatives from the senior interest groups spoke).[58] AARP forged informal ties with members of Congress, and a spokesperson from the organization boasted that the Nixon administration "wouldn't make a move on a major old-age issue without first consulting AARP."[59] The group increasingly turned its attention from service to political activism, achieving a major victory in 1978 with the abolition of mandatory retirement before age 70.

The 1971 White House conference not only increased the willingness of lawmakers to listen to AARP but also stimulated interest in aging issues among elderly members of the mass public. These influences, along with long-term growth in the factors that lead to interest group membership—

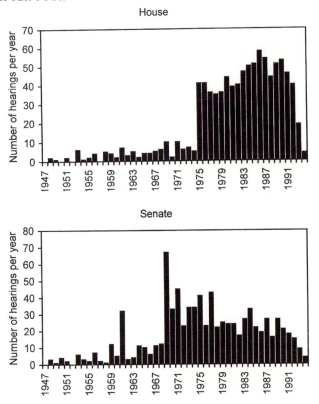

Figure 4.8 Congressional hearings on senior issues, 1947–94. Number of hearings per year on elderly issues and assistance programs, including Social Security (topic code 1303), Medicare and Medicaid (code 303), elderly health issues (code 311), elderly nutrition (code 1301), and elderly housing (code 1408). (Frank Baumgartner and Bryan Jones, U.S. Congressional Hearings Dataset, Policy Agendas Project, Center for American Politics and Public Policy, University of Washington.)

income and general political interest—spurred interest group membership growth. The NCSC grew from 100,000 to 250,000 members from 1971 to 1973.[60] AARP experienced its highest sustained growth rate from 1969 to 1973. The total number of aging interest groups increased as well.[61]

The developing political importance of senior citizens is perhaps most evident in the substantial Social Security benefit increases of the early 1970s, the largest in the program's history. The congressional committees in charge of Social Security, which had long emphasized fiscal responsibility in increasing the program, were overwhelmed by the program's popularity and seniors' growing electoral importance.[62] Benefits were boosted 15 percent in 1970, 10 percent in 1971, 20 percent in 1972, and 11 percent in 1974. The politics behind the unprecedented 20 percent increase in 1972 are particularly telling. Several presidential candidates engaged in a bidding war to claim credit for a generous increase in benefits. President Nixon proposed an increase of 5 percent in late 1971, which was bid up shortly before the New Hampshire primary to 15 percent by Maine senator Edmund Muskie and then to 20 percent by Ways and Means chairman Wilbur Mills, who was also a candidate. AARP opposed the 20 percent increase as inflationary, but the NCSC championed the increase and made a strategically shrewd move in securing Mills's support, with his reputation as both an authority on Social Security and a fiscal conservative.[63] Muskie met the 20 percent figure and then Senator Hubert Humphrey proposed 25 percent shortly after the New Hampshire primary. In July 1972 the House and Senate approved a 20 percent increase, which Nixon threatened to veto but ultimately signed in September. When the checks containing the 20 percent increase were mailed out on October 1, an accompanying note said that the increase was "enacted by the Congress and signed into law by President Richard Nixon."[64]

Seniors' growing political relevance was also manifested in the 1972 legislation to index Social Security benefits, commencing in 1975. Indexation, which led to the trust fund's fiscal crisis of the late 1970s and early 1980s, was supported by Republicans, who generally advocated fiscal restraint but who were tired of congressional Democrats claiming credit for Social Security benefit increases in election years.[65] Nine of the thirteen benefit increases enacted from 1950 to 1976 took place in election years, usually in the middle of the year shortly before election day rather than at the beginning of the year.[66] Any political advantage from indexing was short-lived, however: emergency legislation was required within two years to shore up the OASI trust fund. And indexation imposed a fiscal commitment that proved politically inconvenient. Rather than pass increases whenever inflation had eroded benefits and time had allowed the trust fund to accumulate—a pattern that was both fiscally responsible and politically popular—politicians under indexation would have to scramble to devise blame-avoiding methods of reining in program growth.[67] The era of "easy votes" on Social Security was over.[68]

During the 1970s Congress strengthened other programs for older persons as well. In 1972, legislation added nutrition programs to the Administration on Aging portfolio. This dramatically increased the AoA's budget and visibility and, as already noted, provided a forum for lower-income seniors to hear about age-related policy developments. In 1973 Congress strengthened the Older Americans Act, gave the AoA more funding, established the Area Administrations on Aging, and federalized Old Age Assistance under Supplemental Security Income (SSI). In 1974 Congress also passed the Employee Retirement Income Security Act

(ERISA), which regulated private pension plans through new legal standards, financial safeguards, and disclosure requirements. After the House established a select committee on aging in 1974, the number of hearings on aging issues increased dramatically (figure 4.8).

In the 1970s seniors came into their own as an important political constituency, enjoying the fruits of the participation-policy cycle. The Social Security expansions of the 1950s had made the program nearly universal, and benefit levels were high enough to have large impacts on senior incomes and in turn on senior interest in politics. The 1971 White House Conference on Aging legitimized the involvement of senior interest groups in the policy process, and the groups grew in size dramatically, both because Social Security over time had given seniors the resources and interest to join voluntary groups and because the White House conference and other events focused national attention on senior issues. Congress showed great interest in senior policy, strengthening several key programs. Finally, the large increases in Social Security benefits, particularly the 20 percent increase in 1972, demonstrated seniors' new political relevance.

Period of Threat, 1981–1989

By the 1980s Social Security coverage was virtually universal, and benefits in 1989 reached $713 per month, two and a half times 1950 levels. The replacement ratio for the average worker peaked at 54.4 percent in 1981, and Social Security made up 39 percent of senior incomes on average.[69] In 1988 seniors were 13 percent more likely than nonseniors to vote and 58 percent more likely to make campaign contributions. AARP continued to grow, beginning the decade with 11.7 million members, increasing to 32 million in 1989—half the U.S. population aged 50 and over. The political parties mobilized seniors at even higher rates, and in 1980 and 1984 the Democrats in particular appealed to seniors in their platform, with 1,500 and 1,200 words respectively.

Against this backdrop of senior political potential, fiscal trouble was brewing. High inflation and high unemployment in the late 1970s meant that the now indexed Social Security payouts were growing rapidly while payroll tax receipts were flat or shrinking. By the early 1980s it was clear that the 1977 tax increases were inadequate, and the trust fund faced another crisis. In May 1981, the Reagan administration proposed cutting benefits for early retirees, tightening disability requirements, delaying a scheduled cost-of-living adjustment, and reducing benefit growth for future retirees. A coalition of 125 interest groups called Save Our Security (SOS) formed to fight the cuts. Both houses of Congress formally denounced the Reagan administration proposals. We take up this story—and seniors' reaction—in the next chapter.

TABLE 4.3
Empirical Indicators of the Participation-Policy Cycle

Period/Year		Social Security		Senior Poverty Rate	Senior/Nonsenior Ratios		Party Platforms		House Hearings
		% Covered	Avg. Benefit		Voting	Contributing	# Words: Dem. + Rep.	AARP Membership	
1950–59	1950	16%	$278						0
	1952				0.98	0.69	279		
	1956				1.05	0.59	270		
	1959			35%				50,000	
1960–70	1960	60%	$394		1.00	0.71	902	300,000	2
	1964				1.00	0.73	725		
	1968				0.94	1.06	395		
	1970	82%	$471	24.5%				1,635,000	2
1971–81	1972				0.93	0.56	994		6
	1976				1.00	0.55	711		41
	1980	93%	$627	15.7%	1.11	1.25	2,260	11,695,416	44
1981–89	1984		$694		1.07	1.21	1,677		50
	1988		$706		1.13	1.58	501	18,075,071	
1990–96	1990	93%	$714	12.2%	1.08	1.40	156	33,150,000	53
	1992								
	1995			10.5%					
	1996		$745		1.12	1.53	1,188	32,578,341	

Sources: Social Security Bulletin Annual Statistical Supplement, various years, for Social Security coverage, benefit levels in constant 1996 dollars, and senior poverty rate; National Election Studies for participation ratios; Donald Bruce Johnson, National Party Platforms (Urbana: University of Illinois Press, 1978), and Congressional Quarterly Almanac for party platforms; AARP for membership; Frank Baumgartner and Bryan Jones, U.S. Congressional Hearings Dataset, Policy Agendas Project, Center for American Politics and Public Policy, University of Washington for hearings data.

SUMMARY

At first Social Security expanded through policy advocacy from within the Social Security Administration. As the program became universal in coverage and as benefit levels increased, pulling seniors out of poverty, the capacity of seniors to participate in politics grew. The fact that these benefits were conferred by the federal government fostered in seniors an interest in public affairs and in Social Security policy specifically. Besides affecting individuals in this direct way, the advent of Social Security gave seniors a political identity as program beneficiaries, and they soon became targets of political party and interest group mobilization. Congress increasingly paid attention to senior issues, both because of lobbying by interest groups and the age-related policy bureaucracy and because of seniors' new electoral relevance. Ultimately the increases in seniors' participatory capacity and lobbying, fed by Social Security, led to yet greater Social Security expansions. Table 4.3 provides empirical indicators of this upward participation-policy cycle: the effects of Social Security growth itself led to more growth. In the next chapter we see the consequences of seniors' new political muscle. Their participatory capacity nurtured by decades of program expansion, seniors were well equipped in the 1980s to fight threats to their programs.

Chapter Five

POLICY THREAT AND SENIORS'
DISTINCTIVE POLITICAL VOICE

During the 1992 presidential campaign, Bill Clinton promised to stimulate the economy by increasing both short-term spending and long-term investment. But once he took office, Federal Reserve chairman Alan Greenspan warned that deficit reduction must take priority. Record budget deficits kept long-term interest rates high, squelching consumer spending and economic growth, he argued. Tackling the deficit now would enhance growth later, allowing Clinton to implement his spending plan. One deficit-fighting idea, promoted by budget director Leon Panetta, was to temporarily freeze the Social Security cost-of-living adjustment (COLA). Benefits were scheduled to increase $19 per month on average, a modest amount per person. But when multiplied over millions of recipients, a one-year freeze would save $15 billion, about 10 percent of the total deficit reduction sought. The administration floated the idea on Capitol Hill in January 1993. It was dead within ten days. Opposition from AARP and resistance from Congress, which had been burned on the Medicare Catastrophic Coverage Act just four years earlier, killed it.[1]

The senior lobby's lightning quick reflexes, and Congress's skittishness on senior issues, are the culmination of the participation-policy cycle spurred by the development of Social Security since 1935. This chapter shows how lawmakers came to interpret senior political activity as Social Security–focused. It uses data about individuals to show seniors reacting to specific policy developments: when seniors' welfare state programs were threatened, they responded with surges in participation, particularly in letter writing to Congress. The most pronounced reaction came with the Reagan proposals of 1981, when seniors objected to the cuts with a force lawmakers could not ignore. Although seniors are in many ways a heterogeneous constituency, their attitudes about Social Security had coalesced by 1981, and they were ready to send a concerted and loud message to lawmakers who tampered with the program.[2] These surges show that seniors not only are interested in Social Security, but also act when their programs are threatened. Hence senior participation carries a particular pro–Social Security message. Seniors' high rates of participation matter, because they send different signals to lawmakers than other participators.

TABLE 5.1
Opinion on Age-Related Policies by Age (in percent)

Source	Item	18–64	65+	Chi-square Test
2000 NES	Federal spending on Social Security			
	Increase	65	63	
	Same	30	35	
	Decrease	5	2	
1992 NES	Federal spending on Social Security			
	Increase	50	44	***
	Same	45	55	
	Decrease	5	1	
	Social Security benefits			
	Too low	63	47	***
	About right	33	52	
	Too high	3	2	
	Taxes on Social Security benefits			
	Favor	13	13	
	Oppose	87	87	
	Expand Medicare to cover nursing home care			
	Favor	86	83	
	Neither (volunteered)	3	6	
	Oppose	12	11	

Chi-square tests: *$p < .05$; **$p < .01$; ***$p < .001$.
Source: National Election Studies, 1992 and 2000.

BEHAVIOR VERSUS ATTITUDES

There are differences between political behavior and political attitudes. Previous researchers have argued that seniors do not appear to have distinctive attitudes on age-related issues.[3] When asked on the 2000 NES whether they wanted federal spending on Social Security increased, decreased, or kept the same, nonseniors were as likely as seniors to say increased (65 versus 63 percent) (table 5.1). In answer to the same question in 1992, nonseniors were *more* enthusiastic about increasing benefits than seniors, 50 percent to 44 percent. Similarly, nonseniors were more likely than seniors to say that Social Security benefits are too low (63 versus 47 percent). The two age groups were equally likely to oppose taxes on Social Security benefits and to favor expanding Medicare to cover nursing home care. It is not the case that seniors want to increase federal spending on

Social Security or increase benefit levels over the objections of younger people; nonseniors are at least as supportive of senior programs as seniors themselves. The implication is that seniors' high rates of participation do not matter because they do not have distinct issue preferences.

But two cautions must be kept in mind. The first is that when it comes to political behavior regarding Social Security, and not just attitudes, seniors are indeed distinctive, as this chapter will show. The second is that these attitude data indicate how widespread societal support for Social Security is and help explain why the growth of Social Security over time has met with little backlash from taxpaying nonrecipients. In short, these opinion data say as much about younger people as they do about senior beneficiaries.

Social Security has enjoyed strong support among people of all ages since its inception. The earliest polls from the 1930s found public support of government old-age pensions at 90 percent or more.[4] Support has remained high over the decades, with large majorities favoring existing or higher levels of government spending on Social Security, continued worker contributions to the program, and indexation of benefits to inflation, while opposing a higher retirement age or broad taxes on benefits.[5] Although confidence in the system slipped somewhat in the 1980s, it rebounded in the 1990s, and support for the existing provisions remains high.[6]

Social Security enjoys strong support for a number of reasons. The primary beneficiaries, senior citizens, are a highly regarded segment of society. In NES "thermometer ratings," in which respondents are asked to rate how warmly they feel toward various groups on a scale from 0 to 100, senior citizens received the highest average rating of any group between 1964 and 1992 except teachers, a category included in just one survey (table 5.2). Seniors also continue to be perceived as needy. Survey respondents tend to believe that more seniors are poor than actually are. A 1985 *Los Angeles Times* survey found that two-thirds of respondents believed the elderly poverty rate had been increasing when in fact it had fallen 3 percent in the preceding five years and 22 percent in the preceding twenty-five years. Only one in ten respondents believed the elderly poverty rate was decreasing.[7] Perceptions had not changed much by 1999, when a Kaiser Family Foundation survey found that just over half of Americans believe the senior poverty rate is increasing.[8] Seniors also fare well compared with other welfare state program beneficiaries. Fay Lomax Cook and Edith Barrett surveyed individuals about their perceptions of Social Security and AFDC recipients. Eighty-nine percent of respondents said Social Security recipients "really need benefits"; only 69 percent said as much about AFDC recipients. Similarly, 89 percent of respondents thought Social Security recipients "use benefits wisely"; only 42 percent thought AFDC recipients did so.[9] Government benefits are not seen as

TABLE 5.2
Average Group Thermometer Scores, 1964–92

Group	Average Score 1964–92	Group	Average Score 1964–92
Teachers	84.1	Republicans	59.7
Elderly	**81.3**	Legal aliens	58.8
Farmers	80.2	Hispanics	58.6
Working men/women	79.9	Chicanos	58.3
Women	78.6	People who work for govt.	57.9
Young people	77.9	Lawyers	57.9
Protestants	76.6	Women's liberation	55.9
Whites	76.1	Big business	55.6
Men	75.4	Congress	55.3
Police	75.2	Political parties	55.3
Middle class	75.1	Labor unions	55.0
College students	74.1	Liberals	54.1
City people	72.2	Feminists	53.1
Environmentalists	71.7	Civil rights leaders	52.7
Poor people	71.3	Christian fundamentalists	52.1
Military	70.0	Federal govt.	51.5
Suburbanites	68.9	People on welfare	50.9
Businessmen/women	68.5	Independents	50.7
Easterners	66.8	Anti-abortionists	50.4
Catholics	65.9	Moral Majority	42.8
Intellectuals	65.2	Protesting ministers	40.1
Blacks	65.1	Palestinians	37.9
Southerners	64.6	Illegal immigrants	36.2
Jews	64.3	Gays/lesbians	33.7
Democrats	64.1	People who smoke marijuana	32.1
City officials	63.7	Vietnam protestors	31.8
Supreme Court	62.4	Radical students	31.5
Conservatives	60.1	Black militants	27.9
Asians	59.8	Urban rioters	16.5

Source: Calculated from National Election Studies data by Frank P. Zinni, Laurie A. Rhodebeck, and Franco Mattei, "The Structure and Dynamics of Group Politics, 1964–1992," *Political Behavior* 19: 253–54.

having detrimental effects on seniors, while they are viewed as undermining the work ethic among welfare recipients.

The reasons for Social Security's popularity go beyond perceptions of seniors as needy and deserving. Nonseniors have stakes in the system as well—as workers, who pay into the system and who wish to receive benefits at retirement—and as retired persons' adult children, for whom Social Security provides emancipation. Largely because of the program, few

TABLE 5.3
Least-Fair Tax

Question: *Which do you think is the worst tax—that is, the least fair—including Social Security?*

Age	Federal Income Tax	Social Security Tax	State Income Tax	State Sales Tax	Local Property Tax	Don't Know
18–24	22%	7%	13%	22%	21%	15%
25–34	30	13	9	14	23	11
35–44	28	15	7	17	23	11
45–65	24	8	9	17	27	15
65+	25	7	9	8	28	29

Source: U.S. Advisory Commission on Intergovernmental Relations, "Changing Public Attitudes on Government and Taxes," cited in Matthew C. Price, *Justice between Generations* (Westport, Conn.: Greenwood, 1997), p. 84.

Americans now support their parents financially—just 3 percent, according to a 1983 Roper survey.[10] In fact, seniors are four times more likely to give regular financial assistance to their adult children than to receive it.[11] Nor do many adults share a household with their elderly parents. From 1940 to 1990, the percentage of seniors living in their children's households dropped from 22 percent to 5 percent.[12]

There are also few signs of backlash against Social Security or its recipients. In a 1999 Gallup poll, two-thirds of respondents said political leaders in Washington pay too little attention to the needs of senior citizens; just 4 percent said seniors get too much attention.[13] There is little resentment toward the payroll taxes that support the system. Survey data show that Social Security taxes are perceived as the least or nearly the least unfair tax among nonseniors, as shown in table 5.3. Younger respondents aged 25 to 44 are somewhat more likely than retirement- and near-retirement-age respondents to believe the Social Security tax is unfair, but they resent it less than the federal income tax, state sales tax, and local property taxes.[14]

Some observers believe that public support for Social Security is eroding and cite opinion data showing that the younger respondents are, the less likely they are to believe that they will receive Social Security benefits in retirement. In 1985, 64 percent of 45- to 59-year-olds, 43 percent of 31- to 44-year-olds, and just 33 percent of 18- to 30-year-olds believed Social Security would exist when it was time for them to retire.[15] Confidence in the system dropped from 65 percent in 1975 to 32 percent in 1982. But during the 1990s confidence stabilized around 40 percent, and appears not to undermine public support for the program, which remains high.[16] Perhaps it is the emancipation argument that keeps support high: an individual in her thirties may doubt she will get Social Security three decades hence, but nonetheless be thankful that her parents are covered now.

For these many reasons, Social Security is popular with the broader public. Seniors are not uniquely supportive of the program; their attitudes are not distinctive. But seniors *are* distinctive when it comes to participatory behavior. The difference is that self-interest does not figure equally in attitudes and behavior. Professing an attitude on a survey is costless, while acting on one's beliefs is costly. Hence only those who are directly affected, whose self-interest is at stake, act.[17] This is true across a variety of issue areas. For example, although whites in general opposed busing to end school segregation, it was whites with school-aged children who engaged in antibusing protests.[18] Although labor force participation did not predict opinions on the Equal Rights Amendment, employed women were more likely than homemakers to become pro-ERA activists.[19] Similarly, although nonseniors may profess support of the Social Security system, it is seniors who act. Laurie Rhodebeck found some evidence of distinctive senior voting behavior—they are more likely than nonseniors to take Social Security and Medicare into account in their congressional and presidential vote decisions.[20] This chapter will provide further evidence of senior distinctiveness in behavior regarding Social Security: when the system was threatened with cuts in the 1980s, it was seniors who acted in its defense. The significance of the attitude data shown in table 5.1 is not that seniors are not distinctively supportive of Social Security, but that they are nearly unanimous in their support of Social Security: *98 percent* of seniors want federal spending on Social Security increased or kept the same, a tremendous degree of consensus. This near unanimity becomes important later in interpreting seniors' political behavior. Although seniors' attitudes may not be distinctive, their behavior is.

SENIORS AND THE COLLECTIVE ACTION PROBLEM

A second topic that must be addressed before we explore seniors' participatory behavior concerning Social Security is how seniors come to be active in the first place. How does the individual senior citizen decide to engage in political activism? Mancur Olson's theory of collective action says that it is irrational for a member of a large group to work toward a collective good, because she will benefit from that good regardless of her individual effort.[21] A senior citizen will gain from the defense of Social Security whether or not she herself writes a letter to Congress. Rather than impose the cost of participation on herself, she decides to free ride.

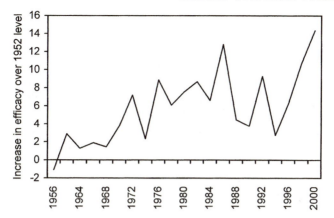

Figure 5.1 Change in seniors' external political efficacy over 1952 level. Level of senior external political efficacy each year (measured on a 100-point scale) over that of 1952. See text. (National Election Studies; full equation in appendix table A.8.)

Nevertheless, many senior citizens do engage in political activism. There are a number of factors that alter the cost-benefit calculation associated with participation. Some of these are characteristics of seniors as individuals and some are characteristics of the social and political context they face.

Among the factors that encourage individuals to engage in political activism are beliefs about the likelihood of success. Steven Finkel, Edward Muller, and Karl-Dieter Opp found that individuals will take part in collective action when they have high levels of personal efficacy and believe their group is likely to succeed.[22] External efficacy reflects how responsive people believe the government is to them and to people like them. Seniors' external efficacy has risen over time. Figure 5.1 shows the level of senior external efficacy from 1956 to 2000 compared with that of 1952: seniors' efficacy rose during the 1970s and 1980s as they were coming into their own politically. On the 100-point scale, senior response to questions about government responsiveness was 13 points higher in 1986 than in 1952.[23] During this period seniors might reasonably have begun to believe in their group's probability of success. Over time the government proved increasingly receptive to them, with the institution of House and Senate special committees on aging, the decennial White House Conference on Aging, and the overt advertising by members of Congress seeking Social Security casework.[24] Seniors also achieved a series of legislative victories, beginning with the elimination of mandatory retirement in 1977, early successes that encouraged more people to join the cause.[25] Seniors' political efficacy then achieved new heights in 1998 and 2000 as senior issues—

"saving" Social Security and introducing prescription drug benefits—reached prominence on the political agenda.

Other characteristics of seniors also help reduce the costs and heighten the benefits associated with political activism. Their participation is facilitated by more-than-adequate resources like time and money as well as proximity to other seniors. Being near others (geographically or through an organizational or professional network) who share your fate reduces informational and other costs associated with action.[26] Many seniors live near other seniors, go to community centers, or belong to mass membership organizations like the NCSC or AARP. Membership groups mobilize seniors when there is a threat, organizing postcard drives that reduce the upfront activity costs for the individual.[27] In all these venues seniors hear news of Social Security and learn how to do something about it. Proximity provides information that highlights seniors' stake and the benefits of action while reducing the costs of action.[28]

Beyond these individual characteristics, the political context that citizens face is important as well.[29] One aspect of context that can influence participation is threat, which increases the benefits of collective action by highlighting the potential for loss. In politics, threat can come from politicians or other policy-relevant actors, can be directed at an individual or a group the individual cares about, and can threaten policy changes that affect the individual's tangible well-being or her values or principles.[30] The literature differs as to whether activism is more likely in times of despair or satisfaction. The more prominent literature says that activism is inspired by a disturbance to the status quo[31] or by a sense of dissatisfaction with circumstances.[32] Another literature says that the desire to defend satisfactory current conditions can also motivate activism.[33] Regardless of which model of activism seems to apply, a threat can motivate action because it implies a change for the worse.[34]

Research in psychology shows that threat is a compelling impetus to action—the "fight or flight" reaction is one example.[35] Threat can powerfully motivate action in politics as well. Both John Mark Hansen and Jack Walker argue that actors are more likely to engage in collective action in the face of threat, which makes the benefits of action more salient.[36] For example, businesses formed interest groups to protect themselves from government regulation and later from threats posed by environmentalists and consumer advocates.[37]

Experimental evidence demonstrates the power of threat to inspire activism among individuals. Joanne Miller, Jon Krosnick, and Laura Lowe found that a "threat" fund-raising letter sent to National Abortion and Reproductive Rights Action League (NARAL) members mentioning three pieces of anti-abortion rights legislation before Congress yielded contributions that were 40 percent higher than a control letter with no such threats. They also found using 1960–96 NES data that the likelihood that respondents would engage in electoral activism (going to political meetings or working for a party or candidate) increased as the threat posed by one's least-liked candidate increased (that is, as the number of dislikes about that candidate increased).[38]

For seniors, threat to Social Security looms large because of the magnitude of the good at stake—over 40 percent of recipients' total income on average. In addition, since Social Security is an earned entitlement, seniors object vociferously to cuts or changes in pension benefits that they have accrued over a lifetime. Martha Derthick asserts that seniors are threatened even by changes proposed for future beneficiaries; perhaps they feel any crack in the system could widen.[39]

In sum, factors at both the individual and the contextual level lower the costs and heighten the benefits of engaging in political activism. Seniors enjoy high degrees of political efficacy and positive perceptions of the potential for group success. High levels of individual resources and proximity to similar others reduce information costs and highlight the benefits of action. Finally, Social Security payments are large and crucial to most seniors. When threats to their programs expose the potential for loss, many seniors ignore the rational calculations of the Olsonian free rider and instead work to defend their programs.[40]

To explore seniors' participatory reaction to the policy threats of the 1980s, we turn to the Roper Social and Political Trends dataset, which includes an item asking respondents whether they have written their congressman or senator in the past year.[41] Previous researchers have tried to link participation and policy using voter turnout.[42] But it is difficult to know what issues are on the voter's mind or what the vote means specifically in terms of policy preferences. This uncertainty—"many issues, one vote," as Raymond Wolfinger puts it—is exacerbated by the vote's fixed schedule.[43] Because voters have their say according to a preestablished electoral cycle, there is little in the timing of the vote to help us discern its issue content. The advantage of the letter-writing item is that contacting is a political activity that can be done at any time, not just during the election season. And the Roper data were collected ten times per year, allowing us to see whether rates of letter writing changed in reaction to specific political and policy events.

Hence the Roper data include the right survey item with a useful degree of granularity. One other characteristic of the data is less fortuitous: we know whether a respondent wrote a letter, but not the content or tenor of the letter. But characteristics of the data and case study overcome this problem. The timing of the letters vis-à-vis policy events helps us to discern the issue stimulus behind them. That seniors are virtually unanimous in their support of Social Security suggests their tenor is pro–Social Secu-

TABLE 5.4
Events in the History of Welfare State Programs for Senior Citizens

Year	Liberalizations
1935	Social Security Act passed.
1939	Coverage extended to dependents and survivors.
1940	First Social Security payments made, two years early.
1950	Coverage extended to nonfarm self-employed. Retirement test improved.
1952	Benefits increased by 12.5 percent. Retirement test liberalized.
1954	Coverage extended to farmers, self-employed members of some professions, farm and domestic employees. Benefits increased by 13 percent. Retirement test liberalized.
1956	Coverage extended to self-employed persons (except physicians), additional farm owners and operators, and certain state and local government employees. Retirement age for widows and female parents lowered to age 62. Military introduced to regular OASDI system.
1958	Benefits increased by 7 percent. Earnings exempt from retirement test increased.
1960	Retirement test liberalized.
1961	Men permitted to retire at age 62 with reduced benefits. Payments to aged widow, widower or surviving dependents liberalized. Retirement test liberalized.
1965	Medicare and Medicaid enacted. Coverage extended to physicians, and wives' and widows' benefits extended to divorced wives when marriage had lasted at least twenty years.
1965	Benefits increased by 7 percent. Retirement test liberalized.
1968	Benefits increased by 13 percent.
1969	Benefits increased by 15 percent.
1971	Benefits increased by 10 percent.
1972	Benefits increased by 20 percent. Benefits for widows and widowers increased. Earnings exempt from retirement test increased. SSI enacted.
1974	Benefits increased by 11 percent.
1975	Automatic cost-of-living adjustments begin.
1977	Supreme Court removed the dependency requirement for aged husbands and widowers on the grounds that none existed for aged wives and widows.

TABLE 5.4
Events in the History of Welfare State Programs for Senior Citizens (*cont'd*)

Year	Threats
1981	Reagan proposes cut in benefits.
1982	Senate Republicans propose $40b cut in Soc. Sec.
1983	"Notch baby" controversy. Taxation of half of OASDI benefits of upper-income recipients. Medicare goes on fixed amounts for hospital care based on 467 diagnosis-related groups (DRGs).
1984	Reagan proposes cut in benefits for well-off.
1985	One-year COLA freeze proposal.
1988	Medicare Catastrophic Coverage Act passed.

Sources: Gerald D. Nash, Noel H. Pugach, and Richard F. Tomasson, eds., *Social Security: The First Half-Century* (Albuquerque: University of New Mexico Press, 1988), pp. 313–21; *New York Times*; *Congressional Quarterly Weekly Report*; and chapter 4.

Note: Only events related to benefits for retired people are included in the chronology; it excludes changes in the disability program, for example, which is also administered by the Social Security Administration.

rity. And analysis of another set of citizen-initiated letters on Social Security and Medicare for which we do have the content shows that seniors are overwhelmingly opposed to cuts in the programs. I performed a content analysis of letters to the editor published in the *New York Times* concerning Social Security and Medicare over the period of threat to seniors' programs, 1981 to 1989. Ninety percent of the letters from writers who could be identified as program beneficiaries opposed the cuts in the programs.[44] Thus the nature of this case study overcomes complications that a different issue, like abortion, would present, where letter writers could come from both the pro-life and pro-choice sides, rendering a tally of letters useless in determining the net direction of opinion.

THREATS TO SENIORS' WELFARE STATE PROGRAMS

A brief history of senior welfare state programs, drawn from chapter 4 and other sources, appears in table 5.4. For the four and half decades following the New Deal, the story of senior programs was one of expansion and liberalization: new categories of seniors were brought into the Social Security program and benefits were increased. Medicare was introduced. The benefits pie grew larger.

By the late 1970s, however, concerns arose about the solvency of both the Social Security and the Medicare trust funds. Rampant inflation caused tremendous growth in the newly indexed Social Security payments. High medical inflation rates caused even greater growth in the size of Medicare. In 1977 President Jimmy Carter signed a bill increasing both the Social Security payroll tax rate and the level of wages that could be taxed. The burden of this rescue legislation fell on wage earners rather than on recipients, but recipients soon faced threats themselves.

The first significant threat to seniors' benefits came in 1981. The 1977 bill had failed to shore up the program, and on May 12, 1981, the Reagan administration announced a plan to reduce benefits for early retirees (two-thirds of Americans retire before age 65), tighten disability requirements, delay a scheduled cost-of-living adjustment, and reduce benefit growth for future retirees.[45] This was the first call for cuts in Social Security benefits since the program's enactment in 1935, and it was met with a firestorm of protest. By the third day after the May 12 announcement, mail poured into Congress and the White House.[46] Besieged by calls from angry constituents, members of both parties attacked the proposals.[47] The Republican-controlled Senate passed, by a 96–0 vote, a nonbinding resolution rejecting the Reagan proposal and promising that Congress would not "precipitously and unfairly penalize early retirees."[48] The House Democrats adopted a resolution accusing the administration of an "unconscionable breach of faith" in reducing earned entitlements.[49] The threatened cuts were a catalyst for Save Our Security (SOS), the coalition of 125 organizations that opposed the proposals.[50]

In the face of this great uproar, President Ronald Reagan effectively withdrew his proposals. In September 1981 he called for a bipartisan commission to make recommendations in 1983 on solving Social Security's financial problems, deferring the politically sensitive issue until after the midterm elections.[51] Controversy continued in 1982, however, as Reagan embraced a Senate Republican plan to make $40 billion in Social Security cuts over three years as part of the fiscal 1983 congressional budget. A bulletin from AARP produced thousands of letters opposing the cuts, and the Republicans withdrew the proposal before the Senate could vote on it.[52] The controversy continued nevertheless, and may have contributed to Republican seat loss in the midterm elections.[53]

After two years of debate, the bipartisan commission produced a package of amendments to the Social Security Act that Congress passed and Reagan signed in July 1983. The amendments raised the retirement age from 65 to 67 by the year 2027, delayed the 1983 COLA for six months, and increased payroll taxes. The final package of amendments was widely accepted, even by senior citizen groups. The larger groups like AARP recognized that some change was inevitable, and approved of the bill because it spread the pain of reform among current recipients, future recipients, and taxpayers.

The most acute political crisis was over, but controversies surrounding seniors' programs continued, fanned by grassroots groups that emerged after Reagan's initial call for benefit cuts. In September 1983, a letter to Dear Abby ignited the so-called notch baby controversy. Seven million people born between 1917 and 1921 did not share in a windfall created by a 1972 legislative miscalculation that overindexed for inflation. In 1977 Congress fixed the formulas in a way that allowed those born between 1917 and 1921 to receive an amount between the correct benefit and the full windfall. At Abby's urging, a half million notch babies wrote their congressman demanding restoration of the full windfall.[54] Despite Abby's partial retraction later in the month admitting that notch babies were not worse off than those coming after them, the controversy lived on for years. As late as 1988, notch babies confronted presidential candidates campaigning in Iowa, and bills restoring the windfall were introduced in the House and Senate, though never passed.[55]

In 1985 Senate Republicans, with the blessing of the White House, introduced a federal budget that included a one-year Social Security COLA freeze. The Senate adopted the budget, but again seniors protested vigorously. The House refused to freeze the COLA, and Congress passed the budget with no changes in Social Security.

Repeatedly stung by senior opposition to proposed Social Security changes, Congress believed it had a winning bill in the Medicare Catastrophic Coverage Act, signed into law in July 1988. The act provided the first major expansion of Medicare since its inception in 1965, protecting Medicare beneficiaries from financial ruin by capping the amount they could be required to pay for hospital care, doctors' bills, and other acute-care services. The act also for the first time provided Medicare coverage for all prescription drugs (after a large annual deductible), mammograms, and respite care for those tending severely disabled Medicare beneficiaries at home. Although the new law did not address the significant issue of long-term care (as did an alternative sponsored by senior advocate Rep. Claude Pepper), public opinion polls showed broad-based support for the measure.[56]

The Medicare expansion was financed not with a payroll tax increase, but with a modest increase in seniors' monthly Medicare premiums and a surtax on the income of the wealthiest 40 percent of seniors. For 25 percent of beneficiaries the surtax would amount to less than $250 per year, another 10 percent would pay between $250 and $800, and the most affluent 5 percent would pay the maximum supplemental premium of $800 per year. Calculations by Price Waterhouse showed that the supplemental premium would not reach the $800 cap until total income reached $45,000 for single seniors and $90,000 for married beneficiaries.[57] Congress congratulated itself for devising a new social program in an era of fiscal constraint. The key, of course, was that the new coverage was funded by seniors themselves.

Strong senior opposition emerged by fall 1988. Wealthier seniors were angered at having to pay for additional benefits that many already had as retirees, either through former employers or through private insurance. Less affluent seniors were frightened by fringe groups' misinformation campaigns claiming that all aged would be subject to the maximum $800 premium.[58]

Public ire continued throughout 1989. In November of that year, Congress repealed the Catastrophic Act. Although seniors would seemingly embrace an expansion of Medicare, they had little interest in financing the expansion themselves. John Rother, the legislative director of AARP, noted, "Many people were not aware of the legislation until after it was enacted. Then they became aware of the price tag without being aware of the benefits."[59] As House members bitterly voted for repeal, Rep. Henry Waxman (D-Calif.) said his fellow congressmen felt the elderly "were ungrateful, so . . . let them stew in their own juices."[60]

Calls for changes in Social Security and Medicare largely ceased after 1989. The period of crisis was over. The 1993 Clinton proposal to freeze the Social Security COLA never had a chance. With little interest in "shared sacrifice," seniors had the participatory wherewithal to defeat the idea immediately.

SENIOR REACTION TO POLICY THREATS

The Roper contacting data illustrate senior reaction to these policy threats. Figure 5.2 shows the rates at which various age groups contacted members of Congress. To reveal the underlying trends, Lowess curves are fitted to the actual data points, which are the proportion of people in a given age group who said that they had written a letter to their congressman or senator in the last year. The senior group starts at age 60 rather than age 65 because of the original Roper coding.[61] The overall period of threat runs from May 1981 (line B in figure 5.2) to November 1989 (line I). Because the data are smoothed somewhat by the question wording (a twelve-month retrospective question), and because many of the 1980s policy threats came in quick succession with overlapping effects, I cannot evaluate separately the participatory reaction to each. I can, however, measure the reaction to two of the specific threats—the initial 1981 proposal to cut Social Security benefits and the 1988 Catastrophic Act. The 1981 threat comes at the beginning of the period and the 1988 threat comes after three years of relative inactivity in aging policy, so they are discrete enough to allow separate analysis. There are thus five time periods:

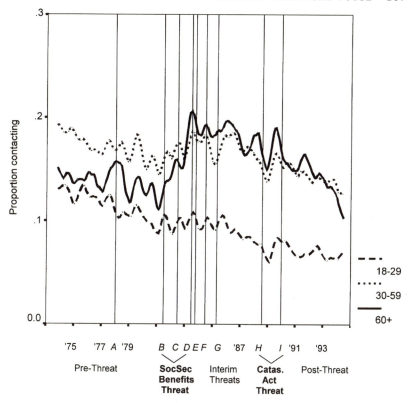

Figure 5.2 Contacting by age, 1973–94. A (Dec. 1977)–President Carter signs Social Security rescue legislation; B (May 1981)–Reagan administration proposal to cut Social Security benefits; C (May 1982)–Senate Republican proposal to cut $40 billion from Social Security over three years; D (July 1983)–Reagan signs 1983 Social Security amendments; E (Sept. 1983)–Notch baby controversy erupts; F (May 1984)–Treasury Secretary Donald Regan suggests reducing Social Security benefits for the well-off on *Meet the Press*; G (Mar. 1985)–One-year COLA freeze proposal; H (July 1988)–Medicare Catastrophic Coverage Act signed; I (Nov. 1989)–Medicare Catastrophic Coverage Act repealed. Proportion contacting means that .1 = 10% of respondents in age group wrote a letter to their congressman or senator in the last year. (Roper Social and Political Trends Archive.)

- *Pre-threat*: From the beginning of the time series in late 1973 to May 1981 (in figure 5.2, from beginning to reference line B).
- *Social Security benefits threat*: From May 1981, when the initial threat to cut Social Security benefits was made, to July 1983, when the 1983 Social Security amendments were signed (reference line B to D).
- *Interim threats*: From July 1983 to July 1988 (reference line D to H).

TABLE 5.5
Change in Contacting Rates for Five Policy Periods

Age	Pre-Threat 9/73–5/81	Social Security Benefits Threat 5/81–7/83	Interim Threats 7/83–7/88	Catastrophic Act Threat 7/88–11/89	Post-Threat 11/89–10/94
18–29	–4.1%	1.9%	–2.3%	2.4%	–1.4%
30–59	–3.5	2.7	–1.4	2.2	–2.4
60+	–2.1	7.3	–2.0	7.9	–4.5

Source: Calculated from the Roper Social and Political Trends Archive; see appendix D.

- *Catastrophic Act threat*: From the July 1988 passage of the Medicare Catastrophic Coverage Act to its November 1989 repeal (reference line H to I).
- *Post-threat*: From November 1989 to the end of the time series in 1994 (reference line I to the end).

I performed a multiple interrupted time-series (MITS) analysis to calculate the slope of participation by each age group in each of the five time periods. This analysis shows how much participation changes as a result of policy events.[62] The changes in contacting rates from the MITS analysis for figure 5.2 are shown in table 5.5. Note that the Lowess curves are calculated differently than the MITS analysis,[63] and so the changes in participation shown by the curves in figures 5.2 through 5.6 may not appear to correspond exactly with the participation changes derived from the MITS analysis.

In the pre-threat period, the rate of contacting for all three age groups declines, with seniors falling 2.1 percent and the younger age groups falling by 3.5 to 4.1 percent as shown in figure 5.2 and table 5.5. This decline in participation squares with other research showing that participation rates in general in the United States have declined over the last three decades. Seniors contacted at higher rates than the youth group, but at lower rates than the more highly educated 30- to 59-year-old group. There is a temporary rise in senior contacting in the period surrounding the 1977 Social Security rescue legislation, which shows that seniors were unique among age groups in focusing on that event and foreshadows seniors' great participatory reaction to the threats of the 1980s. The 1977 bump also demonstrates the sensitivity of these data to specific policy events.

With the initial threat to Social Security in May 1981, the pattern of contacting changes abruptly, at least for seniors. Seniors dramatically increased the rate at which they wrote letters to their congressmen and senators, beginning with the first Roper survey conducted after the May 12

Reagan administration threat (reference line B in figure 5.2). The initial surge lasted until the July 1983 signing of the Social Security amendments, when the urgency introduced by Reagan's initial threat dissipated somewhat (reference line D). During this initial acute period of threat, senior contacting rose 7.3 percent (table 5.5), from around 13 percent to 20 percent, overtaking the 30- to 59-year-old group. The contacting rate of the younger groups rose much more modestly, 2.7 percent for the middle group and 1.9 percent for youth.

During the interim threat period, from the July 1983 signing of the Social Security amendments to the July 1988 adoption of the Medicare Catastrophic Coverage Act (reference lines D to H), senior contacting remained high, above that of younger citizens, as other, albeit less urgent, threats continued (the Senate proposal to cut $40 billion from Social Security, the notch baby episode, and so on). Senior contacting surged again in reaction to the Catastrophic Act, rising 7.9 percent between the act's passage and its repeal in November 1989 (lines H to I in figure 5.2). Again nonsenior reaction was much less, a little over 2 percent for the middle and youth groups. After the Catastrophic Act repeal, which signaled an end to the threats and alarm, the senior contacting rate declined. During this post-threat period, senior contacting fell by 4.5 percent, returning to pre-1981 levels of approximately 13 percent.

The Roper data tell us whether a respondent contacted a member of Congress, not the content of the letter. But the timing of the senior surge suggests strongly that many seniors were writing letters to protest proposed changes to their programs. That the increase in contacting was far greater for seniors than for younger groups also supports this notion. By further breaking down the age groups we can get an even better idea of the relationship between age and participatory reaction to the Social Security threats. Starting in 1977, finer age categories are available in the Roper data, allowing the calculation of changes in contacting rates for age groups in five-year intervals starting at age 40. As people get closer to retirement we might expect they would be more focused on age-related issues, and this is confirmed in these data. With the exception of the 55- to 59-year-old group, the size of the participatory reaction to Social Security threat increases with age. The contacting rate of 40- to 44-year-olds, who are probably little focused on Social Security, increased just 1.3 percent from May 1981 to July 1983, about the same as the under-30 youth group in table 5.5. The contacting increases are larger as age goes up: 4.2 percent for 45- to 49-year-olds, 4.4 percent for 50- to 54-year-olds, 5.4 percent for 60- to 64-year-olds, and 8.4 percent for respondents aged 65 and over (for the contacting changes for all subgroups in all time periods, see appendix D).

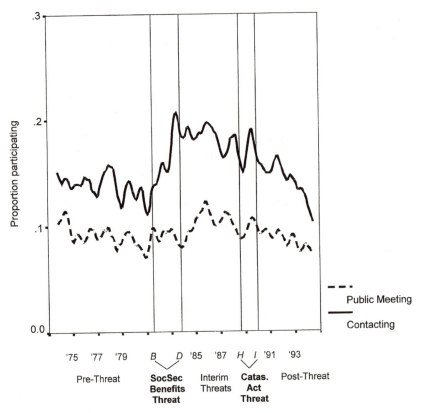

Figure 5.3 Senior contacting and public meeting attendance, 1973–94. Seniors are respondents aged 60 and over. (Roper Social and Political Trends Archive.)

Yet another piece of evidence indicates that seniors wrote letters in response to Social Security threats. Senior participation increased dramatically in an act aimed at politicians with influence over Social Security and Medicare—contacting congressmen and senators—while seniors' participation in an act with no relevance for these federal programs—attending public meetings on town or local affairs—did not rise. In figure 5.3 the rate at which seniors attended such local public meetings remains virtually flat, around 10 percent over the 1973–94 time period; the kind of participatory surge seen in contacting is absent. This is confirmed by analysis of the slope of participation during each time period. At no point does the public meeting attendance rate increase dramatically as did seniors' congressional contacting rate. Indeed, meeting attendance declines modestly over most of the two-decade period. During the initial period of threat, when senior contacting rose by 7.3 percent, for example, senior public meeting attendance fell by .8 percent. Thus the pattern of senior contacting shown in figures 5.2 and 5.3 appears to be a reaction to national policy events, with mobilized and vigilant seniors springing into action to protect their federal benefits from threat by increasing their letter writing to Congress.

VARIATIONS AMONG SENIORS

The analysis in chapter 3 suggests that seniors' reactions to policy events should vary with their level of dependence on government benefits and with the nature of the threat. We would expect less-privileged seniors in general to contact at lower rates, since they possess fewer political resources. But precisely because of their greater dependence on government programs and more limited access to private alternatives, we might expect them to react more vehemently to policy threats.

For example, retired seniors in general contact at much lower rates than their working counterparts, as shown in figure 5.4. But they also have fewer alternatives to Social Security and Medicare than working seniors, who derive income and in many cases health insurance from their employers. Thus retired seniors reacted much more strongly to the two major policy threats, their contacting surging 8.9 percent and 9.2 percent compared with 5.6 percent and 4.2 percent among working seniors. Similarly, female seniors have lower incomes, are less likely to work, and derive a greater portion of their income from Social Security than their male counterparts.[64] Senior women contact at lower rates than do senior men. But again, women's reaction to the policy threats was greater, at 8.0 and 9.2 percent, compared with 6.5 percent for both threats for senior men (figure 5.5).

High-income seniors also contact at much higher rates than do low-income seniors. Extending the government dependency argument to income subgroups, I would have expected low-income seniors to react more strongly to the 1981–83 threat to Social Security benefits, since they derive such a high share of total income from the program. Instead, contacting increased 5.4 percent for low-income seniors compared with 7.5 percent for high-income seniors (figure 5.6). But low-income seniors are also less educated and less likely to belong to interest groups that mobilize seniors, so perhaps the fact that their reaction was nearly as great as that of high-income seniors is notable.

The significance of income for the Catastrophic Act threat is different. Here it was primarily high-income seniors who were threatened, facing the possibility of paying for benefits they already had. And their reaction

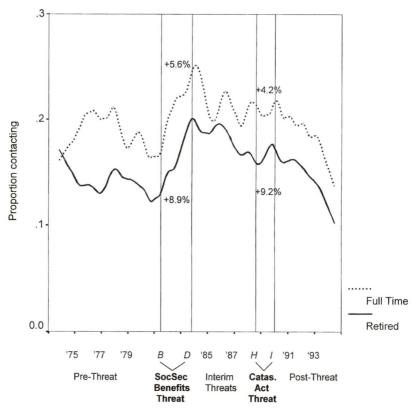

Figure 5.4 Senior contacting by work status, 1973–94. Seniors are respondents aged 60 and over. (Roper Social and Political Trends Archive.)

was quite vociferous. Their contacting increased 17.2 percent, nearly three times as much as low-income seniors at 6.6 percent.

SUMMARY

Senior citizens, when faced with proposals during the 1980s to cut their Social Security and Medicare programs, vigorously defended those programs with surges in letter writing to federal policymakers, as several pieces of evidence attest: seniors' contacting surge coincided precisely with the period of program threat; the great majority of *New York Times* letters to the editor concerning Social Security and Medicare over the same period protested changes in programs; contacting by younger, non-recipient age groups was largely unaffected by these program threats;

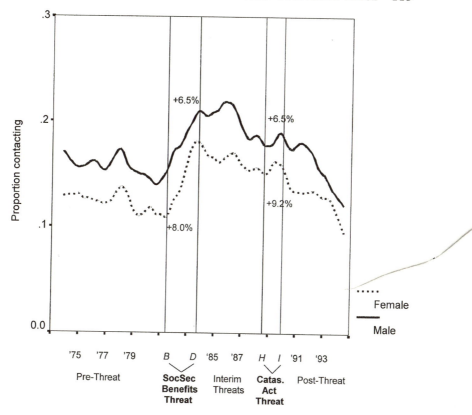

Figure 5.5 Senior contacting by gender, 1973–94. Seniors are respondents aged 60 and over. (Roper Social and Political Trends Archive.)

threats to these federal senior programs had no effect on the rate at which seniors attended local meetings; and responses to specific threats reflect the self-interests of senior subgroups, with retired and female seniors responding most vigorously to the 1981 threat to Social Security benefits, affluent seniors to the Catastrophic Act.

Senior citizens participate in politics at high rates. They are also quite attentive to news of public affairs, especially Social Security. For participation to influence policy outcomes, however, more is required than high participation rates or professed interest in a certain issue area. The group's participatory message must be clear, strong, and distinctive. Seniors' swift and decisive participatory reaction to proposed changes and cuts in their programs during the 1980s admonished lawmakers: do not tamper with Social Security and Medicare. Seniors showed they not only are vigilant about their programs but also are prepared to act when necessary.

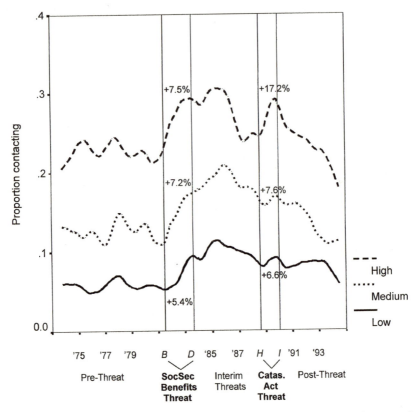

Figure 5.6 Senior contacting by income, 1973–94. Seniors are respondents aged 60 and over. (Roper Social and Political Trends Archive.)

The cycle that began with the development of Social Security policy, which over several decades spawned interest groups and created a political identity for seniors, yields in the 1980s an empowered, vigilant constituency able to defend its programs. Government policy fundamentally transformed its target population, in this presumably inadvertent way: program beneficiaries have the resources to participate and do so with vehemence when there is a threat. In the next chapter we see how lawmakers respond to this active and vocal constituency and how policy outcomes are affected, continuing the cycle.

Chapter Six

CONGRESSIONAL RESPONSIVENESS

THE 1980s, a decade filled with threats to senior programs, came to an end with virtually no fundamental policy changes affecting current recipients. There were some changes in Social Security over this period, but they fell either onto taxpayers (increases in the payroll tax rate and wage base subject to taxation) or onto recipients in the distant, politically safe, future (the 1983 amendments, for example, raised the retirement age from 65 to 67, effective forty-four years later). The 1983 amendments required that upper-income seniors report half of their Social Security benefits as taxable income, but this "cut" in benefits did not provoke much protest, because it came as a package of changes that spread the impact of reform and because it seemed a relatively mild change after the policy scares of 1981–82. Changes in Medicare tended to fall not on program beneficiaries, but on care providers, in the form of cuts in physician- and hospital-reimbursement rates.[1]

Thus at the macro level, senior participation successfully thwarted undesirable proposals. The volume and tenor of seniors' participatory message succeeded in shaping policy outcomes. This chapter further examines the participation-policy link at the level of the individual lawmaker. It studies the responsiveness of members of Congress to active constituencies—how seniors' message was heard and transformed into policy by Congress. On age-related policy roll-call votes, senior constituencies successfully shape the behavior of lawmakers who are not otherwise likely to vote in a pro–welfare state direction. Democratic lawmakers vote to maintain or expand senior programs the majority of the time, while Republican lawmakers vote in favor of seniors at lower rates. But the more senior constituents Republicans have, the more likely they are to vote pro-senior. Thus seniors' high level of activity and distinctive voice are rewarded in the policy arena, and the participation-policy cycle comes full circle.

CONGRESS AND ITS CONSTITUENTS

There is an extensive literature on the connection between constituency preferences and legislator behavior. For the most part, researchers have failed to find much of a relationship.[2] Warren Miller and Donald Stokes in their classic 1963 study found that there was little connection between legislators' roll-call votes and their constituents' issue positions.[3] Subsequent research has tried to improve upon the Miller-Stokes study and to address a host of methodological problems via new measures and new data.[4] There are too few constituents per district for national surveys to measure their preferences, so researchers have used other measures like referendum voting,[5] opinion simulations,[6] and presidential voting.[7] Some studies have used data from exit polls or the NES to more directly estimate constituency preferences.[8] But these attempts have largely failed to find a relationship between constituent positions and legislator behavior.

Gary Jacobson's work on congressional elections shows that few voters know much about candidate issue positions and that few elections turn on them, which suggests that there is little reason for legislators to abide by constituent opinions.[9] Studies of legislator behavior based on interviews with members of Congress, however, find that they worry constantly about the electoral consequences of their decisions.[10] John Kingdon offers this solution to the puzzle: legislators anticipate the electoral effects of their roll-call votes and adjust them as necessary. They consider how to explain votes at home and try to avoid votes that will provide fodder for potential challengers. In short, members of Congress anticipate future public opinion and vote accordingly.[11] Thus there is a relationship between legislator behavior and constituent issue positions, but the correspondence is less with current opinion than with the public's "potential preferences."[12]

To anticipate constituent desires, legislators engage in extensive information gathering. Mark Peterson notes that legislators need three kinds of information to make policy decisions: policy-analytic knowledge, distributional knowledge, and ordinary knowledge.[13] Policy-analytic knowledge is objective information about policy goals and effects. Distributional knowledge tells the legislator about the impact of policy options on various groups and communities and the intensity of response from the relevant organized interests. Ordinary knowledge is "the perspective and attitude formed through everyday observation and interaction."[14] This is subjective information, a gut instinct about how the general public would likely react to a policy proposal.

Policy-analytic knowledge often comes from executive agencies, interest group research, policy experts from think tanks and universities, and congressional agencies like the Congressional Budget Office and General Accounting Office. Distributional knowledge typically comes from political advisors, lobbyists, interest group research, and constituents. Ordinary knowledge comes from legislators' personal experience, home travel, and constituent letters and calls. These latter two types of information—distributional and ordinary—tell a legislator about the political consequences of various policy options. Although Congress is often accused of being out of touch, as an institution it is extremely well primed to absorb this kind of political information.[15]

Ordinary knowledge about some issues, like Social Security, is abundant. Common sense and constituent letters tell legislators that seniors are focused on the program. There are two kinds of constituent letters: casework requests and issue letters. Casework is important not only as a service promoting reelection,[16] but also as an information source for legislators. Such letters inform them which program clienteles are sufficiently politically aware to make casework requests—which clienteles see a connection between legislator action and program benefits.

Issue letters spell out constituents' policy concerns. Legislators use issue-letter volume to measure intensity of opinion.[17] The surges in senior letter writing during the period of threat to Social Security and Medicare during the 1980s showed members of Congress that seniors are vigilant about Social Security and will act politically to defend their programs.

CONGRESS AND SENIOR CITIZENS

Members of Congress hear more from seniors than from nearly any other mass constituency. How responsive are they? I examine roll-call votes on Social Security and Medicare during the 1981–89 period, when these programs were embattled and when senior contacting surged. I assess whether there is a relationship between legislators' roll-call behavior on these issues and pressure from their elderly constituents as measured by the size of senior constituencies and their contacting rates. That such a relationship exists for Republicans but not Democrats suggests that a large senior presence in a district or state can influence lawmakers to vote against their ideological predispositions to satisfy their constituency.

During this period there were thirty-two roll-call votes in the House and seventy-five in the Senate on Social Security and Medicare. For the analysis here I retained twelve House and twenty-seven Senate roll-call votes after eliminating unanimous votes and votes on technical aspects of the programs that did not appear to have a clearly pro- or antisenior side to them.[18] I also treat the votes on the 1989 repeal of the Medicare Catastrophic Coverage Act separately, as part of an analysis of those lawmakers who switched their votes on the act. The roll-call votes retained took place from 1983 to 1988 (see appendix table A.9). For analysis purposes, I coded all the roll-call votes so that 1 = pro-senior vote, meaning an expansion or preservation of the existing programs, and 0 = anti-senior vote.

TABLE 6.1
Correlations between Percentage of Senior Constituents and Pro-Senior Votes on
Social Security and Medicare Roll Calls, 1983–88

	House	Senate
Total	0.07***	0.16***
	(4,998)	(2,564)
Democrats	0.01	0.07**
	(3,009)	(1,225)
Republicans	0.09***	0.14***
	(1,989)	(1,339)

*$p < .05$; **$p < .01$; ***$p < .001$.
Sources: Roll-call votes from the Congressional Quarterly's Congressional Roll Calls, various years; see appendix table A.9; % seniors by congressional district from Politics in America, various years; % seniors by state from U.S. Statistical Abstract, various years.
Note: Number of cases in parentheses.

I begin examining whether elderly constituencies influence lawmaker behavior by assessing the influence of the size of those constituencies. As hypothesized, there is a positive relationship between size of senior constituencies and pro-senior roll-call votes by legislators. For the twenty-seven Senate roll-call votes (2,564 cases total), the correlation between the percentage of seniors in each state and senators' roll-call votes on age-related issues was .16 ($p < .001$), as shown in table 6.1. For the twelve roll-call votes in the House (4,998 cases total), the correlation between percentage of seniors in each congressional district and representatives' roll-call votes was .07 ($p < .001$). It is not appropriate to compare the correlations in the two chambers, since they are based on different sets of votes. In each chamber, however, legislators are more likely to vote in a pro-senior direction when there are more senior constituents in their districts or states.

This relationship is much stronger for Republicans than for Democrats. In the House, the correlation between district senior population and votes on senior issues was a statistically and substantively insignificant .01 for Democrats, but .09 for Republicans ($p < .001$). In the Senate, the correlation for Democrats was .07 ($p < .01$), but twice as high for Republicans, .14 ($p < .001$; see table 6.1). Another way to look at this is to divide districts and states into quartiles by senior population and calculate the proportion of pro-senior votes among legislators in each quartile (table 6.2).[19] Overall, Republicans are much less likely than Democrats to vote in a pro-senior direction, doing so 35 percent of the time versus 76 percent in the House, 46 versus 80 percent in the Senate. More interestingly, as the senior population rises from the low quartile through the high

TABLE 6.2
Proportion of Pro-Senior Roll-Call Votes by Senior Population Quartile, 1983–88.

| | Total | Senior Population Quartile | | | | Difference of Means Test: Low vs. High |
		Low			High	
House						
Democrats	0.76	0.76	0.76	0.76	0.76	
Republicans	0.35	0.28	0.35	0.37	0.42	***
Senate						
Democrats	0.80	0.78	0.79	0.81	0.83	
Republicans	0.46	0.42	0.37	0.52	0.57	***

| | Senior Population Quartile Ranges in 1985 | | | |
	Low			High
House	3%–9.5%	9.6%–11.0%	11.1%–12.7%	12.8%–28.0%
Senate	3%–10.4%	10.5%–11.9%	12.1%–13.2%	13.3%–17.6%

$*p < .05; **p < .01; ***p < .001.$

Sources: Roll-call votes from the *Congressional Quarterly's Congressional Roll Calls*, various years; % seniors by congressional district from *Politics in America*, various years; % seniors by state from *U.S. Statistical Abstract*, various years.

Note: Figures in cells are the proportion of lawmakers of the corresponding description voting in a pro-senior direction on the included roll-call votes; for example, 28 percent of the time House Republicans representing low-senior-population districts (from 3 to 9.5 percent seniors) voted in a pro-senior direction. See appendix table A.9 for a list of roll-call votes. The number of cases each cell is based on varies from 304 to 836.

quartile, the proportion of House Democrats voting in a pro-senior direction remains unchanged at .76 while the proportion of House Republicans voting in a pro-senior direction increases monotonically. In the lowest senior population quartile, House Republicans voted in a pro-senior direction 28 percent of the time while House Republicans in the highest senior population quartile voted in a pro-senior direction 42 percent of the time (this difference is statistically significant at $p < .001$). In the Senate we see a similar story. Across the senior population quartiles, the proportion of Senate Democrats voting in a pro-senior direction remains unchanged (the difference between .78 and .83 in the lowest and highest quartiles is not statistically significant) while the proportion of Senate Republicans voting in a pro-senior direction increases from .42 to .57 ($p < .001$). Multivariate analysis shows that these relationships hold, even controlling for legislators' political ideology.[20]

The more pronounced effect of senior constituency size on Republican lawmaker behavior is reflected in the decision to repeal the Medicare Cat-

TABLE 6.3
Proportion of House Medicare Catastrophic Act Switchers by Senior Population Quartile

Total	Senior Population Quartile				Difference of Means Test: Low vs. High
	Low			High	
Democrats	0.68	0.65	0.64	0.62	
	(57)	(57)	(59)	(60)	
Republicans	0.22	0.21	0.26	0.48	*
	(46)	(39)	(39)	(33)	

*p < .05; **p < .01; ***p < .001.

Sources: Switchers calculated from the *Congressional Quarterly's Congressional Roll Calls,* various years; % seniors by congressional district from *Politics in America,* various years.

Note: Top figures in cells represent the proportion of House members of the corresponding description switching from support to repeal of the Medicare Catastrophic Coverage Act; for example, 22 percent of House Republicans representing low-senior-population districts switched their position. Figures in parentheses represent number of cases.

astrophic Coverage Act. This was an instance in which members changed their minds in response to senior pressure. The House, which had passed the law 302–127 in July 1987, voted to repeal it 360–66 in October 1989. It is particularly interesting to look at the switchers, the 195 members (151 Democrats, 44 Republicans) who voted for both the House and the conference report versions and who subsequently voted to repeal. In particular we can compare the 195 switchers with the 195 members (82 Democrats, 113 Republicans) who did not change their vote to see whether the size of district senior populations influenced representatives' decisions to switch their Catastrophic Act vote (excluded are the 45 members who did not vote on all three bills). This analysis is limited to the House; in the Senate the repeal vote was unanimous and so there are no nonswitchers to compare with the switchers.

Table 6.3 shows the proportion of members switching their Catastrophic Act vote by senior population quartile. In a pattern very similar to that of earlier analyses, Democratic representatives were equally likely to abandon their support of the Catastrophic Act, regardless of the proportion of seniors in their districts (the difference between .68 and .62 is not statistically significant). By contrast, Republican representatives in high senior-population districts were much more likely to switch their vote than their counterparts in low-senior districts. Almost half of the Republican members in high-senior districts switched their vote on the act compared with only 22 percent of GOP members from low-senior

TABLE 6.4

Proportion of Medicare Catastrophic Act Switchers by Senior Population Quartile and Median Home Value

Median Home Value	Senior Population Quartile				Difference of Means Test: Low vs. High
	Low			High	
Low	0.52	0.50	0.51	0.54	
	(29)	(50)	(57)	(57)	
High	0.46	0.43	0.46	0.61	*
	(74)	(46)	(41)	(36)	

$*p < .05;$ $**p < .01;$ $***p < .001.$

Sources: Switchers calculated from the *Congressional Quarterly's Congressional Roll Calls,* various years; % seniors by congressional district from *Politics in America,* various years; median home value from *Politics in America,* various years.

Note: Top figures in cells represent the proportion of lawmakers of the corresponding description switching from support to repeal of the Medicare Catastrophic Coverage Act; for example, 46 percent of House members representing more affluent low-senior-population districts (from 3 to 9.5 percent seniors, median home value over $44,300 in 1985) switched their position. Figures in parentheses represent number of cases.

districts ($p < .05$). Multivariate analysis controlling for lawmaker ideology yields the same results.[21] Again we see Republican lawmakers sensitive to the size of their senior constituency.

There is further evidence of a link between constituency pressure and switching on the Catastrophic Act. We would expect the highest rate of switching in districts with affluent seniors. According to both journalistic accounts of the protests against the act and the analysis of senior contacting in chapter 5, it was affluent seniors who objected to the act most vociferously. Unfortunately data on senior incomes by congressional district are unavailable and I rely instead on a proxy measure: median home value. These are data for median home value for the entire district population, not just senior citizens, but district median home value and senior citizen incomes are probably highly correlated. Seniors living in Pennsylvania's First District (inner-city Philadelphia), where the median home value in 1985 was $16,600, are probably less affluent than seniors in California's Twelfth District (Silicon Valley) with a median home value of $150,000. Table 6.4 shows the proportion of members switching their vote on the Catastrophic Act across the four senior-population categories and two home-value categories (I split the median home value measure into a high-low measure rather than quartiles to maintain cell size). As expected, the affluent high-senior-density districts have the highest proportion of switchers, 61 percent.[22]

These analyses show that members of Congress are sensitive to the size of their senior constituencies. We see the effect among Republican representatives and senators. Democrats tend to vote in a pro-senior direction over three-quarters of the time, doing so regardless of the size of their senior constituencies. Republicans are less ideologically predisposed to vote in a pro-senior direction, doing so only 35 percent of the time in the House and 46 percent of the time in the Senate on average. But that likelihood varies with the size of Republicans' senior constituencies, even after controlling for lawmakers' political ideology. The tendency of Republicans to vote for the maintenance or expansion of Social Security and Medicare increases monotonically with the proportion of seniors in the legislators' districts or states. Republican House members were also more likely to switch from supporting the Medicare Catastrophic Coverage Act to voting for its repeal the more seniors there were in their district.

It also seems reasonable to suppose that roll-call voting is correlated with seniors' contacting—that members of Congress who receive more letters from senior constituents are more likely to vote in a pro-senior direction. This is my expectation, although the decision to write a letter may be partly strategic—there may be no letters to those members who are known as stalwarts or who are completely hopeless.

To examine the relationship between seniors' contacting and roll-call voting, I calculated the correlation between switching one's vote on the Medicare Catastrophic Coverage Act and the rate of senior contacting in one's state during the seventeen-month period between the act's 1988 enactment and its 1989 repeal. I expected that members from states in which senior contacting was greater during this period would be more likely to switch from support to repeal. This correlation, which I expected to be positive, was negative ($-.23$; $p < .001$; $n = 340$). So too was the correlation between switching and the percentage change in senior contacting for each state from the twelve-month period before the act's passage to the seventeenth-month period between enactment and repeal ($-.06$; n.s.; $n = 340$); here the hypothesis was that members from states in which senior contacting after enactment increased the most over preenactment levels would be more likely to switch from support to repeal. But instead I found no statistically significant relationship.[23]

Several empirical and theoretical limitations hinder this analysis. The Roper contacting data are by state, not by congressional district, so the measure of contacting, especially for House members, is imprecise at best. In addition, despite the large number of cases in the Roper data (approximately 24,000 per year), the data were never intended to be used as state samples, so there could be severe bias in state-level analysis. Finally, the greatest limitation may be that citizens do not write letters to legislators who are on their side, but rather contact those members who are leaning the other way in an attempt to persuade them. When those lawmakers remain steadfast and vote antisenior, the relationship between contacting and pro-senior roll-call voting is negative.

Evidence for this last proposition is provided by an analysis of Senate roll-call voting. For each of the Senate roll-call votes, I calculated the average rate of senior contacting by state for the twelve months preceding the vote on the bill.[24] The correlation between senior contacting over the previous twelve months and senators' votes on senior issues across all twenty-seven bills was −.06 ($p < .05$; $n = 1,752$). Analysis by party suggests that antisenior senators were more likely to be contacted: the correlation is 0 for Democrats, −.05 for Republicans, who are more likely to vote antisenior.

SUMMARY

Members of Congress are electorally sensitive to their senior citizen constituencies; we see this in particular in the behavior of Republican legislators. Democrats tend to vote in a pro-senior direction on bills in the House and Senate regardless of the size of their senior constituency. Republicans are less likely to do so overall, but are more likely if there are more seniors in their district or state. Senior presence in the electorate influences congressional roll-call voting. I also tried to assess the influence of a particular kind of participation, contacting, on congressional roll-call voting. My efforts here were hampered by data limitations and also by the notion that letter writers probably write to persuade those members who are not on their side to join them. When the antisenior members remain antisenior, the correlation between letter writing and roll-call voting is negative.

At a more macro level, however, there seems little doubt that the 1980s contacting surge was recognized by members of Congress and interpreted as a senior citizen effort to protect their programs. It was seniors who appeared at legislators' home visits to protest Reagan administration proposals, seniors who turned up at campaign events as late as 1988 to highlight the notch baby issue,[25] and a senior citizen who in 1989 threw herself on the hood of House Ways and Means chairman Dan Rostenkowski's car to protest the Medicare Catastrophic Coverage Act.[26]

Indeed, after the 1989 repeal of the Catastrophic Act, attempts to change or cut senior programs largely died out. It seems to be this episode in particular that both frustrated lawmakers—who in a Burkean sense felt the act was beneficial to the majority of seniors despite what those seniors thought—and reinforced for them seniors' political activism and tenacity. As the political analyst Kevin Phillips noted, the older people "shook more than Rosty's car. They shook the willingness of politicians to confront retirees."[27]

Thus congressional responsiveness to the senior constituency completes the participation-policy cycle. The development of senior programs enhances their political activity levels. With participatory spikes, seniors express their objections to unwanted policy change. Realizing that seniors make up a large share of the electorate, lawmakers are loath to cross them. Some legislators—like the majority of Democrats—tend to vote in a pro-senior direction generally. For Republicans, who are less ideologically predisposed to embrace these large welfare state programs, senior presence makes a real difference, changing lawmaker behavior. And it is not simply that heavily senior districts and states are more likely to elect moderate rather than conservative Republicans. If we control for lawmaker ideology, we find that Republicans who must answer to a large senior constituency are more likely to vote pro-senior. Hence we see the participation-policy cycle in action: government policy creates a constituency, and gives it the means to participate in public affairs along with a compelling interest in doing so, with the result that the constituency and the political influence it wields can shape policy outcomes. The next chapter looks at these participation-policy effects across programs, examining the political ramifications of different program designs.

Chapter Seven

THE RECIPROCAL PARTICIPATION-POLICY

RELATIONSHIP ACROSS PROGRAMS

SOCIAL Security is not unique; it is but one example of the participation-policy cycle. And while data limitations do not allow analysis of other programs exactly comparable to the one in the preceding pages, this chapter begins to look across programs to see under what conditions policy-feedback mechanisms exist and where participation influences policy outcomes. I look briefly at six other policy areas, including both means-tested and non-means-tested programs, examining the participation of recipients in these program areas, their influence on policymaking, and policy outcomes.

I focus on two programs in particular: veterans' benefits, as an example of another non-means-tested program, and public assistance, or "welfare," representative of means-tested programs. Like Social Security, veterans' benefits have positive effects on recipients, enhancing their participation, while welfare undermines the low level of participatory resources its recipients possess through its negative effects on their political efficacy. Groups benefiting from positive policy feedbacks successfully direct their enhanced participatory capacity toward program preservation or expansion. Groups suffering from negative feedbacks become increasingly marginalized, their quiet voices further dampened by the enervating effects of their programs. Hence policy design influences the amount of voice client groups have in the political arena. Government policy itself helps determine the distance between citizen and government, exacerbating the problem of differential group influence on democratic outcomes.

RECIPIENT PARTICIPATION

The Citizen Participation Study asked respondents not only whether someone in their household receives Social Security, but also whether someone receives veterans' benefits, Medicare, Medicaid, food stamps, housing subsidies, or public assistance (AFDC, General Assistance, General Relief, or Supplemental Security Income).[1] Three of these programs are not means tested, meaning that qualification is based not on economic need but on other categorical forms of eligibility. Retired persons aged 65

TABLE 7.1
Political Interest and Demographic Characteristics of Program Recipients

Programs	Political Interest (8-pt. scale)	Family Income (average)	Education (years)	Age (median)
Non-means-tested				
Social Security	5.8	$26,600	11.9	67
Medicare	5.8	$26,000	11.9	69
Veterans' benefits	5.8	$34,300	13.0	57
Means-tested				
Public assistance	4.7	$13,200	10.5	38
Food stamps	4.7	$ 9,600	10.8	35
Housing assistance	4.8	$10,900	11.0	47
Medicaid	4.8	$13,000	10.6	45

Source: Citizen Participation Study.

and over, of nearly every occupation, are eligible for Social Security (reduced benefits available at age 62); most persons aged 65 and over are automatically eligible for Medicare; and military veterans are eligible for veterans' benefits, some of which are means tested, although the income tests are not always rigorously enforced.[2] By contrast, eligibility for public assistance, food stamps, housing subsidies, and Medicaid is determined by income, along with some other factors. These are welfare programs intended to benefit the poor, as opposed to Social Security, an insurance program aimed at virtually all workers. The data allow comparison of the levels of participatory factors—engagement, resources, and mobilization—as well as recipient activity levels across programs.

Social Security and veterans' benefits recipients are more interested in public affairs than are welfare recipients, as table 7.1 shows, but the gulf between the groups is not large (5.8 versus 4.7 on an 8-point interest scale, comparable to the difference between respondents who graduated from high school and those who did not).[3] Including both their cash and their in-kind benefits—AFDC recipients are automatically eligible for Medicaid, and 85 percent also receive food stamps[4]—welfare recipients may be even more dependent on the government than Social Security recipients on average. But as Seymour Martin Lipset notes, "[economic] need alone does not appear to be sufficient" to spur political participation.[5] When we compare the participatory resource levels of means-tested and non-means-tested beneficiaries, large differences appear. Social Security recipients have roughly double the family income of public assistance

Table 7.2
Institutional Affiliations and Civic Skills of Program Recipients

Programs	% Belong to Institution and Practice Skills There		Average Number of Skills Practiced	
	Nonpolitical Organization	Church	Nonpolitical Organization	Church
Non-means-tested				
Social Security	51	31	1.3	1.5
Medicare	51	29	1.3	1.5
Veterans' Benefits	58	28	1.2	2.1
Means-tested				
Public assistance	30	18	0.8	1.4
Food stamps	23	20	0.7	1.2
Housing assistance	31	19	0.6	1.3
Medicaid	26	20	1.1	1.8

Source: Citizen Participation Study.

recipients—$26,600 versus $13,200—partly reflecting differences in benefit levels. In 1996 the average Social Security benefit for a retired worker was $745; the mean AFDC benefit was $134, or $374 for the average recipient family of 2.8 persons.[6] Social Security benefits are high enough to lift most recipients above the poverty line,[7] while AFDC benefits are not;[8] AFDC benefits are intentionally kept low lest they provide a disincentive to work.[9] Non-means-tested recipients also possess higher levels of two other resources relevant for participation, education and civic skills. Social Security recipients have an average of 11.9 years of schooling compared with 10.5 for public assistance recipients. This difference is striking, since Social Security recipients are so much older than public assistance recipients (average age 67 versus 38) and come from less-educated cohorts. AFDC recipients also fail to make up for low levels of formal education with skill development in nonpolitical arenas. They have fewer civic skills than Social Security recipients, and are both less likely to have nonpolitical institutional affiliations and less likely to practice skills within those institutions. Fifty-one percent of respondents in Social Security households belong to non-political voluntary organizations, and they practice an average of 1.3 skills there. By contrast, only 30 percent of AFDC recipients belong to such organizations, and they practice just .8 skills (table 7.2). In church, AFDC recipients practice the same number of civic skills as Social Security recipients, around 1.4 out of 4, but only 18 percent of AFDC recipients belong to churches and get skills there as

TABLE 7.3
Mobilization of Program Recipients

| Programs | Percentage of Program Recipients Asked to | | | |
	Work/Contribute to a Campaign	Contact	Engage in Community Activity	Protest
Non-means-tested				
Social Security	33	26	14	8
Medicare	32	26	14	8
Veterans' benefits	29	27	20	8
Means-tested				
Public assistance	17	10	10	11
Food stamps	11	8	4	9
Housing assistance	17	8	3	11
Medicaid	16	10	6	10

Source: Citizen Participation Study.

opposed to 31 percent of Social Security recipients. Thus even church, an institution that would seem more readily available to AFDC recipients than the workplace or voluntary organizations, is not a significant source of skills across recipients.[10]

Public assistance recipients not only have low levels of resources and skills but also are far less likely to be mobilized to political activity. As table 7.3 shows, Social Security recipients are more likely than welfare recipients to be asked to contribute (33 versus 17 percent), to contact elected officials (26 versus 10 percent), and to engage in informal community activity (14 versus 10 percent). The one activity to which AFDC recipients are more likely to be recruited is protest (11 percent versus 8 percent for Social Security recipients). Data from the 1992 NES show that 21 percent of Social Security recipients were mobilized by one of the political parties during the election campaign compared with just 8 percent of AFDC recipients.[11]

Public assistance recipients also do not benefit as much from the interest, information, and mobilization effects of membership in groups organized around their programs. While AARP, the largest voluntary organization in the country, represents seniors, there have been no notable mass membership groups for public assistance recipients since the National Welfare Rights Organization (NWRO) of the 1960s.[12] There are interest groups that work in defense of AFDC and similar programs, but they tend

TABLE 7.4
Membership in Program-Related Organizations

Programs	% Recipients Belonging to Organization Concerned with Their Program
Non-means-tested	
Social Security	24
Medicare	22
Veterans' benefits	35
Means-tested	
Public assistance	2
Food stamps	< 1
Housing assistance	3
Medicaid	4

Source: Citizen Participation Study.

to be proxy liberal groups like the Children's Defense Fund rather than recipient membership groups.[13] This dearth of welfare groups is reflected in the Citizen Participation Study data. Twenty-four percent of Social Security recipients said they belonged to a group concerned with Social Security (this figure rises to 31 percent if we include Social Security–receiving AARP members who failed to say they belong to a group concerned with Social Security); 35 percent of veterans belong to a veterans' group (table 7.4). By contrast just 2 percent of public assistance recipients belong to organizations concerned with their program.

The low participatory factor levels among means-tested recipients are in part due to their backgrounds and life experiences. But the absence of participation-enhancing positive policy feedbacks also matters. AFDC benefit levels are too low to boost participation as Social Security benefits do. Welfare policy has clearly not encouraged interest group activity the way Social Security and Medicare have.

Indeed, welfare has negative feedback effects on its recipients. Joe Soss shows that the way in which welfare is administered dampens the external political efficacy and participation rates of AFDC recipients. Because AFDC benefits are conferred through ongoing meetings with caseworkers who ask questions about private matters and who appear to have great discretion over benefits, recipients come to believe that the agency is an invasive, threatening, and capricious force in their lives. And they feel that the government in general is as unresponsive as the welfare agency.[14]

Analysis of 1992 NES data in which Social Security and welfare recipients are identified reveals the very different external political efficacy lev-

TABLE 7.5
Participation Rates of Program Recipients

| Programs | Percentage of Program Recipients Who | | | | |
	Vote	Contribute	Contact	Work on Campaigns	Protest
Non-means-tested					
Social Security	78	20	33	7	2
Medicare	81	22	31	8	2
Veterans' benefits	76	29	33	9	5
Means-tested					
Public assistance	43	6	27	6	5
Food stamps	39	5	18	4	5
Housing assistance	44	3	20	5	5
Medicaid	46	6	25	5	3

Source: Citizen Participation Study.

els of these two groups. With respondents' education, income, and other sociodemographic characteristics held constant, AFDC recipients have lower levels of external efficacy than the American public, as Soss found, while Social Security recipients have higher levels (see appendix table A.10).[15] The rise in seniors' external efficacy over time (shown in figure 5.1) suggests that the relationship may be causal—that seniors' external efficacy has risen because of government responsiveness to the group.

Given their low levels of participatory resources, mobilization opportunities, and group membership, as well as negative program effects, it is not surprising to see in table 7.5 that the recipients of means-tested programs participate at much lower rates than do those of non-means-tested programs—78 percent of Social Security recipients and 76 percent of veterans' benefits recipients voted, compared with just 43 percent of those receiving public assistance. Similarly, 20 percent of Social Security recipients and 29 percent of veterans' benefits recipients made campaign contributions versus 6 percent of public assistance recipients. Contacting rates across programs are more comparable, although non-means-tested program recipients still contact at higher rates than do means-tested program recipients. Only when we look at protesting, an activity that requires fewer economic resources and is therefore more available to the poor[16]—and an activity to which they are more likely to be recruited—do we see the participation rate for public assistance recipients (5 percent) rise above that of Social Security recipients (2 percent).

TABLE 7.6
Participation in Regard to Program

Programs	Percentage of Program Recipients Who Participate Specifically with Regard to Their Program		
	Vote	Contribute	Contact
Non-means-tested			
Social Security	25	6	7
Medicare	26	5	6
Veterans' benefits	27	6	14
Means-tested			
Public assistance	10	<1	6
Food stamps	12	<1	3
Housing assistance	12	<1	<1
Medicaid	10	<1	3

Source: Citizen Participation Study.

Non-means-tested program recipients are also more likely to partici-pate in ways specifically focused on their program. As table 7.6 shows, 25 percent of Social Security recipients and 27 percent of veterans' benefits recipients voted with their program in mind compared with just 10 per-cent of those on public assistance. Similarly, 6 percent of Social Security recipients and veterans' benefits recipients contributed money with regard to their program compared with less than 1 percent of public assistance recipients.

If we turn to contacting, we find that public assistance recipients are about as likely as Social Security recipients to complain about their pro-gram to an elected official, but the reason for the low levels of complaints probably differs.[17] Social Security is run quite efficiently by the Social Se-curity Administration. The SSA calculates benefits using precise formulas and sends the monthly checks, often by direct deposit into recipients' bank accounts, to a well-defined and stable population.[18] The distribution of public assistance is a far more complex operation. Recipients enter and exit the system, move more frequently than Social Security recipients, and are required to meet regularly with caseworkers in order to continue re-ceiving benefits. This complexity is reflected in administrative costs; while Social Security administration totaled just .8 percent of benefits in 1996, AFDC administration equaled 16 percent of benefits.[19] Given the intrica-cies of AFDC administration and the fractious nature of recipient-case-worker relations, one might think that welfare recipients would have a lot more to complain about than the 7 percent grievance rate suggests. Indeed, veterans' benefits recipients, who also must deal with a program more complex than Social Security, though less intrusive than AFDC, complain at double the rate of welfare recipients: 14 percent.

INFLUENCE ON POLICYMAKING

Recipients of means-tested and non-means-tested programs participate in politics at dramatically different rates. We now turn to their influence on policymaking, which requires us to examine whether elected officials have an incentive to pay attention to each group. Such incentives could come from three sources. There may be societal support for the program and its recipients that exerts political pressure on lawmakers. Politicians may feel political pressure from a group itself because of its electoral significance, its lobbying efforts, or both. Or regardless of the group's ongoing political activity level, the group may react vociferously to certain policy events, showing politicians that the group members are watchful, defensive, and readily mobilized.

Elected officials certainly feel less ongoing pressure from welfare constituents than from Social Security recipients. In 1996 there were 27 million retired workers receiving Social Security compared with 12.6 million AFDC recipients, of whom only 4 million were adults of voting age.[20] Social Security recipients not only outnumber adult welfare recipients seven to one, but also make up an even larger share of the electorate. In the 1992 NES data, Social Security recipients are 27 percent of the NES sample, 28 percent of voters, and 32 percent of contributors. By contrast AFDC recipients were 4 percent of the sample, 2 percent of voters, and less than 1 percent of contributors. Not surprisingly, members of Congress receive fewer letters from AFDC recipients than from Social Security recipients. In the Citizen Participation Survey, respondents from Social Security households constituted 21 percent of all contactors while AFDC households constituted just 4 percent. Veterans who get benefits are a fairly small group—just 3.3 percent of the 1992 NES sample—but a vocal one. Next to the Social Security Administration, the Veterans Administration generates the most casework requests, according to Obey Commission interviews of House members.[21] By contrast, out of the nineteen agencies named as generating casework, only one serving the poor, Housing and Urban Development, was mentioned (and infrequently at that). Neither welfare nor any other program for the poor was mentioned.

Popular support levels for the programs differ as well. Welfare is unpopular with the public.[22] While only 4 percent of 1992 NES respondents

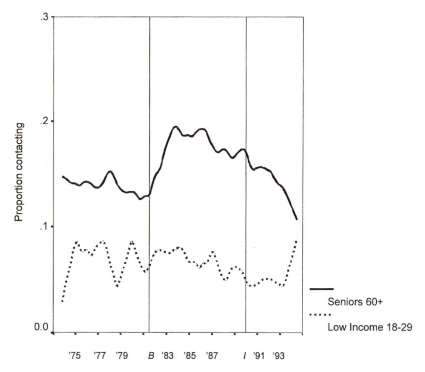

Figure 7.1 Contacting by seniors and low-income youth, 1973–94. Seniors are respondents aged 60 and over. (Roper Social and Political Trends Archive.)

wanted federal spending on Social Security decreased, 42 percent wanted spending on welfare decreased, the most for any of the sixteen issue areas on the survey.[23] On group feeling thermometers, where the elderly scored the highest, "people on welfare" averaged 51 points, the eleventh lowest out of fifty groups (groups ranking lower included illegal aliens, homosexuals, and lawyers). There is no NES feeling thermometer score for veterans, but they are generally a revered group. There are also many veterans in Congress. Their numbers are dwindling—the percentage of House members who are veterans dropped from 75 percent in 1971 to 25 percent in 1999—but there are nonetheless many more veterans in Congress than former welfare recipients.[24]

As we saw in chapter 5, Social Security recipients reacted dramatically to threats to their programs in the 1980s. Welfare programs were also threatened during the 1980s, but recipients did not react in a comparable way. The Roper dataset does not identify welfare recipients, so I examined the participation of very low income people aged 18 to 29.[25] Figure 7.1 compares their contacting rates with those of senior citizens. Seniors of course display the surge around 1981 in response to the Reagan administration threats. For the low-income young people it is difficult to discern any particular participatory reaction during the Reagan years. Perhaps there is a small increase from 1981 to 1982, but that just brings these respondents back up to their 1970s contacting rate. Unfortunately the Roper data do not extend to 1996, when AFDC was replaced with the Transitional Assistance for Needy Families (TANF) program, but given the 1980s results, I suspect there was no contacting surge by welfare recipients in 1996 either.

I also cannot isolate veterans in the Roper data. However, journalistic accounts of veterans legislation suggest that lawmakers do feel political pressure from the group. In a 1996 interview, Senator Alan Simpson, Republican of Wyoming and chairman of the Veterans' Affairs Committee, said, "You mention the word 'veterans,' and you're supposed to pitch forward on your sword." The veterans' lobbies "raise tremendous amounts of money" and "tell their public this Congress doesn't care about their vets."[26] Veterans have substantial support among the public and face little political opposition. Edward J. Derwinski, secretary for veterans affairs in the George H. W. Bush administration, was forced to resign in 1992 after he suggested that nonveterans be admitted to some underutilized VA hospitals. He said, "With welfare, abortion, gun control, the death penalty, you've got legitimate pro and con positions. But there's no anti-vet lobby. No one's going to come in and say, 'Don't waste any more money on veterans.' "[27]

POLICY OUTCOMES

If participation influences policymaking, and elected officials feel different levels of electoral pressure from these groups, then we would expect differential policy outcomes. As this study shows, seniors not only successfully defeated the policy threats of the 1980s, but also now experience proposed and actual benefit expansions. In 2000 the Senate and House voted unanimously to abolish the earnings penalty for Social Security recipients. In 2002, the addition of prescription drug benefits to Medicare was vigorously debated in the two chambers, and a measure was passed in the House (although not in the Senate, to the disappointment of many lawmakers who dreaded explaining the defeat to seniors in the fall elections).[28]

Veterans are also a politically potent group. Originally the American Medical Association opposed extending benefits to non-service-connected illness, but the veterans' lobby prevailed.[29] Edward Tufte also found that veterans' benefits followed an electoral cycle similar to that of Social Security. Prior to their indexation in 1979, payments to veterans rose during election years.[30] Now veterans' numbers are declining as the World War II generation dies off,[31] but veterans still form a strong lobby with much support because of their service to the nation. Organizations like the American Legion and Veterans of Foreign Wars champion veterans' interests "unchallenged by other groups."[32] Nor does the decline in the number of veterans in Congress seem to have an impact on policymaking; William Bianco and Jamie Markham found that with demographic and political factors controlled for, veterans and nonveterans vote similarly on military matters, including Veterans Administration (VA) funding.[33] Measures concerning veterans usually go through the House on the suspension calendar, which is reserved for noncontroversial matters. Even on contested bills, veterans typically win lopsidedly.[34]

In 1988 veterans achieved several victories, including broadened health care, an appeals process for benefits decisions, and elevation of the VA to Cabinet status.[35] In the 1990s the veterans' health system escaped the hospital closings that plagued the civilian sector. While the rest of the industry faced consolidations as a result of market pressures and declines in Medicare reimbursements and federal research funding, the Department of Veterans Affairs expanded its hospital system and saw its budget increased. The system's 172 hospitals and 23,000 beds are estimated to be twice as many as needed, but politically "you're talking about something that would be worse than base closings," according to Bob Stump (R-Ariz.), Chairman of the House Veterans' Affairs Committee.[36] The department has only closed two hospitals since the 1960s, and both of those were for earthquake hazard.[37]

Throughout his presidency, Bill Clinton aggressively courted veterans, many of whom had criticized him for failing to serve in Vietnam. The GOP-controlled Congress approved VA spending increases during the 1990s. Like Social Security, veterans' benefits is an issue area where it can be difficult to tell Republicans and Democrats apart. In 1999 the Disabled American Veterans organized a protest at the VA Medical Center in Manhattan, calling for increased veterans' health spending. In attendance was Republican representative Rick Lazio, who later took Mayor Rudolph Giuliani's place in the 2000 New York Senate race against Hillary Clinton. He told the crowd, "Staff reductions and unnecessary hospital closings are the problems that are most troubling. It's very clear that the President's budget is totally inadequate to meet the minimal needs of veterans."[38] And this despite the fact that Clinton had called for $17.3 billion for health care for veterans, an increase of $6 billion over 1990 levels.[39]

In contrast to Social Security and veterans' benefits, welfare benefits have tended to fall in the last two decades. During the 1980s the Reagan administration successfully cut a variety of welfare programs. Compared with projected outlays under pre-Reagan policy baselines, outlays in fiscal year 1985 were down 14 percent for AFDC, 14 percent for food stamps, 28 percent for child nutrition, 11 percent for housing assistance, and 8 percent for low-income energy assistance.[40] Between 1970 and 1996 the average AFDC benefit per person dropped by 29 percent, from $189 to $135 (in 1996 dollars); during the same period the average Social Security benefit rose 59 percent, from $470 to $745.[41] Welfare benefits languished in part because they were never indexed to inflation at the national level.[42] And unlike Social Security or veterans' benefits, there is no electoral cycle for welfare. Benefit levels have stayed flat or decreased over time, contrary to the increase that we would see if benefits were ratcheted up during election years.[43]

Most significant, Congress and the president eliminated AFDC in 1996, replacing it with the Transitional Assistance for Needy Families program, which ended family entitlement to aid and introduced work requirements and time limits. TANF funds will decline in real terms over time because the block grants to the states are fixed in nominal terms, equal to the 1996 amount of federal spending on AFDC benefits and administration and the cost of the job opportunities and basic skills (JOBS) program.[44]

SUMMARY

The evidence across programs shows that participation influences policy outcomes. High participation groups like seniors and veterans success-fully fend off retrenchment efforts. These groups are able to participate at high rates—and the poor participate at low rates—in large part because of the characteristics they bring to the political arena. But policy feedback effects operate in addition to these preexisting characteristics. The design of programs themselves—benefit levels and the manner in which they are administered—can have enhancing or dampening effects on the participa-tion of recipient groups. Compared with Social Security recipients, AFDC recipients are multiply damned—they have low levels of resources to begin with; the meager program benefits fail to bring them above a partici-patory threshold; the experience of getting the benefits disengages and disempowers them politically; and public opinion is not on their side. Veterans currently share many of the politically salutary characteristics of Social Security recipients, although one can imagine veterans losing their political clout and facing program reduction and hospital closings as their numbers dwindle, and especially as the number of honored World War II vets falls.

This brief look across social welfare programs shows that the effect of program design on democratic citizenship must be considered, lest some groups be permanently marginalized while other are elevated in the participatory arena. Evaluations of policy instruments should acknowledge the potential that government programs have to alleviate or aggravate political inequality. When limited to technical matters such as program efficiency or efficacy, policy evaluations do a disservice to clients by ignoring the significant effects programs have on their ability to enjoy the full rights of citizenship. Without voice such clients become victims of a democratic system in which the vocal and the organized prevail.

Chapter Eight

PARTICIPATION, POLICYMAKING, AND
THE POLITICAL IMPLICATIONS OF
PROGRAM DESIGN

THE ENACTMENT and development of Social Security and Medicare have fundamentally altered the American democratic landscape. The programs helped transform seniors from the poorest, most beleaguered age group to the most comfortable. In supplying seniors with income, health, and free time, the programs have materially enhanced their participatory capacity. The programs' cognitive effects have heightened senior constituents' interest in and vigilance over the political process, a watchfulness of which elected officials are keenly aware. Interest groups arose to fill service niches created by the programs, and as a by-product, the groups serve as informational networks for seniors, alerting them of policy actions. Political parties clamor to mobilize seniors, and elected officials concentrate their casework efforts on them. Seniors learn that they matter politically and that policymakers are receptive. Seniors' political efficacy rises over time as they draw positive lessons about government responsiveness and about themselves as citizens.

These effects have combined to produce the feedback loop described in chapter 4: in its early years, Social Security expanded through the urgings of the Social Security Administration; as these program expansions enhanced seniors' participatory capacity, seniors began to exert political pressure themselves to achieve further expansions. Finally, when Social Security and Medicare were threatened in the 1980s, seniors' participatory capacity, thanks largely to the programs themselves, had grown to such a formidable degree that seniors were able to beat back the threats. Crucially, the design of Social Security meant that seniors had no moral qualms about defending the program. That Social Security is both universal and self-contributory is a major factor in seniors' individual sense of entitlement. As one elderly woman said, "We supported these programs, we paid for these programs, and now it's time to collect."[1] Hence government policy enhanced senior participation levels over time, and seniors, through this participation, have been able to shape policy outcomes.

One observer, writing in 1942, warned, "The demands of the old are rapidly increasing. . . . They are beginning to expect much more of life because of the expansion of programs designed to give them a more enjoyable old age." He predicted that "these growing desires" coupled with "the likelihood of their becoming an increasingly effective pressure group" would create tensions between their needs and those of children, youth, and the middle-aged. Indeed, he even warned that there might be "movements put on foot during this generation to disfranchise those who reach retirement age, in order to protect the interest of other age groups in the population."[2]

It hasn't come to that. There is no credible movement to disenfranchise senior citizens. Even the debate among elites about generational equity—whether the elderly get more than their fair share of society's resources—has never become a focus for the greater public.[3] But other aspects of this early warning have come to fruition. Seniors' participation shapes government outputs. Their programs have largely escaped retrenchment efforts and continue to grow both in terms of spending per recipient and as a share of the federal budget. Through seniors' participation, their aging-policy preferences are fulfilled.

One other aspect of that sixty-year-old prediction has come true: because seniors are a politically dominant group, their preferences on other issues also matter. Policy effects spill over: if seniors' participatory capacity is enhanced by their programs, and if politicians and parties work to mobilize seniors rather than other groups, then issue areas beyond Social Security are affected. Analysis by the economist James Poterba shows that per student education spending is lower in states with a greater proportion of senior citizens.[4] In her history of retirement, Dora Costa argues that seniors lower the price of recreation for themselves by congregating geographically and substituting senior centers and golf courses for playgrounds and public schools.[5] The demographer Samuel Preston noted in 1984 that starting in the late 1950s there had been a sharp decline in the child population and large increase in the elderly population. Demographers would probably predict that such a change would have "favorable consequences for children and troubling ones for the elderly," as fewer children competed for benefits earmarked for them and more elderly competed for resources directed at their group.[6] But as we know, the opposite occurred, perhaps best encapsulated by the divergent trends in poverty rates. Thus while age-related programs have had laudable effects like the reduction in senior poverty, they have also significantly redistributed public sector resources to the elderly, at all levels of government, crowding out other expenditures.[7]

In addition to these concerns about the allocation of societal goods, we must consider the nature of expenditures as well. Spending on children represents both consumption and investment, while spending on the elderly is primarily consumption.[8] Arguably it is in the collective interest to invest in the future, but American democracy is more responsive to organized interests like the elderly. Some might counter that large programs for the elderly are in the interest of the nonelderly, since they relieve younger people of financial burden. But whether that benefit trumps other interests or not, there is little prospect for meaningful debate on the subject, given the political dominance of the organized and highly participatory senior citizen constituency.[9]

As the brief look at veterans and welfare recipients in chapter 7 demonstrated, other groups gain or lose from governmental action depending upon the force of their participation. That some groups participate less and suffer policy disappointments as a result is problematic for political equality and democratic governance. Robert Dahl concludes that "if a group is inactive, whether by free choice, violence, intimidation, or law, the normal American system does not necessarily provide it with a checkpoint anywhere in the process."[10] Participatory quiescence can lead to policy disaster.

Indeed, we can add government policy to Dahl's causes of group inactivity. The design of social welfare programs can enhance recipient participation, as with Social Security, or hinder it, as with welfare. Government policy magnifies groups' participatory advantages or disadvantages, affecting the ability of groups to voice their preferences, therefore influencing subsequent policymaking. Groups get on upward or downward policy trajectories, and advantages or disadvantages accrue.

Democratic theory is predicated on the equal proximity of citizens to government. But public policy itself can undermine this foundation. As Sidney Verba and Gary Orren note, American history is marked by extensions of political equality but not of economic equality.[11] In the latter realm, Americans have traditionally let market outcomes prevail, preferring individualism and self-determination to redistribution. But the lack of economic equality undermines our nominal political equality, muting the voice of the poor. And government programs can make matters worse by elevating some groups over others in the political arena.

Indeed, the effects of policy on recipients and their political participation provide yet another argument for universal social welfare programs. Scholars such as Theda Skocpol and William Julius Wilson assert that targeted, income-tested programs like welfare lack public support because members of the middle class see themselves only as taxpayers, not as potential beneficiaries.[12] Added to this taxpayer consciousness is an association in the United States between such programs and race.[13] Wilson advocates replacing means-tested programs with universal programs to which "the more advantaged groups of all races can positively relate." Skocpol argues for "targeting within universalism," giving extra benefits and services to the poor within larger, publicly supported programs, just as Social

Security redistributes income to poor seniors in a relatively hidden, non-stigmatizing way. In either case, including the poor in universal programs is touted as the key to winning the battle for public approval.

This study shows that the merits of universal programs extend beyond the public support they enjoy. These programs incorporate low-income recipients, minorities, women, and other disadvantaged groups into democratic citizenship on an equal footing with the more affluent. Rather than subject prospective beneficiaries to the stigma and bureaucratic red tape associated with means-tested programs, universal programs treat their recipients with dignity and respect. The programs are set up to ease the way for recipients to secure the benefits they have "earned," rather than face a demeaning process of proving eligibility. The programs have institutionalized appeals processes to dispute benefits decisions. The interactions between government and beneficiary are marked by professionalism and the equal application of well-publicized standards. The result is increased individual efficacy vis-à-vis the government, which enhances participation levels. The degree to which universal programs would enhance the participation rates of the disadvantaged depends on many factors, including benefit levels, but at a minimum the citizenship lessons learned would not actively decrease participation as is the case under welfare's current means-tested design.

More than a Civic Generation

This book has argued that the development of Social Security and Medicare in part fueled the rise in senior participation since the 1950s. Alternatively, Robert Putnam asserts that there is a unique "civic generation" of Americans born between 1910 and 1940 that was socialized to politics in the crucible of the Great Depression and World War II.[14] Perhaps the rise in political activity we see is simply this highly participatory generation's aging and constituting greater proportions of the senior population over time.

Certainly these generational effects operate, which is why I have argued that Social Security and Medicare have *in part* enhanced senior participation over time. But this alternative explanation cannot account for the entire increase. Government programs for the aged have also played a large role.

Consider the counterfactual situation, that Social Security and Medicare were never passed.[15] Members of Putnam's civic generation would still exhibit participatory norms arising from their early socialization experiences. But they would not have the stake in government activity that comes from getting half their income from a government program; the cohort would possess a strong sense of civic duty but not the large and tangible self-interest in public policy. Nor would the cohort have the same resources of time, money, and health. Without Social Security and Medicare, there would be greater senior poverty, less disposable income, a lower retirement rate, and less access to health care. Participatory capacity would be diminished. Perhaps most important, there would be less senior mobilization in the absence of Social Security and Medicare. Without a government policy conferred on the basis of age, there is no politically meaningful senior "group," merely a demographic category. There would be no basis for appeals by political parties and interest groups. Indeed, interest groups of the aged would be less likely to exist without policy niches like medigap insurance to fill. Without Social Security and Medicare, seniors—even those in the civic generation—would have less participatory capacity, less interest in contemporary policymaking, and fewer mobilization opportunities. Hence the generational argument is an incomplete explanation of increased senior activity.

THE FUTURE DESIGN OF SOCIAL SECURITY

Sometime in the coming decades, Social Security will go "bankrupt," unable to pay full benefits under current law. The projected date changes with each shift in national economic circumstances, but one fact remains: the current system is unsustainable. Social Security reform is inevitable.

The key question is what form the new design of Social Security will take. The most prominent reform proposals "privatize" Social Security by investing a portion of the payroll tax receipts in stocks and bonds through either the trust fund or individual accounts (the latter is what most people mean by "privatization.") The choices might be "market organized," allowing individuals to invest in mutual funds, certificates of deposit, and other financial instruments offered by private firms, similar to 401(k) investing, or they might be "government organized," permitting individuals to choose from a fixed number of government-designated options, including stock and bond index funds. In either case a portion of Social Security would become a defined-contribution program (as opposed to the current defined-benefit system with its cost-of-living adjustments and partial redistribution from high-wage to low-wage workers).[16]

A great deal has been written about the economic consequences of various designs: Would privatized benefit levels be higher or lower than current benefits? What would be the effect of different market conditions? How would outcomes differ across individuals?[17] The economic arguments have a normative dimension as well, with actors on either side of the issue maximizing different values and goals. Advocates of private accounts argue that they will restore the confidence of younger people in the system, permit different degrees of risk tolerance, encourage individual responsibility and choice, add to national savings since they may be financed with additional resources, and prevent trust-fund raiding for alternative purposes like an increase in benefits or other spending. Opponents counter that private accounts would expose workers to market risks and the risk of poor investment choices; divert resources from the trust fund, leaving the remaining deferred benefit portion inadequately funded; and increase administrative costs, effectively decreasing benefits.[18]

The findings of this study suggest that this economic focus is too narrow—the political consequences of program change must also be considered. Reform has significant implications for democratic citizenship, altering both Social Security's political engagement and its resource effects. Individual management of Social Security assets could break the tie between senior citizens and the government. Seniors would be less interested in what the government does, since the government would be responsible for a smaller portion of their retirement income. This cognitive link, this interest in public affairs that animates senior participation, would be diminished. The break would be most abrupt for low-income seniors, whose well-being is so closely tied to government action.

Privatization could also have deleterious effects on senior resource levels, and again the effects would be most severe for low-income seniors. Because their income security is so fragile, the less affluent are particularly vulnerable to the kinds of concerns privatization opponents voice.[19] Reducing the defined-benefit portion of Social Security, for example, disproportionately affects low-income seniors, who have few other assets. At retirement, median wealth holdings are only $50,000 in home equity, $16,000 in employer-provided pensions, and $14,000 in personal financial assets.[20] The net worth of new retirees in the poorest income quartile is less than $6,500, including home equity.[21] There is also considerable concern about the treatment of subgroups that are highly dependent on Social Security. Most privatization proposals reduce benefits compared with current law, with advocates arguing that increased income from equity investments would offset the reductions.[22] But such income is not enough to maintain benefit levels for the disabled under the major proposals, a General Accounting Office study found.[23] Leaders of the women's movement argue that divorced women would be harmed by individual accounts because the diverted money in a man's private account might be out of reach to his former wife (under current law, a divorced woman who was married at least ten years has rights to a share of her ex-husband's Social Security benefits).[24] Finally, individuals' decision making regarding their personal retirement savings reinforces concerns about behavior under privatization. In their 401(k) investments, many individuals make poor choices in terms of diversification and age-appropriate risk.[25] And if under privatization there is pressure to make the 401(k)-like account balances available as lump sums upon retirement, surviving spouses might be left with inadequate retirement income: studies show that 40 percent of individuals use lump-sum pension distributions for consumption rather than for savings.[26]

It is possible that privatization would empower poor citizens by giving them a sense of control over their retirement, which would in turn enhance their feelings of internal efficacy and therefore their political participation levels. But demobilization is more likely, both because the tie with government activity is broken and because resource levels are reduced.

Divisions by age and income are already apparent. Public opinion polls show seniors are less supportive of privatization than younger citizens, and low-income seniors are the most wary. One poll by Zogby International in 1999, representative of many others, shows that preference for changing the Social Security system to allow those "who want the choice of investing their Social Security taxes through individual accounts similar to IRAs or 401(k) programs" decreases with age, falling from 88 percent among 18- to 29-year-olds to 80 percent for 30- to 49-year-olds, 60 percent for 50- to 64-year-olds, and just 34 percent among senior citizens.[27] Only 25 percent of seniors with incomes under $25,000 support privatization. Individual accounts are more popular among affluent seniors—supported by 47 percent of those with incomes over $50,000—but still have less appeal than among younger age groups. When asked whether they would invest their Social Security tax money in their own accounts given the option, just 26 percent of lower-income seniors say they would be likely to do so compared with 57 percent of affluent seniors (and nearly three-quarters of those under 50).

These poll results suggest that the poor and affluent are divided when it comes to Social Security privatization, a significant development. Until recently, seniors have been fairly united when it comes to age-related policy; the fight has been characterized by a "benefits for all" approach. But recent policy proposals highlight differential class interests in a way that may provide retrenchment proponents with a divide-and-conquer strategy. The Medicare Catastrophic Coverage Act episode first exposed this potential division; in that instance, both low- and high-income seniors opposed the act, but, crucially, did so for different reasons reflecting their divergent economic situations. With Social Security privatization, class differences among seniors become even starker. Low-income seniors prefer the current defined-benefit structure. By contrast, affluent seniors can afford market risk; indeed their retirement is already privatized, because private pensions, not Social Security, are their main source of retirement income.[28] This divide promises to worsen over time. Although baby boomers have higher real incomes and greater wealth than their parents at comparable ages, they are not saving enough to maintain their standard of living in retirement, and the problem is particularly acute among low-income boomers.[29] Hence economic inequality and attitudinal divisions will likely increase among future cohorts of senior citizens.

Age-related policy advocates fear that conservatives want to trim the growth of Social Security and Medicare with a means test, which will divide the senior constituency. But it isn't necessary to go so far as means testing: proposals that simply have differential impacts across income groups may undermine senior solidarity. The current design of Social Security has differential impacts too, but impacts that reduce inequality—both economic and political—among seniors. The new breed of privatization proposals exacerbate rather than ameliorate economic inequality and so threaten to unmake seniors' relative political equality.

Conclusion

This book addresses a number of the fundamental political questions summarized by Lasswell's famous query: "Who gets what, when, how?"[30] First, high-participation groups do prevail in the policy arena; this study supports the assumption behind decades of participation research—that participatory inputs influence policy outputs. Second, existing policies do structure subsequent political processes. And these feedback effects are pronounced for the mass public and are certainly not limited to state or interest group capacities. Finally, self-interest is an impetus to political activity, when the stakes are high, the informational barriers low, and moral or social reservations absent. We saw this particularly in the activity of low-income seniors with regard to Social Security. But the cross-program comparison showed that interest is not enough; individuals must have at least minimal resources for participation. In the case of senior citizens, these means come in part from government programs. Welfare state programs laudably mobilize a low-income group—poor seniors—which is a rarity in American politics. But senior programs also serve to elevate the participation of seniors in general over that of other groups. These normative effects of welfare state programs cannot be ignored.

Policy studies typically evaluate policy instruments in terms of their "efficiency, effectiveness and feasibility of adoption and implementation."[31] This book shows that the design of social programs has significant implications for politics as well. Politically relevant aspects of program design include the size and characteristics of the beneficiary group, the level of benefits, the funding mechanism, and the method of conferring benefits. These program characteristics influence electoral politics, the politics of distribution, and the politics of retrenchment. Over time Social Security itself has enhanced the participation rates of a large group of people. Benefits are high enough to have tangible effects on senior participatory capacity and to heighten their interest in a program that provides such a large share of their income. Because the program is self-contributory, seniors confront no welfare stigma in receiving benefits, feel no moral compunction exercising their self-interest in defending their benefits, and have faced little backlash from the rest of the public. Social Security is a highly regarded and effective program that seniors rationally and unequivocally defend. It is also a program that because of its very design has led to disproportionate senior influence on electoral politics and on policymaking. Seniors get more out of the government than less-participatory groups, in part because of the structure of their welfare state programs. This presumably unintended consequence shows that both economic *and* political implications must be considered when designing social programs.

Appendix A

SUPPLEMENTARY TABLES

Table A.1
Explaining the Participation of All Respondents: Logistic Regression Results for Figure 3.4

	Voting	Contributing	Contacting	Campaign Work	Protest
Education	0.391***	0.361***	0.219***	0.182***	0.254***
Income	0.021***	0.025***	0.002	0.009#	0.005
Income-squared	−0.000068**	−0.000066***	−0.0000027	−0.000015	−0.000010
Male	−0.162	0.144	0.247*	−0.092	−0.202
Married	0.204#	0.040	0.161	−0.056	−0.363#
Black	0.112	0.328	−0.390*	0.706**	0.539#
Working	0.506***	0.273#	−0.079	0.163	−0.204
Retired	0.777**	0.139	−0.205	0.758*	0.073
Political interest	0.423***	0.480***	0.372***	0.544***	0.522***
Age	0.041***	0.019***	0.004	−0.007	−0.040***
Constant	−5.6345***	−7.6487***	−4.0782***	−6.8777***	−5.3906***
N	2,259	2,259	2,259	2,259	2,259
−2 log likelihood	2189.24	1972.08	2650.82	1149.74	855.43
Goodness of fit	2241.53	2172.78	2303.20	2213.37	2171.46
% correctly predicted	76.1%	79.9%	69.0%	91.8%	94.6%

#$p < .10$; *$p < .05$; **$p < .01$; ***$p < .001$.
Source: Citizen Participation Study.
Note: Figures in cells are logistic regression coefficients.

TABLE A.2
Explaining Social Security Participation by Seniors: Logistic Regression Results
for Figure 3.5, Contacting and Contributing

	Social Security–Oriented Participation	
	Contacting	Contributing
Education	0.355*	−0.007
Income	−0.020[a]	0.080[a]
Income-squared	0.000037[a]	−0.0011000[a]
Male	1.534*	−0.236
Married	−1.177[#]	−0.308
Black	−0.143	1.030
Working	0.901	−0.190
Retired	1.192	0.732
Political interest	0.609*	0.712**
Age	0.033	0.007
Constant	−11.2171**	−9.3308*
N	234	233
−2 log likelihood	113.16	109.64
Goodness of fit	458.64	248.98
% correctly predicted	93.1%	94.2%

[#]$p < .10$; *$p < .05$; **$p < .01$; ***$p < .001$.
Source: Citizen Participation Study.
Note: Results are for respondents aged 65 and over. Figures in cells are logistic regression coefficients. For Social Security voting, see two-stage model in appendix B.
[a] Income and Income-squared are jointly significant ($p < .001$).

TABLE A.3
Civic Voluntarism Model, Seniors versus Nonseniors: Logistic Regression Results for Table 3.9, Citizen Participation Study Data

	Voting 18–64	Voting 65+	Contributing 18–64	Contributing 65+	Contacting 18–64	Contacting 65+	Working on Campaigns 18–64	Working on Campaigns 65+
Resources								
Education	0.168***	0.166*	0.173***	0.127#	-0.043	0.122*	-0.020	-0.085
Income	0.061*	1.043***	0.101***	0.183*	0.002	-0.220**	0.064*	-0.040
Retired	2.282**	-0.078	-0.177	0.918*	0.842*	-0.203	1.350**	1.702#
Working	0.588***	-2.521**	0.068	-0.578	-0.244	0.167	0.103	1.292
Free time	0.003	-0.124#	-0.018	-0.013	0.013	-0.058	0.040	0.104
Civic skills	0.048#	0.129	0.042	0.170*	0.111***	0.181*	0.100*	0.339***
Engagement								
Political interest	0.368***	0.290*	0.265***	0.159	0.179***	0.275*	0.300***	0.641**
Political information	0.160***	0.055	0.025	0.115	0.015	0.050	-0.092	0.395*
Political efficacy	0.039	-0.066	0.106***	0.122#	0.145***	-0.002	0.140***	-0.004
Mobilization								
Activity recruitment	0.196**	0.681*	0.677***	0.352*	0.656***	0.675***	0.534***	0.439#
Other characteristics								
Male	-0.205#	-0.149	0.338*	-0.945*	0.047	1.153**	-0.295	-0.342
Black	0.188	0.707	0.650**	0.038	-0.358#	-0.660	0.827**	1.276
Hispanic	-0.005	0.770	0.022	1.126	-0.741*	-0.353	0.772#	2.082
Married	0.327**	0.168	0.104	0.353	-0.103	0.858**	-0.239	0.844
Age	0.039***	0.031	0.025***	0.010	0.005	0.017	0.001	-0.025
Citizen	1.462***	1.023	-0.022	0.779	-0.129	0.626	1.073*	-0.711
Constant	-8.396***	-5.579#	-8.996***	-8.311**	-3.371***	-6.630**	-7.619***	-9.476*
N	2,124	287	2,123	287	2,124	287	2,123	287
-2 log likelihood	1965.57	209.46	1615.20	282.15	2186.39	309.53	985.17	123.85
Goodness of fit	1995.30	220.62	1931.07	625.31	2093.85	409.19	2048.37	1173.78
% correctly predicted	77.0%	83.7%	82.9%	79.8%	74.8%	79.5%	91.7%	93.8%

#$p < .10$; *$p < .05$; **$p < .01$; ***$p < .001$.
Source: Citizen Participation Study.
Note: Figures in cells are logit coefficients.

TABLE A.4
Civic Voluntarism Model, Seniors versus Nonseniors: Logistic Regression Results for Table 3.9, 1992 and 1996 National Election Studies Data

	Voting		Contributing		Working on Campaigns	
	18–64	65+	18–64	65+	18–64	65+
Resources						
Education	0.355***	0.312*	0.082	0.413***	0.043	0.244
Income	0.009**	0.016	0.015***	0.015*	0.000	0.013
Retired	0.179	1.121**	−0.137	−0.368	−1.523	−0.976
Working	0.014	1.657**	0.229	−0.297	0.088	−1.377
Engagement						
Political interest	1.866***	1.278**	2.050***	1.291*	2.242***	0.623
Political information	0.503***	0.739*	−0.265	−0.433	0.841#	0.776
Political efficacy	0.842***	0.936	0.558	0.768	1.320**	0.993
Mobilization						
Party mobilization	0.942***	1.006**	0.610***	0.854**	1.386***	0.592
Other characteristics						
Male	−0.334**	−0.576#	0.189	0.289	−0.383	0.352
Black	0.096	0.562	−1.632**	0.133	0.264	0.244
Hispanic	−0.158	0.085	0.432	0.823	−0.816	−4.667
Married	0.407**	0.763*	−0.088	0.317	−0.373	−0.488
Age	0.029***	0.015	0.031***	0.033	0.016	−0.046
Constant	−3.625***	−3.693*	−6.838***	−7.781***	−7.565***	−2.480
N	2,290	510	2,290	510	2,288	510
−2 log likelihood	1842.97	344.77	1077.73	307.08	600.52	118.89
Goodness of fit	2260.48	477.07	2349.30	463.76	2339.30	625.22
% correctly predicted	81.6%	85.7%	92.0%	88.4%	96.4%	97.1%

#$p < .10$; *$p < .05$; **$p < .01$; ***$p < .001$.
Source: National Election Studies, 1992 and 1996.
Note: Figures in cells are logit coefficients.

TABLE A.5
Civic Voluntarism Model, Seniors versus Nonseniors: Logistic Regression Results for Table 3.9, Roper Survey 8108 Data

	Voting		Working on Campaigns		Petition Signing	
	18–64	65+	18–64	65+	18–64	65+
Resources						
Education	0.387***	0.405*	0.470***	0.295	0.377***	0.449*
Income	0.012	0.052*	0.015	0.048	0.013	0.050*
Retired	0.287	1.785*	−6.244	−0.557	0.411	0.276*
Working	0.505*	1.731	−0.010	−7.965	0.097*	0.139
Engagement						
Political interest	0.625***	0.146	0.421#	1.564	0.296***	−0.083
Social Security interest	0.204	1.697*	0.601*	0.212	0.265	1.019*
Other characteristics						
Male	−0.273	−0.672	−0.624*	0.369	−0.119	0.294
Black	−0.949*	−7.043	0.726	−6.015	−1.199*	−0.401
Married	0.060	0.081	−0.072	−1.441#	−0.103	−0.305
Age	0.109**		0.108#		−0.031**	
N	1,378	201	1,378	201	1,378	201
−2 log likelihood	918.07	128.81	410.11	61.51	1630.17	181.79
Goodness of fit	1371.16	141.72	1359.68	123.80	1349.01	185.19
% correctly predicted	87.5%	83.6%	96.0%	95.0%	65.9%	77.1%

#$p < .10$; *$p < .05$; **$p < .01$; ***$p < .001$.
Source: Roper Survey 8108.
Note: Figures in cells are logit coefficients.

TABLE A.6
Influences on Senior Participation, Including Mobilization: Logistic Regression
Results for Table 4.2, NES Data, 1952–96

	Voting	Contributing	Campaign Work
Mobilization			
Party mobilization	0.921***	0.712***	1.078***
Resources			
Education	0.246***	0.343***	0.093*
Income	0.043***	0.040***	0.010
Engagement			
Political interest	0.479***	0.549***	0.773***
Other characteristics			
Male	0.220**	0.035	0.431*
Black	0.083	−.278	0.016
Married	0.315***	0.342**	0.102
Age	−.008	0.012	−.041**
Constant	−1.139*	−6.999***	−3.863***
N	4,215	4,206	4,015
−2 log likelihood	4408.48	2251.11	1275.69
Goodness of fit	4497.11	3882.58	4300.52
% correctly predicted	76.2%	90.8%	95.9%

#$p < .10$; *$p < .05$; **$p < .01$; ***$p < .001$.
Source: National Election Studies, 1952–96.
Note: Figures in cells are logit coefficients.

TABLE A.7
Influence of AARP Membership on Respondent Participation: Logistic Regression Results for Chapter 4 "Senior Citizen Interest Groups" Section

	Voting	Contributing	Contacting	Campaign Work	Social Security Voting	Social Security Contributing	Social Security Contacting
Education	0.415***	0.383***	0.214***	0.182***	0.181*	0.088	0.187
Income	0.009***	0.011***	0.002	0.006**	-.012*	-.001	-.017
Male	-.144	0.141	0.246*	-.098	0.649*	0.076	0.267
Married	0.329**	0.148	0.124	-.089	0.365	-.242	-.069
Black	0.119	0.320	-.378*	0.716**	0.172	0.396	-.375
Working	0.599***	0.308#	-.130	0.122	-.597#	0.082	-.086
Retired	0.764**	0.289	0.017	0.991*	-.548#	1.150	0.377
Political interest	0.425***	0.477***	0.366***	0.536***	0.529***	0.493**	0.410**
Age 35–44	0.424**	0.366*	0.247*	0.242	0.782	6.229	0.779
Age 45–54	0.855***	0.647***	0.178	-.006	1.877#	5.601	0.980
Age 55–64	1.321***	0.289	0.382*	0.082	2.491**	5.572	-.355
Age 65+	1.795***	0.627*	-.276	-.744#	2.142*	5.355	-.607
AARP membership	0.569#	0.233	0.429*	0.355	-.200	0.513	0.852*
Constant	-4.4942***	-6.927***	-3.9422***	-7.0011***	-6.774***	-12.6428	-5.5745***
N	2,258	2,258	2,258	2,258	419	422	423
–2 log likelihood	2193.24	1982.44	2633.44	1143.54	458.08	165.27	226.66
Goodness of fit	2219.96	2154.44	2300.67	2199.20	472.24	429.95	530.24
% correctly predicted	74.9%	79.8%	69.9%	91.8%	75.5%	95.1%	92.5%

# $p < .10$; * $p < .05$; ** $p < .01$; *** $p < .001$.
Source: Citizen Participation Study.
Note: Figures in cells are logistic regression coefficients.

TABLE A.8
External Political Efficacy of Senior Citizens over Time: Basis of Figure 5.1

	External Efficacy		External Efficacy
Demographics		1994	−40.197***
Education	6.220***	1996	−37.701***
Income	3.049***	1998	−35.077***
Male	−.155	2000	−13.090***
Black	−5.163***	Year * Senior	
South	−2.987***	1956 * Age 65+	−1.085
Strength of partisanship	3.334***	1960 * Age 65+	2.901
Age	−.060**	1964 * Age 65+	1.292
Age 65+	−7.252**	1966 * Age 65+	1.902
Year dummies		1968 * Age 65+	1.452
1956	3.758**	1970 * Age 65+	3.791
1960	4.443**	1972 * Age 65+	7.207*
1964	−2.361	1974 * Age 65+	2.346
1966	−6.282***	1976 * Age 65+	8.886*
1968	−12.548***	1978 * Age 65+	6.099#
1970	−11.785***	1980 * Age 65+	7.576#
1972	−16.074***	1982 * Age 65+	8.704#
1974	−15.797***	1984 * Age 65+	6.629#
1976	−21.473***	1986 * Age 65+	12.813**
1978	−22.136***	1988 * Age 65+	4.495
1980	−20.911***	1990 * Age 65+	3.773
1982	−23.202***	1992 * Age 65+	9.294**
1984	−11.361***	1994 * Age 65+	2.746
1986	−28.769***	1996 * Age 65+	6.280#
1988	−25.089***	1998 * Age 65+	10.720**
1990	−38.048***	2000 * Age 65+	14.363***
1992	−23.592***	R-squared	0.17
		N	35,292

# $p < .10$; * $p < .05$; ** $p < .01$; *** $p < .001$.
Source: National Election Studies.
Note: Figures in cells are unstandardized OLS regression coefficients. 1952 and 1952 * Age 65+ are the reference categories. The year dummies are included to control for the secular decrease in external political efficacy over time.

Figure 5.1 graphs the Year * Age 65+ coefficients. These coefficients show how many points (on a 100-point scale) seniors' external political efficacy has risen over 1952 levels. See chapter 5 for further discussion. External political efficacy (vcf0648 from NES cumulative file) scale (0 to 100) constructed from these items: "People like me don't have any say about what the government does" (v6102); "I don't think public officials care much what people like me think" (v6103). Higher values indicate greater external efficacy.

TABLE A.9
House and Senate Roll-Call Votes on Social Security and Medicare Included in Chapter 6 Analysis (Tables 6.1 and 6.2)

Program	Year	Date	Item	Description	Reject/ Adopt	Yea– Nay	Correlation with %65+ in District or State
House							
SS	1983	9-Mar	HR 1900	SS Act amendments of 1983: Amdt. to raise retirement age to 67	A	228–202	0.08#
SS	1983	9-Mar	HR 1900	Amdt.: substitute payroll tax increase for long-term benefit cuts in the cmte bill	R	132–296	0.06
SS	1983	9-Mar	HR 1900	Amdt.: raise retirement age to 67	A	230–200	0.08#
SS	1983	9-Mar	HR 1900	Passage: 1983 SS amendments	A	282–148	0.12**
SS	1983	24-Mar	HR 1900	Conf. report: 1983 SS amendments	A	243–102	0.07
SS	1985	23-May	H Con Res 15	Amdt. to eliminate COLA , etc.	R	56–372	0.07
M	1987	22-Jul	HR 2470	Medicare catastrophic coverage bill. Provide for floor consideration of bill (substitute in compromise pkg.)	A	248–174	0.07
M	1987	22-Jul	HR 2470	Amdt. striking encouragement of generic drugs	R	161–265	–.11*
M	1987	22-Jul	HR 2470	Amdt. to substitute text of more limited version	R	190–242	0.07
M	1987	22-Jul	HR 2470	Passage of Medicare catastrophic coverage bill (House version)	A	302–127	0.13**
M	1988	2-Jun	HR 2470	Adopt rule so can consider catastrophic conf. report	A	269–129	0.07
M	1988	2-Jun	HR 2470	Conf. report: Medicare catastrophic coverage bill passed (final version)	A	328–72	0.19***
Senate							
SS	1983	17-Mar	HR 1900	Amdt.: move to 1983 (not 1988) automatic decrease in COLA when trust fund falls below certain level	R	25–72	0.18#
SS	1983	22-Mar	HR 1900	Amdt. to move up by 2 years phaseout of earnings limitation	R	44–49	0.09
SS	1983	22-Mar	HR 1900	Amdt.: index income threshold at which SS benefits subject to taxation	R	22–74	0.06
SS	1983	23-Mar	HR 1900	Amdt.: change threshold for taxation to reduce marriage penalty in SS benefits taxation	R	34–62	0.16
SS	1983	23-Mar	HR 1900	Amdt.: strike provision requiring tax exempt interest income to be included in calculation	R	44–52	–.09

# $p < .10$; * $p < .05$; ** $p < .01$; *** $p < .001$.

Source: Congressional Quarterly's Congressional Roll Calls, various editions.

Note: Con Res–concurrent resolution; HR–House resolution; J Res–joint resolution; M–Medicare; SS–Social Security.

TABLE A.9
House and Senate Roll-Call Votes on Social Security and Medicare Included in Chapter 6 Analysis (Tables 6.1 and 6.2) (cont'd)

Program	Year	Date	Item	Description	Reject–/Adopt	Yea–/Nay	Correlation with %65+ in District or State
Senate							
SS	1983	23-Mar	HR 1900	Passage: 1983 SS amendments	A	88–9	0.14
SS	1983	24-Mar	HR 1900	Conf. report: 1983 SS amendments	A	58–14	0.26*
SS	1984	1-May	HR 2163	Deficit reduction Amdt.: freeze COLAs for entitlements	R	38–57	0.16
M	1984	9-May	HR 2163	Motion to kill elimination of Part B premium increases	A	58–36	0.21*
M	1984	9-May	HR 2163	Motion to kill elimination of delay in Medicare eligibility	A	59–36	0.10
SS	1984	9-May	HR 2163	Substitute plan capping COLAs	R	23–72	0.06
M	1984	17-May	HR 2163	Amdt. to restore some Medicare savings	R	44–50	0.19#
SS	1985	1-May	S Con Res 32	Amdt. retaining existing COLAs	A	65–34	0.38***
M	1985	2-May	S Con Res 32	Amdt. to restore some funding to Medicare	A	93–6	0.09
SS	1985	9-May	S Con Res 32	Amdt. including elimination of 1986 COLA	A	50–49	0.21*
SS	1985	9-May	S Con Res 32	Motion to kill amdt. restoring full COLA	A	51–47	0.15
M	1985	9-May	S Con Res 32	Motion to kill amdt. restoring Medicare funding	A	54–44	0.16
M	1985	9-Dec	H J Res 465	Maneuver re: increasing Medicare hospital deductible	A	53–37	0.30**
M	1985	9-Dec	H J Res 465	Maneuver re: capping hospital deductible	A	45–41	0.34**
SS	1986	12-Mar	S J Res 225	Motion re: bar cutting SS benefits to balance budget	A	57–42	0.36***
M	1987	6-May	S Con Res 49	Motion to kill amdt. raising Medicare, Medicaid funding	A	69–29	–.02
M	1987	27-Oct	S 1127	Medicare catastrophic coverage bill amdt. adding drug coverage	A	88–9	0.04
M	1987	27-Oct	S 1127	Amdt. permitting Medicare beneficiaries to opt out of new catastrophic benefits without giving up Part B	R	18–77	0.26*
M	1987	27-Oct	S 1127	Motion to kill sense of Senate amdt. that federal taxes shouldn't be increased	A	65–32	0.21*
M	1987	27-Oct	HR 2470	Passage of Medicare catastrophic coverage bill (Senate version)	A	86–11	0.10
SS	1987	10-Dec	S 1920	Budget reconciliation motion killing amdt. restricting COLAs to 2%	A	71–25	0.09
M	1988	8-Jun	HR 2470	Conf. report: Medicare catastrophic coverage bill passed (final version)	A	86–11	0.13

#$p < .10$; *$p < .05$; **$p < .01$; ***$p < .001$.

Source: Congressional Quarterly's Congressional Roll Calls, various editions.

Note: Con Res–concurrent resolution; HR–House resolution; J Res–joint resolution; M–Medicare; SS–Social Security.

TABLE A.10
External and Internal Political Efficacy of Program Recipients—Social Security,
Veterans' Benefits, and AFDC—for Efficacy Discussion in Chapter 7, "Recipient
Participation" Section

	External Efficacy	Internal Efficacy
Education	.312***	0.652***
Income	0.043**	0.039
Male	−.102	1.603***
Black	0.044	0.704**
South	−.095	0.218
Age	−.011*	0.005
Strength of partisanship	0.195***	0.374***
Get Social Security	0.428*	−.187
Get AFDC	−.496*	1.454***
Get veterans' benefits	0.273	0.356
R-squared	0.08	0.16
N	1,958	1,952

$^{#}p < .10$; $^{*}p < .05$; $^{**}p < .01$; $^{***}p < .001$.
Source: National Election Study, 1992.
Note: Figures in cells are unstandardized OLS regression coefficients.

External efficacy scale (1 to 10) constructed from these items: "People like me don't have
any say about what the government does" (v6102); "I don't think public officials care much
what people like me think" (v6103). Higher values indicate greater external political efficacy.

Internal efficacy scale (1 to 20) constructed from these items: "I feel that I have a pretty
good understanding of the important political issues facing our country" (v6105); "I consider myself well qualified to participate in politics" (v6106); "I feel that I could do as good
a job in public office as most other people" (v6107); "I think that I am better informed
about politics and government than most other people" (v6108). Higher values indicate
greater internal political efficacy.

TABLE A.11
Respondents Reporting Voting for Whom No
Record of Voting Could Be Found

	18–34	35–64	65+
1964	20%	18%	16%
1976	22	13	15
1978	34	22	16
1980	21	14	14
1984	16	13	11
1986	24	18	10
1988	19	15	9
1990	26	17	10

Source: National Election Study cumulative file.
Note: Variable 9151 = 1.

TABLE A.12
Voter Turnout in 2000 by Age

	18–34	35–64	65+
Did not vote	18%	12%	12%
Thought about it, but didn't	19	5	< 1
Usually vote, but didn't	5	5	8
I am sure I voted	58	78	80
Total	100%	100%	100%

Columns may not total 100 due to rounding.
Source: National Election Study, 2000.

TABLE A.13
Work Status among Seniors by Gender

	Men	Women
Working full time	6.0%	2.3%
Working part time	6.7	6.1
Retired	84.6	47.9
Keeping house	2.0	40.8
Permanently disabled	0.7	1.9
Other (student, full time volunteer)	0	1.0

Source: Citizen Participation Study.

TABLE A.14
Senior/Nonsenior Mobilization Ratios, All Respondents versus
Registered Respondents

Year	All Respondents	Registered Respondents
1956	0.97	0.96
1960	0.67	0.63
1964	0.67	0.66
1968	0.74	0.75
1972	0.93	0.96
1976	1.02	1.03
1980	1.23	1.23

Source: National Election Studies.

TABLE A.15
Number of Roper Survey Respondents by Age

Age	Minimum	Maximum	Median
18–29	319	616	534
30–59	679	1,283	1,019
60+	249	493	427

Source: Roper Social and Political Trends Archive.

TABLE A.16
Predicting Pro-Senior Roll-Call Voting

	House		Senate	
	Democrats	Republicans	Democrats	Republicans
% 65 +	−0.0004	0.0616***	0.106*	0.059*
ADA score	0.0223***	0.0013#	0.014***	0.017***
Constant	−0.4434#	−1.3406***	−0.794	−1.176***
N	2,751	1,774	1,184	1,322
−2 log likelihood	2901.94	2272.42	1140.34	1758.76
Goodness of fit	2761.41	1772.13	1190.55	1322.88
% correctly predicted	76.9%	64.7%	80.6%	59.5%

#$p < .10$; *$p < .05$; **$p < .01$; ***$p < .001$.
Sources: Roll-call votes from the *Congressional Quarterly's Congressional Roll Calls*, various years; ADA scores and % seniors by congressional district from *Politics in America*, various years; % seniors by state from *U.S. Statistical Abstract*, various years.
Note: Figures in cells are logit coefficients.

TABLE A.17
Predicting Medicare Catastrophic Act Vote Switching in the House

	Democrats	Republicans
% 65 +	−0.048	0.212***
ADA Score	−0.005	0.040***
Constant	1.559#	−4.331***
N	233	155
−2 log likelihood	300.96	153.05
Goodness of fit	232.92	154.14
% correctly predicted	64.8%	74.8%

#p < .10; *p < .05; **p < .01; ***p < .001.
Sources: Switchers calculated from the *Congressional Quarterly's Congressional Roll Calls*, various years; ADA scores and % seniors by congressional district from *Politics in America*, various years.
Note: Figures in cells are logit coefficients.

TABLE A.18
Predicting Medicare Catastrophic Act Vote Switching with Home Value

	Democrats	Republicans
Median home value	0.019	−0.043**
Median home value × % 65+	−0.001	0.004**
ADA Score	−0.009	0.039***
Constant	0.848	−1.733**
N	233	155
−2 log likelihood	299.39	154.14
Goodness of fit	232.96	150.18
% correctly predicted	64.8%	75.5%

#p < .10; *p < .05; **p < .01; ***p < .001.
Sources: Switchers calculated from the *Congressional Quarterly's Congressional Roll Calls*, various years; ADA scores, % seniors by congressional district, and district median home values from *Politics in America*, various years.
Note: Figures in cells are logit coefficients.

Appendix B

TWO-STAGE SOCIAL SECURITY
PARTICIPATION MODEL

ALTHOUGH THE Citizen Participation Study included questions asking whether respondents have ever contacted, voted, or made campaign contributions with regard to Social Security, the Social Security–oriented activity reported by respondents is probably contaminated by non–Social Security activity. This is particularly likely for voting, which is often done for many reasons, even when respondents say they voted with regard to Social Security. The following model "purges" Social Security voting of non–Social Security activity.

There are two ideal types of participatory activity—participation that is oriented toward Social Security and participation that is not. Non–Social Security–oriented participation, P_i^N, is a function of socio-structural factors like education, income, race, gender, and work status, designated as X, and other factors, O, plus error.

$$P_i^N = \alpha_1 + \alpha_2 X + \alpha_3 f(O) + \text{error.} \tag{B.1}$$

Since we do not know what the other factors are that influence participation, we include $f(O)$ in the error term and estimate P_i^N as a function of the socio-structural factors X.

Social Security participation, P_i^{SS}, is also a function of socio-structural factors X, other factors O, and error.

$$P_i^{SS} = \beta_1 + \beta_2 X + \beta_3 f(O) + \text{error.} \tag{B.2}$$

I hypothesize that the other factor O that influences Social Security participation is self-interest in the program. One plausible measure of self-interest with regard to Social Security is income, since those with lower incomes are more dependent. I believe that this model, in which Social Security participation is a function of socio-structural factors and income, is complete. There is no reason to include ideology, for example. Ideology does not influence Social Security participation or attitudes independent of income; NES data show that liberal and conservative seniors have the same opinion on Social Security (the difference between their answers to the question, "Should federal spending on Social Security be increased, decreased or kept the same?" is not statistically significant). Unlike an issue such as abortion, where there are two ideologically opposed sides, virtually no seniors are against Social Security.

Thus Social Security participation, P_i^{SS}, is a function of socio-structural factors X and self-interest, which I measure with income. The difficulty is that income not only measures self-interest vis-à-vis Social Security but also serves as a proxy for other factors, like the propensity to participate in general. To isolate the self-interest aspect of income, I must control for the other effects of income.

$$P_i^{SS} = \gamma_1 + \gamma_2 \, Q_i + \gamma_3 \, f(O) + \text{error.} \tag{B.3}$$

Social Security participation, P_i^{SS}, is a function of the propensity to participate in general without Social Security in mind, Q_i, and other factors, O, for which I am using income.

The best estimate of Q_i is P_i^N from equation (B.1), non–Social Security–oriented participation. I ran a two-stage analysis. One cannot simply put P_i^N in equation (B.4) for Q_i, because there could be some variable left out that influences both P_i^N and P_i^{SS}, such as a taste for participation. In equations (B.1) and (B.2), such variables are in the error term. If I substituted (B.1) for Q_i in (B.4) and there was a common omitted variable, the error from equation (B.1) would then be an included variable in (B.4), and there would be correlation between that included variable and the error, resulting in biased estimates of the coefficients. Instead I ran a two-stage analysis:

$$P_i^{SS} = \gamma_1 + \gamma_2 \, Q_i + \gamma_3 \, \text{income} + \text{error.} \tag{B.4}$$

Social Security participation, P_i^{SS}, is a function of income (the sole measure of $f(O)$) and non–Social Security–oriented participation, Q_i, which is instrumented with education, income, gender, race, work status, political interest, and age. Estimations of equation B.4 using a two-stage process produced the results in figures 3.5b and 3.6.

In the Citizen Participation voting analysis shown in figure 3.5b, I created an index of participatory activities that seemed least likely to be contaminated by Social Security: informal community activity and board membership/meeting attendance (the index ranges from 0 to 2). In the first stage of the analysis I estimated this non–Social Security participation index with OLS, using a variety of demographic variables (education, income, male, married, black, working, retired, political interest, age—that is, the instruments). In the second stage I regressed Social Security voting on the estimated non–Social Security participation index from the first stage, income, and income-squared, using logistic regression (Social Security voting is a 0–1 variable; table B.1).

TABLE B.1

Logistic Regression Estimate of Social Security Voting, Seniors Only (Figure 3.5b)

	B	S.E.
Estimated non-SS participation	3.2224	0.8184***
Income	−0.0027	0.0134
Income-squared	−0.00005	0.00007
N	231	
−2 log likelihood	315.41	
Goodness of fit	284.91	
% correctly predicted	73.0%	

***$p < .001$.

Source: Citizen Participation Study.

This analysis shows the self-interest effect of income on Social Security participation: the income coefficients for Social Security voting are negative (the hypothesized direction). Income and income-squared are jointly significant ($p < .10$). Thus voting related to Social Security decreases with income, in sharp contrast to what we usually see in participation research. I also performed the analysis with the 2SLS procedure as a further check on the standard errors (not shown). The results from 2SLS were the same. I show the logit results here and in figure 3.5b because the 2SLS results predict activity outside the 0–1 bound.

I performed a similar analysis with the Roper data, applying the purging technique to the regular contacting item to isolate Social Security–oriented contacting. Analysis of the Social Security contacting item from the Citizen Participation Study shown in figure 3.5a and appendix table A.2 yielded income and income-squared coefficients that were jointly significant but not individually significant. The much larger N in the Roper data overcomes that problem. In the first stage I estimated non–Social Security participation—a 0-to-4 index of local public meeting attendance, good government group membership, local organization committee membership, and club or organization officer—using as instruments education, income, male, black, married, retired, and working. Then in the second stage I estimated (Social Security) contacting with non–Social Security participation, income, and income-squared (table B.2).

The income and income-squared coefficients are highly statistically significant, and while the income coefficient is positive, the income-squared coefficient is negative, so that the likelihood of contacting with regard to

TABLE B.2
Logistic Regression Estimate of Roper (Social Security) Contacting,
Seniors Only (Figure 3.6)

	B	S.E.
Estimated non-SS participation	4.6667	0.1106***
Income	0.0225	0.0032***
Income-squared	−0.0006	0.00005***
N	60,174	
−2 log likelihood	47020.37	
Goodness of fit	59433.81	
% correctly predicted	84.95%	

***$p < .001$.

Source: Roper Social and Political Trends Archive.

Social Security (more precisely, the likelihood of contacting controlling for the propensity to participate in general) is lower at high-income levels. Again, I also ran the analysis using 2SLS with exactly the same results (not shown)—non–Social Security participation, income, and income-squared were highly statistically significant (t-values of 12 or more), and the income coefficient was positive and the income-squared coefficient negative so Social Security contacting was lower at high-income levels. I show the logistic regression results here and in figure 3.6 because the 2SLS results predicted activity outside the 0–1 bound.

Appendix C

SENIOR/NONSENIOR MOBILIZATION
RATIOS BY PARTY, 1956–96

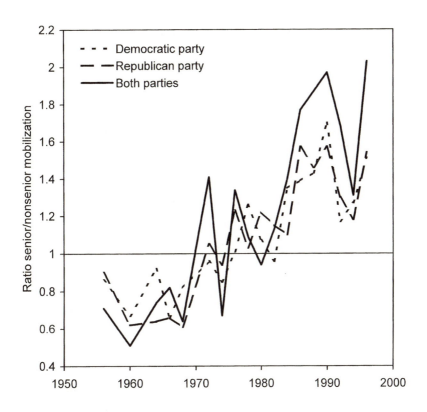

Appendix D

MULTIPLE INTERRUPTED TIME-
SERIES ANALYSIS

I PERFORMED a multiple interrupted time-series (MITS) analysis of the participatory trends in the Roper data to assess how participation rates change with policy events (and how the changes differ across population subgroups). This analysis uses a series of counter and dummy variables to delineate the policy events and intervening time periods. Proper combination of the resulting parameters yields the slope of participation before, during, and after the two major policy events. This analysis forms the basis for table 5.5 and figures 5.2–5.6.

Following the example of Lewis-Beck and Alford (1980), I performed a dummy variable analysis, estimating the following equation:

$$P_t = b_0 + b_1X_{1t} + b_2X_{2t} + b_3X_{3t} + b_4X_{4t} + b_5X_{5t} + b_6X_{6t}$$
$$+ b_7X_{7t} + b_8X_{8t} + b_9X_{9t} + e_t,$$

where P_t = mean level of participation in each survey, that is, the proportion of, say, seniors who said they wrote a letter to their congressman or senator in the past year. The independent variables are counters and dummy variables for the various time periods. X_{1t} = a counter for surveys from 1 to 204 which equals the number of observations; X_{2t} = a dichotomous variable scored 0 for observations before Reagan's May 12, 1981, threat and 1 for observations after the threat; X_{3t} = a counter for surveys, scored 0 for observations before May 12, 1981, and 1, 2, 3 . . . for observations after the threat; X_{4t} = a dichotomous variable scored 0 for observations before the July 1983 signing of the Social Security amendments and 1 for observations after that; X_{5t} = a counter for surveys, scored 0 for observations before July 1983, and 1, 2, 3 . . . for observations after that; X_{6t} = a dichotomous variable scored 0 for observations before the July 1988 passage of the Medicare Catastrophic Coverage Act and 1 for observations after that; X_{7t} = a counter for surveys, scored 0 for observations before July 1988, and 1, 2, 3 . . . for observations after that; X_{8t} = a dichotomous variable scored 0 for observations before the November 1989 repeal of the Medicare Catastrophic Coverage Act and 1 for observations after that; X_{9t} = a counter for surveys, scored 0 for observations before November 1989, and 1, 2, 3 . . . for observations after that.

Table D.1
MITS Analysis Coefficients for Contacting by Age (ARIMA Results)

	Contacting		
	18–29	*30–59*	*60+*
b_1	−0.000527	−0.000452	−0.000278
b_3	0.0014089	0.001718	0.003743
b_5	−0.0013421	−0.001539	−0.003859
b_7	0.0021464	0.000181	0.006046
b_9	−0.0020223	−0.002099	−0.006727

I originally estimated the coefficients with OLS, but the Durbin-Watson statistics and Box-Jenkins analysis of the autocorrelation (ACF) and partial autocorrelation (PACF) functions of the residuals indicated the presence of positive autocorrelation for some of the age-participation equations. I replicated the analysis using an ARIMA (1 0 0) model (the Box-Jenkins analysis indicated a first-order autoregressive process). The ARIMA and OLS results are nearly identical; I report the ARIMA results here.

Contacting rates by age will serve as an example of converting the parameter estimates into changes in participation. Table D.1 contains the slope coefficients (b_1, b_3, b_5, b_7, b_9) for contacting by the three age groups.

The slope for the period from the beginning of the time series to May 1981 is b_1, from May 1981 to July 1983 is $(b_1 + b_3)$, from July 1983 to July 1988 is $(b_1 + b_3 + b_5)$, from July 1988 to November 1989 is $(b_1 + b_3 + b_5 + b_7)$, and from November 1989 to the end of the time series in October 1994 is $(b_1 + b_3 + b_5 + b_7 + b_9)$. To calculate the percentage change in contacting for each time period and age group, I multiplied the slope coefficients by the number of surveys in each time period and then multiplied this product by 100 to convert from a proportion to a percentage. For example, the calculation for the change in the contacting rate of seniors during the threat to Social Security benefits from May 1981 to July 1983 is

$$(b_{1\text{seniors}} + b_{3\text{seniors}})(21)(100) = (-.000278 + .003743)(21)(100) = 7.3\%.$$

TABLE D.2
Changes in Participation Rates, All Subgroups, All Time Periods

	9/73–5/81	Social Security Benefits Threat 5/81–7/83	7/83–7/88	Catastrophic Act Threat 7/88–11/89	11/89–10/94
Contacting by age					
18–29	−4.1	1.9	−2.3	2.4	−1.4
30–59	−3.5	2.7	−1.4	2.2	−2.4
60+	−2.1	7.3	−2.0	7.9	−4.5
40–44[a]	−4.6	1.3	1.2	5.0	−2.1
45–49	−3.8	4.2	−1.8	3.0	−3.5
50–54	−1.2	4.4	−2.7	5.8	−1.9
55–59	−3.1	−0.3	−2.3	3.3	−2.7
60–64	−2.7	5.4	−2.9	3.8	−3.1
65+	−3.7	8.4	−1.5	9.3	−5.0
Public meeting attendance					
60+	−2.1	−0.8	1.9	3.3	−1.7
Senior contacting by income					
Low	−0.4	5.4	−0.3	6.6	0.1
Medium	−0.7	7.2	0.6	7.6	−6.2
High	−1.0	7.5	−5.7	17.2	−6.7
Senior contacting by work status					
Retired	−3.3	8.9	−2.9	9.2	−5.1
Work full time	−1.8	5.6	−4.5	4.2	−3.0
Senior contacting by gender					
Female	−2.5	8.0	−2.1	9.2	−2.9
Male	−1.8	6.5	−2.3	6.5	−6.2

Source: Roper Social and Political Trends Archive.
Note: "Seniors" are age 60+. Cells contain the percentage change in the participation rate of the specified group during each time period.
[a] For five-year age increments, data begin in January 1977.

NOTES

CHAPTER ONE
INTRODUCTION: THE RECIPROCAL PARTICIPATION-POLICY RELATIONSHIP

1. Frances Fox Piven and Richard A. Cloward, *Why Americans Don't Vote* (New York: Pantheon, 1989); Howard L. Reiter, "Why Is Turnout Down?" *Public Opinion Quarterly* 43 (1979): 297–311; Walter Dean Burnham, "The Turnout Problem," in *Elections American Style*, ed. A. James Reichley (Washington, D.C.: Brookings, 1987); E. E. Schattschneider, *The Semisovereign People: A Realist's View of Democracy in America* (New York: Holt, Rinehart and Winston, 1960).

2. Sidney Verba, Kay Lehman Schlozman, and Henry E. Brady, *Voice and Equality: Civic Voluntarism in American Politics* (Cambridge: Harvard University Press, 1995).

3. Joe Soss, "Lessons of Welfare: Policy Design, Political Learning, and Political Action," *American Political Science Review* 93 (1999): 363–80.

4. Robert A. Dahl, *On Democracy* (New Haven: Yale University Press, 1998), chap. 4.

5. Soss, "Lessons of Welfare."

6. Sidney Verba, "Thoughts about Political Equality: What Is It? Why Do We Want It?" Paper prepared for the Inequality Summer Institute, Harvard University, 13–14 June 2001.

7. Piven and Cloward, *Why Americans Don't Vote*.

8. Kim Quaile Hill and Jan E. Leighley, "The Policy Consequences of Class Bias in State Electorates," *American Journal of Political Science* 36 (1992): 351–65. Also see Kim Quaile Hill, Jan E. Leighley, and Angela Hinton-Anderson, "Lower-Class Mobilization and Policy Linkages in the U.S. States," *American Journal of Political Science* 39 (1995): 75–86. The authors confirm the relationship between lower-class turnout and generosity of welfare benefits across states and time, using a pooled time-series analysis of the fifty states from 1978 to 1990.

9. Sidney Verba and Norman H. Nie, *Participation in America: Political Democracy and Social Equality* (New York: Harper & Row, 1972).

10. Theda Skocpol, *Protecting Soldiers and Mothers: The Political Origins of Social Policy in the United States* (Cambridge: Harvard University Press, 1992), and *Social Policy in the United States: Future Possibilities in Historical Perspective* (Princeton: Princeton University Press, 1995); Paul Pierson, "When Effect Becomes Cause: Policy Feedback and Political Change," *World Politics* 45 (1993): 595–628, and *Dismantling the Welfare State? Reagan, Thatcher, and the Politics of Retrenchment* (Cambridge: Cambridge University Press, 1994); Sven Steinmo, Kathleen Thelen, and Frank Longstreth, eds., *Structuring Politics: Historical Institutionalism in Comparative Analysis* (Cambridge: Cambridge University Press,

1992); and Peter A. Hall, *Governing the Economy: The Politics of State Intervention in Britain and France* (Oxford: Oxford University Press, 1986).

11. Exceptions to the dearth of empirical work on mass public feedback effects are Soss, "Lessons of Welfare"; Suzanne Mettler, "Bringing the State Back In to Civic Engagement: Policy Feedback Effects of the G.I. Bill for World War II Veterans," unpublished paper, Syracuse University, 2001; and Suzanne Mettler and Eric Welch, "Policy Feedback and Political Participation: Effects of the G.I. Bill for World War II Veterans over the Life Course," paper presented at the annual meeting of the American Political Science Association, 2001.

12. Pierson, "When Effect Becomes Cause," p. 621.

13. Helen Ingram and Anne Schneider, "Constructing Citizenship: The Subtle Messages of Policy Design," in *Public Policy for Democracy*, ed. Helen Ingram and Steven Rathgeb Smith (Washington, D.C.: Brookings, 1993), p. 89. These effects are predicted by theories of participatory democracy that emphasize the influence of institutional arrangements on the individual. See John Stuart Mill, *Considerations on Representative Government*, in *John Stuart Mill: Three Essays*, ed. Richard Wollheim (1861; Oxford: Oxford University Press, 1975), and Carole Pateman, *Participation and Democratic Theory* (Cambridge: Cambridge University Press, 1970).

14. Amartya K. Sen, "Rational Fools: A Critique of the Behavioral Foundations of Economic Theory," *Philosophy and Public Affairs* 6 (1977): 314–44; Aaron Wildavsky, "Choosing Preferences by Constructing Institutions: A Cultural Theory of Preference Formation," *American Political Science Review* 81 (1987): 3–21; Laura Stoker, "Interests and Ethics in Politics," *American Political Science Review* 86 (1992): 369–80.

15. Neal E. Cutler, "Demographic, Social-Psychological, and Political Factors in the Politics of Aging: A Foundation for Research in 'Political Gerontology,' " *American Political Science Review* 71 (1977): 1011–25.

16. Suzanne Mettler, *Dividing Citizens: Gender and Federalism in New Deal Public Policy* (Ithaca, N.Y.: Cornell University Press, 1998), p. 9.

17. T. H. Marshall, *Class, Citizenship, and Social Development* (Chicago: University of Chicago Press, 1964).

18. See Seymour Martin Lipset, Introduction to Marshall, *Class, Citizenship, and Social Development*.

19. Gøsta Esping-Andersen, *The Three Worlds of Welfare Capitalism* (Princeton: Princeton University Press, 1990); Peter Taylor-Gooby, *Public Opinion, Ideology, and State Welfare* (London: Routledge & Kegan Paul, 1985); Skocpol, *Social Policy in the United States*; Pierson, *Dismantling the Welfare State?* and *"The New Politics of the Welfare State,"* *World Politics* 48 (January 1996): 143–79.

20. Saul Friedman, "Are Golden Years Much Too Golden?" *Newsday*, 6 February 2001, p. B16; Andrew Sullivan, "Golden Oldies? Pandering to Well-Off Senior Citizens Is the New Political Pastime," *Pittsburgh Post-Gazette*, 8 October 2000, p. E1; Robert J. Samuelson, "Pampering the Elderly," *Washington Post*, 21 November 1990, p. A19; Henry Fairlie, "Talkin' 'bout My Generation," *The New Republic*, 28 March 1988, pp. 19–22.

21. For one example, see Robin Toner, "Older Voters' Shift to G.O.P. Is Democrats' 2000 Challenge," *New York Times*, 31 May 1999, p. A1.

22. Kenneth Janda, Jeffrey M. Berry, and Jerry Goldman, *The Challenge of Democracy: Government in America* (Boston: Houghton Mifflin, 1995).

23. For two recent examples, see Matthew C. Price, *Justice between Generations: The Growing Power of the Elderly in America* (Westport, Conn.: Greenwood, 1997), and Lawrence A. Powell, John B. Williamson, and Kenneth J. Branco, *The Senior Rights Movement: Framing the Policy Debate in America* (New York: Twayne, 1996).

24. During the 1960s and 1970s there was a great deal of interest among political scientists in aging and politics. Studies examined life-cycle and cohort effects on participation and attitudes, asking, for example, whether older people are more conservative or whether age causes disengagement from social life. See Angus Campbell, "Politics through the Life Cycle," *The Gerontologist* 11 (1971): 112–17; Norman H. Nie, Sidney Verba, and Jae-on Kim, "Political Participation and the Life Cycle," *Comparative Politics* 6 (1974): 319–40; Norval D. Glenn, "Aging and Conservatism," *Annals of the American Academy of Political and Social Science* 415 (1974): 176–86; M. Kent Jennings, "Another Look at the Life Cycle and Political Participation," *American Journal of Political Science* 23 (1979): 753–71; Paul R. Abramson, "Developing Party Identification: A Further Examination of Life-Cycle, Generational, and Period Effects," *American Journal of Political Science* 23 (1979): 78–96; M. Kent Jennings and Richard G. Niemi, *Generations and Politics* (Princeton: Princeton University Press, 1981); John Creighton Campbell and John Strate, "Are Old People Conservative?" *The Gerontologist* 21 (1981): 580–91. Such work tapered off during the 1980s, although some studies continued the work of the earlier research. See M. Kent Jennings and Gregory B. Marcus, "Political Involvement in the Later Years: A Longitudinal Survey," *American Journal of Political Science* 32 (1988): 302–16; John M. Strate, Charles J. Parrish, Charles D. Elder, and Coit Ford III, "Life Span Civic Development and Voting Participation," *American Political Science Review* 83 (1989): 443–64. More recent work has centered on seniors as an interest group—see Christine L. Day, *What Older Americans Think: Interest Groups and Aging Policy* (Princeton: Princeton University Press, 1990); Henry J. Pratt, *The Gray Lobby* (Chicago: University of Chicago Press, 1976) and *Gray Agendas: Interest Groups and Public Pensions in Canada, Britain, and the United States* (Ann Arbor: University of Michigan Press, 1993)—or on senior attitudes (Christine L. Day, "Older Americans' Attitudes toward the Medicare Catastrophic Coverage Act of 1988," *Journal of Politics* 55 (1993): 167–77; Laurie A. Rhodebeck, "The Politics of Greed? Political Preferences among the Elderly," *Journal of Politics* 55 (1993): 342–64; Susan A. MacManus, *Young v. Old: Generational Combat in the 21st Century* (Boulder, Colo.: Westview Press, 1996). There is little recent research on seniors' participatory behavior. Steven A. Peterson and Albert Somit in *The Political Behavior of Older Americans* (New York: Garland, 1994) use 1987 General Social Survey data to examine some forms of senior participation, but their analysis is limited to cross-sectional data and therefore does not take up the important issue of senior participatory growth. Also, their models leave out some explanatory variables, like income, that are crucial for understanding senior behavior. Eric M. Uslaner uses data from a 1992 survey conducted for AARP to look at senior participation, but the number of both independent and dependent variables

is limited, and again the data are cross-sectional ("Discount Drugs and Volunteering: Does the AARP Produce Social Capital?" paper presented at the annual meeting of the Midwest Political Science Association, Chicago, 1997). Robert Binstock, who is careful to note the diversity among seniors, has written an article about senior voting behavior after each of the last several presidential elections ("Older Voters and the 1992 Presidential Election," *The Gerontologist* 32 (1992): 601–6; and "The 1996 Election: Older Voters and Implications for Policies on Aging," *The Gerontologist* 37 (1997): 15–19).

25. I define senior citizens as those aged 65 and over, although occasionally I must use age 60 as the cutoff because data are coded or published that way. I use the terms "senior citizens," "seniors," "the elderly," "older Americans," and "the aged" interchangeably. Nonseniors are aged 18 to 64 (or 18 to 59 when the senior category starts at 60).

26. Cutler, "Demographic, Social-Psychological, and Political Factors in the Politics of Aging," p. 1012; Administration on Aging, U.S. Administration of Health and Human Services, "A Profile of Older Americans: 2000" (Washington, D.C.: U.S. Government Printing Office, 2000), p. 3.

27. U.S. Bureau of the Census, *Statistical Abstract of the United States 1998* (Washington, D.C.: U.S. Government Printing Office, 1998), pp. 16–17; author's analysis of the 1996 National Election Study.

28. U.S. Bureau of the Census, *Statistical Abstract of the United States 1998*, p. 339.

29. Philip E. Converse, "The Nature of Belief Systems in Mass Publics," in *Ideology and Discontent*, ed. David Apter (New York: Free Press, 1964).

30. Even in 1952, seniors made up 13 percent of National Election Study respondents, 235 cases—plenty for analysis.

31. James M. Poterba, "Demographic Structure and the Political Economy of Public Education," *Journal of Policy Analysis and Management* 16 (1997): 48–66.

32. Claudia Goldin and Lawrence Katz, "Why the United States Led in Education: Lessons from Secondary School Expansion, 1910–1940," National Bureau of Economic Research Working Paper no. 6144, 1997; Caroline M. Hoxby, "How Much Does School Spending Depend on Family Income? The Historical Origins of the Current School Finance Dilemma," unpublished paper, Department of Economics, Harvard University, 1997.

33. Also see Mettler, *Dividing Citizens*, which examines these welfare state policy and citizenship issues from the perspectives of gender and federalism.

34. Sidney Verba, Kay Lehman Schlozman, Henry E. Brady, and Norman Nie, American Citizen Participation Study, 1990 [computer file]. ICPSR version. Chicago: University of Chicago, National Opinion Research Center (NORC) [producer]. Ann Arbor, Mich.: Interuniversity Consortium for Political and Social Research [distributor], 1995.

35. In *Mobilization, Participation, and Democracy in America* (New York: Macmillan, 1993), Steven Rosenstone and John Mark Hansen used national marginals from the published Roper Reports and several tables created for them by the Roper Center at the University of Connecticut.

CHAPTER TWO
OVERVIEW: RISING SENIOR PARTICIPATION AND THE
GROWTH OF THE AMERICAN WELFARE STATE

1. Robert D. Putnam, *Bowling Alone: The Collapse and Revival of American Community* (New York: Simon & Schuster, 2000), chap. 2.

2. Ruy Teixeira, *Why Americans Don't Vote: Turnout Decline in the United States, 1960–1984* (Westport, Conn.: Greenwood Press, 1987) and *The Disappearing American Voter* (Washington, D.C.: Brookings, 1992); Walter Dean Burnham, "The Turnout Problem," in *Elections American Style*, ed. A. James Reichley (Washington, D.C.: Brookings, 1987); Richard Brody, "The Puzzle of Political Participation in America," in *The New American Political System*, ed. Anthony King (Washington, D.C.: American Enterprise Institute, 1978); Steven J. Rosenstone and John Mark Hansen, *Mobilization, Participation, and Democracy in America* (New York: Macmillan, 1993); Robert D. Putnam, "Bowling Alone: America's Declining Social Capital," *Journal of Democracy* 6 (1995): 65–78, and "Tuning In, Tuning Out: The Strange Disappearance of Social Capital in America," *PS: Political Science and Politics* 28 (1995): 664–83.

3. Teixeira, *The Disappearing American Voter.*

4. Rosenstone and Hansen mention the mobilization of senior citizens around Social Security that occurred in the mid-1980s. See *Mobilization, Participation, and Democracy in America*, pp. 115–17.

5. Amanda S. Barusch, *Older Women in Poverty: Private Lives and Public Policies* (New York: Springer, 1994), p. 5.

6. Sheridan Downey, *Pension or Penury* (New York: Harper and Brothers, 1939), pp. 23–28; see also Jackson K. Putnam, *Old-Age Politics in California* (Stanford: Stanford University Press, 1970); California Department of Social Welfare, *Old Age Dependency* (1928), cited in Abraham Epstein, *Insecurity: A Challenge to America* (New York: Random House, 1943).

7. W. Andrew Achenbaum, *Old Age in the New Land: The American Experience since 1790* (Baltimore: Johns Hopkins University Press, 1978); James T. Patterson, *America's Struggle against Poverty, 1900–1994* (Cambridge: Harvard University Press, 1994).

8. David Hackett Fischer, *Growing Old in America* (Oxford: Oxford University Press, 1978).

9. The Social Security Act also included grants to the states for unemployment compensation administration, Aid to Dependent Children, and aid to the needy blind.

10. SSI provides monthly cash payments to blind and disabled persons as well as to needy seniors.

11. Gerald D. Nash, Noel H. Pugach, and Richard F. Tomasson, *Social Security: The First Half-Century* (Albuquerque: University of New Mexico Press, 1988).

12. Patterson, *America's Struggle against Poverty*, p. 73.

13. Coverage was extended to dependents and survivors in 1939; to the non-farm self-employed in 1950; to farmers, self-employed members of some professions, and farm and domestic employees in 1954; to additional self-employed

persons except physicians, additional farm owners and operators, and certain state and local government employees in 1956; and to physicians and certain divorced wives in 1965. See Nash, Pugach, and Tomasson, *Social Security*, pp. 313–21. Today over 90 percent of the workforce is covered. The only large categories of workers still outside the system are some state and local government employees, most federal civilian employees hired before 1984, and low-earnings casual workers. See Nash, Pugach, and Tomasson, *Social Security*, p. 17; U.S. House Committee on Ways and Means, *1998 Green Book: Overview of Entitlement Programs* (Washington, D.C.: U.S. Government Printing Office, 1998).

14. U.S. House Committee on Ways and Means, *1998 Green Book*, p. 3.

15. Congress passed the first benefit increase of 12.5 percent in 1952, and the legislation of the 1950s served chiefly to replace the real value of benefits eroded by inflation since payments had begun 1940. Congress greatly increased benefits during the Nixon administration, with increases of 15, 10, 20, and 11 percent between 1970 and 1974. Legislation in 1972 put automatic cost-of-living adjustments (COLAs) into place beginning in 1975.

16. AFDC, the federal entitlement program for low-income mothers and children, no longer exists, replaced in the 1996 welfare overhaul (HR 3734, P.L. 104–93) by a state block grant program providing temporary assistance for needy families (TANF). The 1996 law gives states control over their own programs within federal guidelines, which include a five-year limit on aid and a work requirement after two years of aid. Chapter 7 discusses some reasons for the differing trajectories of Social Security and AFDC.

17. U.S. House Committee on Ways and Means, *1998 Green Book*, p. 38.

18. Ibid., p. 1032.

19. Henry J. Pratt, *Gray Agendas: Interest Groups and Public Pensions in Canada, Britain, and the United States* (Ann Arbor: University of Michigan Press, 1993); Nan L. Maxwell, *Income Inequality in the United States, 1947–1985* (New York: Greenwood Press, 1990).

20. William G. Bowen and T. Aldrich Finegan, *The Economics of Labor Force Participation* (Princeton: Princeton University Press, 1969).

21. Achenbaum, *Old Age in the New Land*, p. 148.

22. Compulsory retirement policies also proliferated, rationalized partly on the grounds of Social Security expansion, although research indicates that the pull of leisure was a stronger incentive than the push of mandatory retirement. See Bowen and Finegan, *The Economics of Labor Force Participation* and Gary S. Fields and Olivia S. Mitchell, *Retirement, Pensions, and Social Security* (Cambridge: MIT Press, 1984). The 1978 amendments to the 1967 Age Discrimination in Employment Act outlawed mandatory retirement prior to age 70. But while individuals can work beyond age 65 if they wish, most choose to retire early. Reduced Social Security benefits at age 62 have been available since 1961 (since 1956 for women). In 1996, 72 percent of new Social Security beneficiaries were people under 65 who chose to take the actuarially reduced early retirement benefits (U.S. House Ways and Means Committee, *1998 Green Book*, p. 21). The reasons retired workers left their last job have changed dramatically over the years. In 1941–42, 56 percent of retirees said their retirement was employer initiated, 34 percent retired because of health problems, and 10 percent retired on their own initiative. In

1982, only 20 percent of retirements were employer initiated, 17 percent were caused by health problems and 63 percent were employee initiated (Virginia P. Reno and Susan Grad, "Economic Security, 1935–85," *Social Security Bulletin* 48 (1985): 18). In her history of retirement, the economist Dora L. Costa argues that income and health have become less important to the retirement decision because of higher income levels, cheaper leisure, and improved health; see *The Evolution of Retirement: An American Economic History, 1880–1990* (Chicago: University of Chicago Press, 1998).

23. W. Andrew Achenbaum, *Social Security: Visions and Revisions* (Cambridge: Cambridge University Press, 1986), p. 53.

24. If there were no Social Security program, people's behavior over their lifetimes would probably change so that the senior poverty rate would not be as high as 50 percent, but it would certainly be much higher than 10.5 percent. Whether and to what degree the existence of Social Security discourages private saving is a subject of much debate. See U.S. Bureau of the Census, "Measuring the Effect of Benefits and Taxes on Income and Poverty: 1992," Current Population Reports, Series P60–186RD (Washington, D.C.: U.S. Government Printing Office, 1993), p. xxii; Patterson, *America's Struggle against Poverty*; Maxwell, *Income Inequality in the United States*; Marilyn Moon and Janemarie Mulvey, *Entitlements and the Elderly: Protecting Promises, Recognizing Reality* (Washington, D.C.: Urban Institute Press, 1996).

25. Furthermore, including the value of government transfers reduces the child poverty rate by only 3 percent, a far cry from the enormous 40-point difference that government cash transfers make to the senior poverty rate. See U.S. Bureau of the Census, "Measuring the Effect of Benefits and Taxes on Income and Poverty: 1992," p. xxii.

26. David M. Cutler, "Reexamining the Three-Legged Stool," in *Social Security: What Role for the Future*, ed. Peter A. Diamond, David C. Lindeman, and Howard Young (Washington, D.C.: National Academy of Social Insurance, 1996), p. 127; *Social Security Bulletin Annual Statistical Supplement* 1997, p. 21. Also, Social Security benefits are linked to the Consumer Price Index while most private pensions are not. Thus for individual retirees, Social Security makes up a larger share of income as age increases. For seniors overall, growth in pension income is expected to slow, because an increasing proportion of U.S. employment is in the service sector, where fringe benefits tend to be less generous than in manufacturing. See Sheila Zedlewski, Robert Barnes, Martha Burt, Timothy McBride, and Jack Meyer, *The Needs of the Elderly in the 21st Century* (Washington, D.C.: Urban Institute Press, 1990).

27. Fischer, *Growing Old in America*, p. 162.

28. "America through the Ages: Studying the Elderly," *Public Opinion* (February/March 1985): 34.

29. NES question wording: "During the past year (have you/has your family living here) been able to buy most of the things you needed and planned on buying or have you had to put off buying these things? In the past year did you (or anyone in your family living here) put off medical or dental treatment because you didn't have the money? In order to make ends meet this past year did (any of) you do any of the following: Borrow money from a bank, a lending institution, or from

relatives or friends? Dip into your savings? Look for a job, look for a second job, or try to work more hours at your present job? Over the past year have you (and your family) been able to save any money? This past year have you (or anyone in your family living here) fallen behind in rent or house payments?"

Citizen Participation Study wording: "These days, many people have been feeling a financial pinch. Here is a list of actions that some people find are necessary to make ends meet. Over the past twelve months have you or any members of your immediate family living with you had to take any of these actions in order to make ends meet?" (Put off medical or dental treatment; delayed paying the rent or making house payments; cut back on amount or quality of food; cut back on spending on entertainment or recreation; worked extra hours or took an extra job; none.)

30. Question wording: "There's been some talk these days about different social classes. Most people say they belong either to the middle class or the working class. Do you ever think of yourself as belonging in one of these classes?" If yes: "Which one?" If no: "Well, if you had to make a choice, would you call yourself middle class or working class?" This question was not asked in the 1996 NES.

31. "White-collar" occupations are those coded 1 and 2 in the NES collapsed occupation codes (executive, administrative and managerial; professional specialty occupations). "Pink-collar" occupations are those coded 3 to 5 (technicians and related support occupations; sales occupations; and administrative support, including clerical). "Blue-collar" occupations are coded 6 to 13 (private household; protective service; service except protective and household; farming, forestry, and fishing; precision production, craft, and repair occupations; machine operators, assemblers, and inspectors; transportation and material-moving occupations; and handlers, equipment cleaners, helpers, and laborers).

32. Odin W. Anderson and Jacob J. Feldman, *Family Medical Costs and Voluntary Health Insurance: A Nationwide Survey* (New York: McGraw-Hill, 1956); LuAnn Aday, Ronald Andersen, and Gretchen V. Fleming, *Health Care in the U.S.: Equitable for Whom?* (Beverly Hills, Calif.: Sage, 1980).

33. Anderson and Feldman, *Family Medical Costs and Voluntary Health Insurance*; Aday, Andersen, and Fleming, *Health Care in the U.S.*

34. Karen Davis, "Medicare Reconsidered," in *Health Care for the Poor and Elderly: Meeting the Challenge*, ed. Duncan Yaggy (Durham, N.C.: Duke University Press, 1984), p. 81.

35. Aday, Andersen, and Fleming, *Health Care in the U.S.*

36. In Britain many medical procedures are explicitly rationed. In Canada and Sweden there are waiting lists for coronary surgery, hip replacement, cataract surgery, and corneal lens transplants. In Germany, health care funds are financed on a pay-as-you-go basis, so there are no reserves to pay the higher costs of elderly patients. As a result, German physicians are more dissatisfied than U.S. doctors with the services available to the elderly; only 15 percent of German physicians said elderly medical services are good or excellent compared with 44 percent in the United States. The United States rations care too, but through limited access for the uninsured nonelderly rather than through limitations on services and procedures for the elderly. See Marie L. Lassey, William R. Lassey, and Martin J.

Jinks, *Health Care Systems around the World: Characteristics, Issues, Reforms* (Upper Saddle River, N.J.: Prentice-Hall, 1997).

37. Davis, "Medicare Reconsidered," p. 83.

38. Question wording: "Of course, everyone is more interested in some things being carried in the news than in others. To take some different kinds of examples—is news about _____ something you have recently been following fairly closely, or just following casually, or not paying much attention to?"

39. Table 2.3 shows percentages for 60+ rather than for 65+ to be consistent with other salience data in this chapter that are available for 60+ only.

40. The percentage of respondents aged 60+ closely following news about Social Security increases dramatically over these three surveys, from 56 percent to 72 percent to 82 percent. Although some of the difference may be due to question wording, 1977 to 1981 was a crisis period for Social Security. The Social Security trust fund was nearing insolvency in 1977, prompting rescue legislation signed by President Jimmy Carter in December of that year. That bill failed to shore up the system, and in May 1981 President Ronald Reagan proposed cutting Social Security benefits for early retirees, the first proposed cuts affecting current recipients in the program's sixty-year history. Seniors' participatory reaction to these threats is the subject of chapter 5.

41. Verbatim question wording: "Here is a list of a number of different considerations that may be more or less important to you in deciding who to vote for for President next Fall. Tell me for each one if it is your number one consideration in who you will vote for, or one of your 2 or 3 most important considerations, or a contributing factor in your decision, or of rather minor importance in deciding who to vote for as President of the United States?" (The economy, foreign policy, social issues, governmental problems, moral questions, law and order, the personal qualities of the candidates). "When you say social issues, are you mainly concerned about education, or health, or women's rights, or poverty, or Social Security, or what?"

42. Robin Toner, "Older Voters' Shift to G.O.P. Is Democrats' 2000 Challenge," *New York Times*, 31 May 1999, p. A10.

43. For a typology of political acts, see Henry E. Brady, "Conceptualizing and Measuring Political Participation," in *Measures of Political Attitudes*, ed. John P. Robinson, Phillip R. Shaver, and Lawrence S. Wrightsman (San Diego: Academic Press, 1999).

44. On the mechanisms behind these activities, see Sidney Verba, Kay Lehman Schlozman, and Henry E. Brady, *Voice and Equality: Civic Voluntarism in American Politics* (Cambridge: Harvard University Press, 1995), as well as the analyses in chapter 3.

45. The 1993 figure for the Roper data is the combined total for the ten surveys taken in 1993, the last full year for which Roper data are available. The question asked was, "Here is a list of things some people do about government or politics. Have you happened to have done any of those things in the past year? Written your Congressman or Senator?" The Roper figure is for respondents aged 60 and over.

46. The proportion of African Americans in the NES who said someone from a political party contacted them during the election season ranged from 13 to 27 percent during the 1956–1996 period, averaging 19 percent; in 2000, 30 percent

of blacks were mobilized. Similarly, among union members between 16 and 33 percent were mobilized prior to 2000, averaging 27 percent; in 2000, 44 percent were mobilized.

47. Sidney Verba and Norman H. Nie, *Participation in America: Political Democracy and Social Equality* (New York: Harper & Row, 1972).

48. Turnout data from the Current Population Survey tell a similar story: voting in the 18–34 age group declined from 60 percent in 1972 to 50 percent in 1988, before rebounding to 58 percent in 1992; turnout for the middle 35–64 group stayed flat at 74 percent; and turnout among seniors increased from 67 percent in 1972 to 76 percent in 1992. Reported turnout is higher in the NES than in the Current Population Survey, probably because the many political cues in the NES exacerbate the social desirability bias generally found in self-reported voting.

49. The addition of 18- to 20-year-olds to the ranks of eligible voters in 1972 (thanks to the Twenty-Sixth Amendment) accounts for part of the youth group's turnout decline. But 21- to 34-year-olds' voting rates declined as well, from 75 percent in 1960, to 69 percent in 1972, to 60 percent in 2000.

50. Vote validation studies were conducted as part of the NES in 1964, 1976, 1978, 1980, 1984, 1986, 1988, and 1990. Seniors were less likely to lie about voting than 18- to 34-year-olds in every year, and less likely to lie than 35- to 64-year-olds every year except 1976. The proportion of misreporters among seniors has decreased over time while staying flat or increasing among nonseniors. For the percentage of respondents from the NES cumulative file who reported voting for whom no record of voting could be found (variable 9151 = 1), see appendix table A.11.

On overreporting by age, also see John M. Strate, Charles J. Parrish, Charles D. Elder, and Coit Ford III, "Life Span Civic Development and Voting Participation," *American Political Science Review* 83 (1989): 443–64. In 2000 the National Election Study changed its turnout question wording to try to reduce overreporting. Rather than being asked whether they had voted or not, respondents were asked which statement best described them: "One, I did not vote (in the election this November); two, I thought about voting this time—but didn't; three, I usually vote, but didn't this time; or four, I am sure I voted." For the results by age, see appendix table A.12.

51. In 1952, 1956, 1960, 1962–68, 1972–78, and 1986, the NES asked a single question about contributions that mentioned both candidates and parties. Starting in 1980 (except for 1986) two questions were asked: one about giving money to candidates and another about giving money to parties. The percentages reported here for the later dates are constructed from the two questions. No contribution question was asked in 1954, 1958, or 1970.

52. NES respondents were asked, "Did you do any [other] work for one of the parties or candidates?" This question was not asked in 1954, 1958, or 1966.

53. See note 45 for question wording. Because of the original coding, the age categories in the Roper data are 18–29 for the youth group, 30–59 for the middle group, and 60 and over for seniors.

54. The right-hand side of figure 2.13 is compressed by a retirement rate ceiling effect.

55. There are fewer data points in figure 2.14 than in figures 2.12 and 2.13 because data on Social Security as a percentage of senior incomes are available for just a few years.

CHAPTER THREE
A MODEL OF SENIOR CITIZEN POLITICAL PARTICIPATION

1. Author's calculations from the 1992 Current Population Survey.

2. Martha Malone [pseud.], interview by author, 30 October 2001.

3. Harry Smith [pseud.], interview by author, 30 October 2001.

4. Charles Smith [pseud.], interview by author, 15 March 2002.

5. David O. Sears and Jack Citrin, *Tax Revolt: Something for Nothing in California* (Cambridge: Harvard University Press, 1982), p. 220. The structure of support for Massachusetts's 1980 property tax initiative was similar. See Helen F. Ladd and Julie Boatright Wilson, "Who Supports Tax Limitations: Evidence from Massachusetts' Proposition 2½," *Journal of Policy Analysis and Management* 2 (1983): 256–79.

6. Sidney Verba and Norman H. Nie, *Participation in America: Political Democracy and Social Equality* (New York: Harper & Row, 1972); Gabriel A. Almond and Sidney Verba, *The Civic Culture: Political Attitudes and Democracy in Five Nations* (Princeton: Princeton University Press, 1963); Samuel Barnes and Max Kaase, *Political Action: Mass Participation in Five Western Democracies* (Beverly Hills, Calif.: Sage, 1979); Lester W. Milbrath and M. L. Goel, *Political Participation: How and Why Do People Get Involved in Politics?* 2d ed. (Chicago: Rand McNally, 1977). For an excellent overview of the participation literature, see Jan E. Leighley, "Attitudes, Opportunities, and Incentives: A Field Essay on Political Participation," *Political Research Quarterly* 48 (1995): 181–209.

7. Wolfinger and Rosenstone found in their examination of turnout that income did not predict voting above the poverty line. See Raymond E. Wolfinger and Steven J. Rosenstone, *Who Votes?* (New Haven: Yale University Press, 1980). The analysis presented here and in Verba, Schlozman, and Brady's *Voice and Equality* does find that income is a positive and statistically significant predictor of turnout. See Sidney Verba, Kay Lehman Schlozman, and Henry E. Brady, *Voice and Equality: Civic Voluntarism in American Politics* (Cambridge: Harvard University Press, 1995), p. 358.

8. David B. Tyack, *The One Best System: A History of American Urban Education* (Cambridge: Harvard University Press, 1974).

9. Paul M. Sniderman, *Personality and Democratic Politics* (Berkeley: University of California Press, 1975).

10. Wolfinger and Rosenstone, *Who Votes?*; Verba, Schlozman, and Brady, *Voice and Equality.*

11. Verba, Schlozman, and Brady, *Voice and Equality;* Norman H. Nie, Jane Junn, and Kenneth Stehlik-Barry, *Education and Democratic Citizenship in America* (Chicago: University of Chicago Press, 1996).

12. Steven J. Rosenstone and John Mark Hansen, *Mobilization, Participation, and Democracy in America* (New York: Macmillan, 1993), p. 10.

13. Wolfinger and Rosenstone, *Who Votes?* p. 20; Steven J. Rosenstone, "Economic Adversity and Voter Turnout," *American Journal of Political Science* 26 (1982): 25–46; Milbrath and Goel, *Political Participation*, p. 98; M. Margaret Conway, *Political Participation in the United States*, 2d ed. (Washington, D.C.: CQ Press, 1991), p. 25.

14. Rosenstone and Hansen, *Mobilization, Participation, and Democracy in America*, p. 12.

15. There can also be a substitution effect in which the wealthy's higher wages raise the opportunity cost associated with participation and other leisure activities; see Verba, Schlozman, and Brady, *Voice and Equality*, pp. 284, 291.

16. Verba, Schlozman, and Brady, *Voice and Equality*, pp. 376–78.

17. Conway, *Political Participation in the United States*.

18. Sixty-three percent of seniors say they are "retired" and another 25 percent "keep house." For the breakdown by gender among seniors, see appendix table A.13.

19. Administration on Aging, U.S. Administration of Health and Human Services, "A Profile of Older Americans: 2000" (Washington, D.C.: U.S. Government Printing Office, 2000), p. 10.

20. Edward E. Duensing, *America's Elderly: A Sourcebook* (New Brunswick, N.J.: Center for Urban Policy Research, 1988).

21. Marilyn Moon and Janemarie Mulvey, *Entitlements and the Elderly: Protecting Promises, Recognizing Reality* (Washington, D.C.: Urban Institute Press, 1996), p. 25.

22. Daniel B. Radner, "Money Incomes of Aged and Nonaged Family Units, 1967–84," *Social Security Bulletin* 50 (1987): 8–28.

23. Seniors on average also have financial assets that help mitigate their low income levels. The median household net worth for seniors was $158,000 in 1999, up from $93,000 in 1984 (constant 1999 dollars). Over the same period median net worth for 45- to 54-year-olds declined from $111,000 to $85,000; see Federal Interagency Forum on Aging-Related Statistics, "Older Americans 2000: Key Indicators of Well-Being" (Washington, D.C.: U.S. Government Printing Office, 2000), p. 67. From 1984 to 1994, the net assets of all U.S. adults decreased by 7.5 percent, but those of the elderly aged 75 and over increased .2 percent and those of seniors aged 65 to 74 increased 22 percent; see Rose M. Rubin and Michael L. Nieswiadomy, *Expenditures of Older Americans* (Westport, Conn.: Praeger, 1997), p. 21.

24. Wolfinger and Rosenstone, *Who Votes?*

25. Herbert F. Weisberg and Bernard Grofman, "Candidate Evaluations and Turnout," *American Politics Quarterly* 9 (1981): 197–219.

26. Wolfinger and Rosenstone, *Who Votes?* pp. 35–36, 60.

27. Rosenstone and Hansen, *Mobilization, Participation, and Democracy in America*.

28. This difference, while statistically significant ($p < .05$), is small compared with the differences in vocabulary knowledge between education levels for the whole sample. The average number of words (out of ten) correctly defined by Citizen Participation Study respondents by education level: less than high school

(4.2); high school graduate (5.7); some college (6.7); college graduate (7.5); and postgraduate (8.0).

29. These explanations of the importance of education to participation assume that education matters in an absolute sense—that the more education one has, the more likely one is to overcome bureaucratic hurdles and register, to be inculcated with American civic values, and to have politically relevant skills. If education matters in this absolute sense, then it is a puzzle that participation rates are declining overall in the United States while education levels are rising; see Richard Brody, "The Puzzle of Political Participation in America," in *The New American Political System*, ed. Anthony King (Washington, D.C.: American Enterprise Institute, 1978). In *Education and Democratic Citizenship in America*, Nie, Junn, and Stehlik-Barry offer a compelling explanation: relative level of education matters, not just absolute level. They find that education has an absolute effect on tolerance, for example; more education leads to greater tolerance, both among individuals in cross-sectional data and in society over time. But for other political attitudes and behavior, education level relative to one's cohort is what matters. Participation in what these authors call "difficult" political activities like contacting, campaign work, and community activity depends on social network centrality, which is determined in part by one's education level relative to one's peers. For yet other political attributes, both the absolute and the relative aspects of education come into play; this is true for voting, political knowledge, and political attentiveness. Because relative education is important for so many of the political attitudes and behaviors focused on here, seniors' low absolute levels of education may not matter so much.

30. The job skill questions were asked of those who were employed. The church skill questions were asked of those who were active members of their churches or who had served on their church board in the past five years. The organization skill questions were asked of respondents' "main" nonpolitical organization (see Verba, Schlozman, and Brady, *Voice and Equality*, appendix B.9 for further explanations of the skills variables).

31. This is a little curious since the few seniors who are still working report having jobs of a similar job level—on a five-level measure of the amount of education and training needed for the job—as nonseniors. Perhaps this measure hides some important differences.

32. Verba, Schlozman, and Brady, *Voice and Equality*.

33. The result showing that seniors are stronger partisans than nonseniors is the same if one adheres to the Keith et al. findings that independent leaners are as partisan as weak identifiers of the same party and codes strong identifiers as 2, weak identifiers and independent leaners as 1, and true independents as 0. See Bruce E. Keith, David B. Magleby, Candice J. Nelson, Elizabeth Orr, Mark C. Westlye, and Raymond E. Wolfinger, *The Myth of the Independent Voter* (Berkeley: University of California Press, 1992).

34. Rather than repetitively spell out differences between seniors and each nonsenior age group, I will often make comparisons with 35- to 49-year-olds (and with 30- to 44-year-olds in the Roper data, following the original coding). This age category is the most appropriate for use as a reference group. Younger respondents aged 18 to 34 are less appropriate because their political participation is so

very low due to life-cycle factors. Other major concerns dominate their lives: finishing school, launching careers, getting married, and establishing families; see Thomas B. Jankowski and John M. Strate, "Modes of Participation over the Adult Life Span," *Political Behavior* 17 (1995): 89–106. Those aged 50 to 64 are more similar to seniors than the very young because they are closer in the life cycle to seniors. But their participatory behavior may already be "contaminated" by old-age policy concerns as the group prepares for retirement.

By contrast, respondents aged 35 to 49 have reached a stage in the life cycle that encourages participation (or at least does not discourage it as with the very young); many of them have children, own homes and are otherwise comparatively established in their personal lives and communities. At the same time, they are unlikely yet to participate in politics with the concerns of retirement and old age in mind. The more forward-looking among them are saving and investing for retirement, but they are far enough from being senior citizens themselves that they are unlikely to vote or contact based on old-age policy issues. Most of this group's parents are senior citizens, and there is a possibility that the adult children participate with their parents' interests in mind. However, despite speculation in this direction (see Leonie Huddy, "Generational Agreement on Old-Age Policies," Ph.D. dissertation, University of California, Los Angeles, 1989; Christine L. Day, *What Older Americans Think: Interest Groups and Aging Policy* (Princeton: Princeton University Press, 1990)), there is little supporting evidence. Analysis in chapter 5 shows that while 35- to 49-year-olds are supportive of Social Security, they do not tend to participate in politics with Social Security in mind.

35. Warren E. Miller and J. Merrill Shanks, *The New American Voter* (Cambridge: Harvard University Press, 1996), chap. 7.

36. The Political Interest 8-point scale is the sum of answers to two questions, with "very interested" scored as 4 and "not at all" as 1: Thinking about your local community, how interested are you in local community politics and local community affairs? Are you Very interested, Somewhat interested, Slightly interested, or Not at all interested? How interested are you in national politics and national affairs?

37. Respondents were asked to name the two senators from their state and the member of Congress from their district. The other five questions concerned the amount of federal spending on NASA versus Social Security, the purpose of the Fifth Amendment, the origin of primary elections, the definition of "civil liberties," and the major difference between democracies and dictatorships. Interestingly, seniors were more likely than nonseniors to believe erroneously that the federal government spends more on NASA than on Social Security. Removing this question from the knowledge scale brings seniors' average score close to those of nonseniors.

38. Both the political interest and the political efficacy scales include national and local questions. Each question offered four responses for a total of sixteen points. Because seniors are recipients of federal programs like Social Security and Medicare, one explanation for seniors' low scores in these areas could be an emphasis by seniors on the national scene at the expense of the local. Looking at the local and national questions separately, however, shows that seniors are not uniquely focused on national politics. They are like nonseniors in being slightly

more interested in national affairs than in local ones while having somewhat higher feelings of efficacy at the local level than at the national.

39. If education were responsible for seniors' lower engagement scores, their scores would be the highest within each education category.

40. Roper Survey 8108, administered in August 1981, is the most recent survey in the dataset assessing Social Security interest.

41. The data shown in table 3.5 are the same as those shown in table 2.3, but in a different format: respondents following news closely are scored as 3, those following news casually as 2, and those paying no attention or don't know (a single category in the original data) as 1.

42. A factor analysis on the news items produces two scales, with the domestic issues (prices, income taxes, interest rates, air traffic controllers' strike, and the Conoco buyout) forming one scale with a Cronbach's alpha of .63 and international issues (royal wedding, Arab-Israeli relations, Polish situation, English riots, and the Irish hunger strikes) forming another with a Cronbach's alpha of .80.

43. These differences are both statistically significant at $p < .001$.

44. These differences are statistically significant at $p < .001$.

45. Note that the analysis of traditional activities is performed on all respondents, while analysis of Social Security activity can only be performed on the 200-plus respondents from Social Security households who were asked about Social Security–specific participation.

46. I estimated the equations for the dichotomous participation variables with logistic regression. The points plotted in figures 3.4 and 3.5 are the probability of performing each activity at each income level while the other independent variables are held at their means.

47. When Social Security voting is modeled the same way as Social Security contacting and contributing, that is, the "regular" way, the income coefficient is positive, but the income-squared coefficient is large and negative so that Social Security voting is less common at high-income levels. When graphed, the pattern of Social Security voting modeled this "regular" way looks similar to the pattern of contacting from the Roper data shown in figure 3.6.

48. Jack Citrin and Donald Philip Green, "The Self-Interest Motive in American Public Opinion," *Research in Micropolitics* 3 (1990): 1–28.

49. Verba, Schlozman, and Brady, *Voice and Equality*.

50. Rosenstone and Hansen, *Mobilization, Participation, and Democracy in America*.

51. Jan E. Leighley, "Attitudes, Opportunities, and Incentives: A Field Essay on Political Participation," *Political Research Quarterly* 48 (1995): 181–209; R. Kenneth Godwin, *One Billion Dollars of Influence: The Direct Marketing of Politics* (Chatham, N.J.: Chatham House, 1988); Rosenstone and Hansen, *Mobilization, Participation, and Democracy in America*, chap. 6.

52. David Knoke, *Organizing for Collective Action: The Political Economies of Associations* (New York: Aldine de Gruyter, 1990); Lawrence S. Rothenberg, *Linking Citizens to Government: Interest Group Politics at Common Cause* (Cambridge: Cambridge University Press, 1992); Verba and Nie, *Participation in America*; Verba, Schlozman, and Brady, *Voice and Equality*.

53. Requests to perform campaign work and to make contributions are counted as a single item in the released dataset.

54. Barnes and Kaase, *Political Action*.

55. Question wording: In the past five years, did someone in authority on the job, in church, or in your organization ever suggest that you: Personally vote for or against certain candidates in an election for public office? Take some other action on a political issue—sign a petition, write a letter, or get in touch with a public official?

56. I use NES data because there is no political party mobilization question in the Citizen Participation Study.

57. While chapter 4 includes a full discussion of recruitment trends over time, I should note here that 1996 was not a unique year in the mobilization of seniors by political parties; senior citizens have been mobilized by the political parties at higher rates than nonseniors since 1976, with the gap increasing over time.

58. Rosenstone and Hansen, *Mobilization, Participation, and Democracy in America*, p. 241.

59. Kelly Lambert [pseud.], interview by author, 14 March 2002.

60. A separate analysis (not shown) reveals that the size of those contributions depends on income and mobilization.

61. It is likely senior participation is driven by health as well. I do not include health in the analyses presented here because neither subjective nor objective measures of health status are included in the Roper, NES, or Citizen Participation Study datasets. However, analysis of other cross-sectional survey data shows that seniors who say they are in good health are more likely to vote; see Mohsen Bazargan, Tai S. Kang, and Shahrzad Bazargan, "A Multivariate Comparison of Elderly African Americans' and Caucasians' Voting Behavior: How Do Social, Health, Psychological, and Political Variables Effect Their Voting?" *International Journal of Aging and Human Development* 32 (1991): 181–98, and Steven A. Peterson and Albert Somit, *The Political Behavior of Older Americans* (New York: Garland, 1994). Unfortunately, no longitudinal datasets that begin before Medicare's passage in 1965 include both participation and health items, so it is not possible to directly test the effect of improved senior health on participation over time. However, because senior health has improved over time with the access to care provided by Medicare (chapter 2) and because good health is correlated with voter turnout, it is reasonable to conclude that Medicare has helped to enhance senior participation since its implementation.

62. Moon and Mulvey, *Entitlements and the Elderly*, p. 29.

63. Farmers, for example, vote at rates far higher than predicted by their education, income, age, and other demographic characteristics (Wolfinger and Rosenstone, *Who Votes?*). They are such active participators in part because their economic fortunes, like senior citizens', are unusually dependent on government action. Government employees also vote at high rates.

64. Sidney Verba, Norman H. Nie, and Jae-on Kim, *Participation and Political Equality: A Seven-Nation Comparison* (New York: Cambridge University Press, 1978); G. Bingham Powell, "American Voting in Comparative Perspective," *American Political Science Review* 80 (1986): 23–37.

65. Theda Skocpol, *Social Policy in the United States: Future Possibilities in Historical Perspective* (Princeton: Princeton University Press, 1995), p. 26.

66. Verba, Schlozman, and Brady, *Voice and Equality*, p. 384.

CHAPTER FOUR
SENIOR CITIZEN PARTICIPATION AND POLICY OVER TIME

1. These are replacement ratios for new retirees getting Social Security, not replacement ratios across all retirees or across all senior citizens.

2. U.S. House Committee on Ways and Means, *1998 Green Book: Overview of Entitlement Programs* (Washington, D.C.: U.S. Government Printing Office, 1998), p. 27.

3. Interest in public affairs question coded "Hardly at all" = 1, "Only now and then" = 2, "Some of the time" = 3, and "Most of the time" = 4.

4. I fit ordinary least-squares regression lines to compare the trends in the two participatory activities.

5. One alternative explanation for the higher rate of senior mobilization could be that seniors are more likely than younger people to be registered to vote. The ratio of senior to nonsenior party mobilization, however, is the same among registered respondents as it is among all respondents. For data comparing the ratios for all the years in which the NES asked respondents whether they were registered to vote, see appendix table A.14.

6. I tabulated the number of column inches devoted to senior citizens, Social Security, and Medicare in the Democratic and Republican party platforms from 1932 to 2000 and divided these by total platform length. Platforms for 1932 through 1976 are from Donald Bruce Johnson, *National Party Platforms* (Urbana: University of Illinois Press, 1978). Platforms for 1980 to 2000 are from various issues of the *CQ Almanac*.

7. Except for the 1944 Democratic and 1948 Democratic and Republican platforms, which mentioned Social Security but did not devote a separate section to the program.

8. Henry J. Pratt, *The Gray Lobby* (Chicago: University of Chicago Press, 1976), p. 57.

9. Ibid., pp. 66–68.

10. See also Peter W. Wielhouwer and Brad Lockerbie, "Party Contacting and Political Participation, 1952–90," *American Journal of Political Science* 38 (1994): 211–29. They show that in general individuals who are contacted by the parties are more likely to vote and engage in other electoral activities.

11. The organization officially adopted the acronym as its name in the late 1990s to increase its appeal to the nonretired.

12. U.S. Bureau of the Census, *Historical Statistics of the United States: Colonial Times to 1970* (Washington, D.C.: U.S. Government Printing Office, 1975), p. 225.

13. David Hackett Fischer, *Growing Old in America* (Oxford: Oxford University Press, 1978), p. 179.

14. Abraham Holtzman, *The Townsend Movement: A Political Study* (New York: Bookman Associates, 1963).

15. Edwin Amenta and colleagues find that in some states the Townsend movement achieved its goal of high pensions for the aged, but had little influence at the national level. See Edwin Amenta, Bruce G. Carruthers, and Yvonne Zylan, "A Hero for the Aged? The Townsend Movement, the Political Mediation Model, and U.S. Old-Age Policy, 1934–1950," *American Journal of Sociology* 98 (1992): 308–39.

16. Calculated from U.S. Bureau of the Census, *Historical Statistics of the United States*, pp. 10, 224.

17. William W. Lammers, *Public Policy and the Aging* (Washington, D.C.: CQ Press, 1983), p. 42.

18. Ibid.; Christine L. Day, *What Older Americans Think: Interest Groups and Aging Policy* (Princeton: Princeton University Press, 1990), p. 18.

19. On the origins of policy alternatives, see John W. Kingdon, *Agendas, Alternatives, and Public Policies*, 2d ed. (New York: Harper Collins, 1995), chap. 6.

20. Jack L. Walker, *Mobilizing Interest Groups in America* (Ann Arbor: University of Michigan Press, 1991).

21. Pratt, *The Gray Lobby.*

22. Charles R. Morris, *The AARP: America's Most Powerful Lobby and the Clash of Generations* (New York: Times Books, 1996), p. 209.

23. Ibid., pp. 10–11.

24. Morris, *The AARP.*

25. For two examples, see Ken Kollman, *Outside Lobbying: Public Opinion and Interest Group Strategies* (Princeton: Princeton University Press, 1998), and Bruce C. Wolpe and Bertram J. Levine, *Lobbying Congress: How the System Works*, 2d ed. (Washington, D.C.: CQ Press, 1996).

26. The SSA also administered Medicare from 1965 until 1977, when the Health Care Financing Administration (HCFA) was created. In 2001 the HCFA was renamed the Centers for Medicare and Medicaid Services. "Aging enterprise" is Carroll Estes's term. *The Aging Enterprise* (San Francisco: Jossey-Bass, 1979).

27. James Q. Wilson, *Bureaucracy: What Government Agencies Do and Why They Do It* (New York: Basic Books, 1989).

28. U.S. House Ways and Means Committee, *1998 Green Book*, p. 81.

29. Pratt, *The Gray Lobby*, pp. 116–17.

30. Lammers, *Public Policy and the Aging*, p. 78.

31. Arnold M. Rose, "Group Consciousness among the Aging," in *Older People and Their Social World: The Subculture of the Aging*, ed. Arnold M. Rose and Warren A. Peterson (Philadelphia: F. A. Davis Company, 1965).

32. David R. Mayhew, *Congress: The Electoral Connection* (New Haven: Yale University Press, 1974); Richard F. Fenno, Jr., *Home Style: House Members in Their Districts* (Boston: Little, Brown, 1978).

33. Here I cite average numbers of seniors across states and congressional districts, but of course senior constituencies vary in size. In 1998, for example, the percentage of seniors in state populations ranged from 4.2 percent in Alaska to 19.1 percent in Florida. The percentage of seniors in congressional district populations ranged up to 32 percent in Florida's twenty-second district. See Michael Barone and Grant Ujifusa, *The Almanac of American Politics 2000* (Washington, D.C.: National Journal, 1999).

34. R. Douglas Arnold, *The Logic of Congressional Action* (New Haven: Yale University Press, 1990), p. 14.

35. Chapter 5 discusses senior attitudes and behavior regarding Social Security. Although some political gerontologists have asserted that seniors are a diverse population, not a cohesive "bloc" (see Robert H. Binstock, "Interest Group Liberalism and the Politics of Aging," *The Gerontologist* 12 (1972): 265–80; and "A Policy Agenda on Aging for the 1980s," *National Journal* 41 (13 October 1979): 1711–17), congressional fear of sanction is real and not unfounded, as chapter 5 demonstrates. That analysis shows that seniors will defend their programs when they are threatened.

36. John R. Johannes, *To Serve the People: Congress and Constituency Service* (Lincoln: University of Nebraska Press, 1984), p. 19.

37. Ibid., pp. 26–27. Johannes performed multivariate analysis on data from the 1978 and 1980 National Election Studies to determine which kinds of people make casework requests. The only consistent finding is that older people generate more casework. Age is the only factor significant in both years; casework requests did not vary with education, income, occupation, economic hardship, or race, and the only variables besides age that were at all significant appeared in the 1978 data, where government employees and people of higher self-ascribed social status were more likely to make casework requests.

38. Robert H. Binstock, "Federal Policy toward the Aging—Its Inadequacies and Its Politics," *National Journal* 40 (11 November 1978): 1838.

39. Robin Toner, "Long-Term Care Merges Political with Personal," *New York Times*, 26 July 1999, p. A1.

40. Arnold, *The Logic of Congressional Action*, pp. 64–65.

41. Johannes, *To Serve the People*, pp. 164, 262. Although casework is an important source of information for members, the relevance of casework for age-related policy extends even further. Casework requests not only generate problem-solving activity by congressional staffs, but also can inspire legislative efforts. Seventy-seven percent of the members of Congress Johannes interviewed said they had made "attempts to generalize about problems discovered in constituency service operations so that some remedial action, such as introduction of legislation, might be taken" (*To Serve the People*, p. 164). Of the fifty-one bills mentioned by members and aides as having been casework inspired, twelve concerned the Social Security program itself and another five concerned Medicare, the Railroad Retirement system, and VA benefits for elderly veterans, for a total of seventeen, or 34 percent of casework-inspired bills benefiting senior citizens (ibid., pp. 164, 262). Just as seniors are the most likely to make casework requests and seniors' programs are the number one source of casework, so senior-related casework generates the most legislative activity. Not surprisingly, these casework-inspired legislative efforts are almost always remedial, making incremental improvements in existing laws rather than major innovations in public policy. But more important for this discussion, the largest proportion of legislation inspired by casework concerns senior citizens.

42. This section draws heavily on Julian E. Zelizer, *Taxing America: Wilbur D. Mills, Congress, and the State, 1945–1975* (Cambridge: Cambridge University Press, 1998), chap. 2. See also Edward D. Berkowitz, "The Historical Develop-

ment of Social Security in the United States," in *Social Security in the 21st Century*, ed. Eric H. Kingson and James H. Schulz (New York: Oxford University Press, 1997). Both works extensively cite the large literature on the early history of Social Security.

43. Zelizer, *Taxing America*, p. 76.

44. Ibid., p. 60.

45. Berkowitz, "The Historical Development of Social Security," p. 26.

46. Quoted in Zelizer, *Taxing America*, p. 78.

47. Pratt, *The Gray Lobby*, p. 26.

48. Martha Derthick, *Policymaking for Social Security* (Washington, D.C.: Brookings, 1979), pp. 62–88.

49. U.S. House Ways and Means Committee, *1998 Green Book*, pp. 58–59.

50. For an excellent account of the trust fund's role in promoting Social Security's autonomy and long-term sustainability, see Eric M. Patashnik, *Putting Trust in the U.S. Budget: Federal Trust Funds and the Politics of Commitment* (Cambridge: Cambridge University Press, 2000), chap. 4. In addition, policymaking from 1940 to the present has been carried out against a background of strong public support for Social Security. Even in the 1930s, before benefit payments commenced, support was in the 90 percent range. See Michael E. Schiltz, *Public Attitudes toward Social Security, 1935–1965*, Social Security Administration, Office of Research and Statistics, Research Report no. 33 (Washington, D.C.: U.S. Government Printing Office, 1970), p. 36.

51. Day, *What Older Americans Think*. Observers disagree about how influential senior interest groups were during this period. Pratt argues in *The Gray Lobby* that the NCSC figured importantly in the fight for Medicare; Marmor's account of Medicare's passage hardly mentions elderly interest groups at all. See Theodore R. Marmor, *The Politics of Medicare* (Chicago: Aldine, 1973).

52. Pratt, *The Gray Lobby*, p. 117.

53. Lammers, *Public Policy and the Aging*, p. 46.

54. Ibid.

55. Day, *What Older Americans Think*, p. 94.

56. U.S. House Ways and Means Committee, *1998 Green Book*, p. 27.

57. Pratt, *The Gray Lobby*.

58. Ibid., p. 133.

59. Ibid., p. 148.

60. Ibid., p. 152.

61. David D. Van Tassel and Jimmy Elaine Wilkinson Meyer, *U.S. Aging Policy Interest Groups: Institutional Profiles* (New York: Greenwood Press, 1992).

62. R. Kent Weaver, *Automatic Government: The Politics of Indexation* (Washington, D.C.: Brookings, 1988), p. 67; Zelizer, *Taxing America*, p. 13.

63. Pratt, *The Gray Lobby*, p. 165.

64. Edward R. Tufte, *Political Control of the Economy* (Princeton: Princeton University Press, 1978), pp. 32–36.

65. Derthick, *Policymaking for Social Security*, pp. 349–57; Weaver, *Automatic Government*.

66. Tufte, *Political Control of the Economy*, p. 30.

67. Weaver, *Automatic Government*. On the fiscal assumptions that provided political cover in the era before indexation, see also Zelizer, *Taxing America*, pp. 72–73.

68. Martha Derthick, "How Easy Votes on Social Security Came to an End," *Public Interest* 54 (1979): 94–105.

69. U.S. House Ways and Means Committee, *1998 Green Book*, p. 27; Social Security Administration Office of Research, Evaluation and Statistics, *Income of the Aged Chartbook, 1996* (Washington, D.C.: U.S. Government Printing Office, 1998), p. 22.

CHAPTER FIVE
POLICY THREAT AND SENIORS' DISTINCTIVE POLITICAL VOICE

1. Bob Woodward, *The Agenda: Inside the Clinton White House* (New York: Simon & Schuster, 1994); Gwen Ifill, "Social Security Won't Be Subject to Freeze, White House Decides," *New York Times*, 9 February 1993, p. A1; James Risen, "White House Backs off Social Security Freeze," *Los Angeles Times*, 9 February 1993, p. A1.

2. For works emphasizing the diversity of senior citizens, see Robert H. Binstock, "Interest Group Liberalism and the Politics of Aging," *The Gerontologist* 12 (1972): 265–80; and Christine L. Day, *What Older Americans Think: Interest Groups and Aging Policy* (Princeton: Princeton University Press, 1990).

3. Day, *What Older Americans Think*.

4. Michael E. Schiltz, *Public Attitudes toward Social Security, 1935–1965*, Social Security Administration, Office of Research and Statistics, Research Report no. 33 (Washington, D.C.: U.S. Government Printing Office, 1970), p. 36.

5. Robert Y. Shapiro and Tom W. Smith, "The Polls: Social Security," *Public Opinion Quarterly* 49 (1985): 561–72; Jennifer Baggette, Robert Y. Shapiro, and Lawrence R. Jacobs, "Social Security—An Update," *Public Opinion Quarterly* 59 (1995): 420–42.

6. Baggette, Shapiro, and Jacobs, "Social Security—An Update."

7. "Poverty in America," *Public Opinion*, June/July 1985, p. 25.

8. Kaiser Family Foundation, National Survey of Americans on Social Security, 20 May 1999, at www.kff.org/content/archive/24, viewed 3 June 2001.

9. Fay Lomax Cook and Edith J. Barrett, *Support for the American Welfare State: The Views of Congress and the Public* (New York: Columbia University Press, 1992), pp. 97–100.

10. Respondents who said they supported their parents financially included 4 percent of 30- to 44-year-olds, 5 percent of 45- to 59-year-olds, and 2 percent of respondents aged 60 and over. Author calculations from the Roper Social and Political Trends Archive.

11. Janet Elder, "Portrait of the Elderly: Still Independent despite Limitations," *New York Times*, 15 January 1987, p. C1.

12. Dora L. Costa, *The Evolution of Retirement: An American Economic History, 1880–1990* (Chicago: University of Chicago Press, 1998), pp. 110–11; see also Frank Levy, *The New Dollars and Dreams: American Incomes and Economic Change* (New York: Russell Sage Foundation, 1998), p. 150.

13. Gallup Poll, 8–9 October 1999, at www.gallup.com/poll/indicators/indsocialsecurity.asp, viewed 3 June 2001.

14. People may not resent Social Security taxes because they feel they are making payments for their own retirement or supporting their parents' retirement. Another possibility is that Social Security taxes are relatively hidden. Harold Wilensky suggests that the degree to which tax burdens are hidden is more important for politics than the actual level of taxation; see *The New Corporatism, Centralization, and the Welfare State* (Beverly Hills, Calif.: Sage, 1976). Social Security taxes are by no means completely obscured, but they are listed on one's paycheck stub as "FICA" and "FICA-HI" rather than as "Social Security" and "Medicare Hospital Insurance"; they do not arrive in the mail as lump-sum bills like property taxes; and one never needs to calculate the yearly total as one does with federal or state income taxes. On the visibility of taxes, see also Anthony Downs, "Why the Government Budget Is Too Small in a Democracy," *World Politics* 12 (1960): 541–63.

15. ABC News/*Washington Post* Poll, 11–16 January 1985, in *Public Opinion*, April/May 1985, p. 22.

16. Lawrence R. Jacobs and Robert Y. Shapiro, "Myths and Misunderstandings about Public Opinion toward Social Security," in *Framing the Social Security Debate*, ed. R. Douglas Arnold, Michael J. Graetz, and Alicia H. Munnell (Washington, D.C.: National Academy of Social Insurance, 1998), pp. 364–65. On the low confidence–high support paradox, see also Karlyn Bowman, "Social Security: A Report on Current Polls," American Enterprise Institute for Public Policy Research, April 1999.

17. Jack Citrin and Donald Philip Green, "The Self-Interest Motive in American Public Opinion," *Research in Micropolitics* 3 (1990): 1–28.

18. Donald P. Green and Jonathan A. Cowden, "Who Protests—Self-Interest and White Opposition to Busing," *Journal of Politics* 54 (1992): 71–96.

19. K. L. Tedin, D. W. Brady, M. E. Buxton, B. M. Gorman, and J. L. Thompson, "Social Background and Political Differences between Pro- and Anti-ERA Activists," *American Politics Quarterly* 5 (1977): 395–408.

20. Laurie A. Rhodebeck, "The Politics of Greed? Political Preferences among the Elderly," *Journal of Politics* 55 (1993): 342–64.

21. Mancur Olson, *The Logic of Collective Action* (Cambridge: Harvard University Press, 1965).

22. Steven E. Finkel, Edward N. Muller, and Karl-Dieter Opp, "Personal Influence, Collective Rationality, and Mass Political Action," *American Political Science Review* 83 (1989): 885–903.

23. The 100-point efficacy scale (variable 648 in the NES cumulative dataset) is constructed from two items: "People like me don't have any say about what the government does" and "I don't think public officials care much what people like me think." Higher values indicate greater external political efficacy. Figure 5.1 graphs the efficacy of seniors over 1952 levels (1952 is the reference point, the coefficients graphed are year x senior dummies). The model controls for education, income, gender, race, region, strength of partisanship, and age, and also includes year dummies to control for the secular decline in external political efficacy. In other words, figure 5.1 shows how much seniors' external efficacy has risen

since 1952, controlling for demographic characteristics and the fact that efficacy has declined in general. See appendix table A.8 for the regression results.

24. For an example of such advertising, see Morris P. Fiorina, *Congress: Keystone of the Washington Establishment* (New Haven: Yale University Press, 1977), p. 46.

25. On the importance of early victories in encouraging potential members to join the civil rights movement, see Dennis Chong, *Collective Action and the Civil Rights Movement* (Chicago: University of Chicago Press, 1991).

26. R. Douglas Arnold, *The Logic of Congressional Action* (New Haven: Yale University Press, 1990).

27. Charles R. Morris, *The AARP: America's Most Powerful Lobby and the Clash of Generations* (New York: Times Books, 1996).

28. See Arnold M. Rose, "Group Consciousness among the Aging," in *Older People and Their Social World: The Subculture of the Aging*, ed. Arnold M. Rose and Warren A. Peterson (Philadelphia: F. A. Davis Company, 1965). An interesting avenue for further research would be to determine whether seniors who live in senior-only communities or housing are more likely to be politically active than those living in mixed-age settings (I refer to age-restricted housing developments for the able-bodied, not nursing homes). Of course it would be necessary in such a study to control for selection effects; those who choose senior communities or housing may be predisposed to activism or especially attuned to senior issues to begin with, so a participation differential could be due to those selection factors, not to the effect of living in a senior community itself. Some sociological and anthropological studies were done when such communities became popular in the 1960s, but I know of none that focus on political participation. In a book chapter on the relatively affluent senior community of Sun City, Florida, the journalist Frances FitzGerald notes that the seniors living there uniformly vote against school bond issues and, despite being conservative Republicans, are strongly defensive of their Social Security benefits. See Frances FitzGerald, *Cities on a Hill: A Journey through Contemporary American Cultures* (New York: Simon & Schuster, 1986). Several senior citizens I interviewed suggested that their counterparts who have moved to senior communities are less likely to participate, having eschewed the rough-and-tumble of regular communities for the homogeneity and worry-free leisure of the age-segmented enclaves.

29. The following discussion of context and threat owes much to Joanne M. Miller, Jon A. Krosnick, and Laura Lowe, "The Impact of Policy Change Threat on Grassroots Activism," Ohio State University, unpublished paper, 1999.

30. Ibid.

31. David Truman, *The Governmental Process* (New York: Alfred A. Knopf, 1951).

32. Samuel Barnes and Max Kaase, *Political Action: Mass Participation in Five Western Democracies* (Beverly Hills, Calif.: Sage, 1979); Jeffrey M. Berry, *The Interest Group Society* (Boston: Little, Brown, 1984); Russell Dalton, *Citizen Politics: Public Opinion and Political Parties in Advanced Western Democracies* (Chatham, N.J.: Chatham House, 1988); William A. Gamson, *The Strategy of Protest* (Homewood, I.L.: Dorsey Press, 1975); Theodore R. Gurr, *Why Men Rebel* (Princeton: Princeton University Press, 1970); Steven J. Rosenstone and

John Mark Hansen, *Mobilization, Participation, and Democracy in America* (New York: Macmillan, 1993).

33. John Mark Hansen, "The Political Economy of Group Membership," *American Political Science Review* 79 (1985): 79–96; Burdett A. Loomis and Allan J. Cigler, "Introduction: The Changing Nature of Interest Group Politics," in *Interest Group Politics*, ed. Allan J. Cigler and Burdett A. Loomis (Washington, D.C.: CQ Press, 1995); Norman J. Ornstein and Shirley Elder, *Interest Groups, Lobbying, and Policymaking* (Washington, D.C.: CQ Press, 1978).

34. Miller, Krosnick, and Lowe, "The Impact of Policy Change Threat on Grassroots Activism."

35. See ibid. for the relevant psychological literature.

36. Hansen, "The Political Economy of Group Membership"; Jack L. Walker, *Mobilizing Interest Groups in America* (Ann Arbor: University of Michigan Press, 1991).

37. Truman, *The Governmental Process*; Walker, *Mobilizing Interest Groups in America*; Loomis and Cigler, "Introduction."

38. Miller, Krosnick, and Lowe, "The Impact of Policy Change Threat on Grassroots Activism."

39. Martha Derthick, "How Easy Votes on Social Security Came to an End," *Public Interest* 54 (1979): 94–105.

40. I am by no means asserting that seniors are exempt from the collective action problem. Rather, the factors mentioned alter the cost-benefit calculation sufficiently for a large enough proportion of seniors that we can see participatory reactions to policy threats.

41. See chapter 2, note 45, for question wording.

42. Frances Fox Piven and Richard A. Cloward, *Why Americans Don't Vote* (New York: Pantheon, 1989); Kim Quaile Hill and Jan E. Leighley, "The Policy Consequences of Class Bias in State Electorates," *American Journal of Political Science* 36 (1992): 351–65. See also Arend Lijphart, "Unequal Participation: Democracy's Unresolved Dilemma," *American Political Science Review* 91 (1997): 1–14.

43. Raymond E. Wolfinger, "Dealignment, Realignment, and Mandates in the 1984 Election," in *The American Elections of 1984*, ed. Austin Ranney (Durham, N.C.: Duke University Press, 1985), p. 293.

44. This statistic is all the more remarkable given the press's well-known proclivity to try to provide "balance" on an issue by including both sides—even when one side is a small minority—and given the press's fascination with "man bites dog"—in this case letters from recipients who oppose Social Security. See Doris A. Graber, *Mass Media and American Politics* (Washington, D.C.: CQ Press, 1997).

Content analysis methodology: I counted letters to the editor in the *New York Times* from May 1981 through November 1989, the period of senior program threat, coding letters explicitly about Social Security or Medicare. I divided the letters into three categories: those written by recipients (as self-identified or obvious from the latent context); those not written by recipients (such as those written by academics, interest group officials, or medical professionals); and those for which the writer's identity was not clear. Within each category I coded the letters as taking a defensive antithreat stand, a pro-change stand, or other. The percentage reported in the text is the proportion of recipient letters that took a defensive antithreat stand.

45. Office of Management and Budget director David Stockman needed $44 billion in savings to meet his budget goals, and he lit on Social Security—big cuts in a big program could make up the gap. Stockman's proposal included reducing benefits for early retirees from 80 percent of full benefits to 55 percent, effective immediately; on January 1, 1982, the average early retiree's monthly check would have been cut from $469 to $310. Reagan, who was still recovering from the March 1981 assassination attempt, apparently did not realize the cuts were immediate when he approved Stockman's plan. But since the plan came from his administration and since Reagan had a history of negative comments about Social Security, dating back to a 1964 television speech for Barry Goldwater in which Reagan raised the idea of a voluntary Social Security system, the media pegged Reagan with the cuts. Over the years Reagan's advisors warned him to avoid the subject, but he continued to inveigh against the program in what his biographer Lou Cannon called "unguarded public moments." See Lou Cannon, *President Reagan: The Role of a Lifetime* (New York: Simon & Schuster, 1991), p. 243.

46. Paul Light, *Artful Work: The Politics of Social Security Reform* (New York: Random House, 1985).

47. "The Social Security Flap," *Congressional Quarterly Weekly Report* 39 (23 May 1981): 896.

48. Light, *Artful Work*, p. 125.

49. Timothy B. Clark, "Saving Social Security—Reagan and Congress Face Some Unpleasant Choices," *National Journal* 13 (13 June 1981), p. 1053.

50. Clark, "Saving Social Security."

51. Pamela Fessler and Harrison Donnelly, "Congress Seeking to Assure Retirement Income Security," *Congressional Quarterly Weekly Report* 39 (28 November 1981): 2333–36.

52. Neal R. Peirce and Peter C. Choharis, "The Elderly as a Political Force: 26 Million Strong and Well Organized," *National Journal* 14 (11 September 1982): 1559–62.

53. Light, *Artful Work*.

54. Henry Fairlie, "Talkin' 'bout My Generation," *The New Republic* (28 March 1988): 19–22.

55. Robert Pear, "Benefits Disparity Made Issue in Iowa," *New York Times*, 1 January 1988, Section 1, p. 36. On the notch controversy, also see R. Kent Weaver, *Automatic Government: The Politics of Indexation* (Washington, D.C.: Brookings, 1988), pp. 80, 87.

56. Julie Rovner, "Conferees Set to Begin Work on Catastrophic-Costs Bill," *Congressional Quarterly Weekly Report* 46 (13 February 1988): 313–15. For an extensive account of the Catastrophic Act, see Richard Himelfarb, *Catastrophic Politics: The Rise and Fall of the Medicare Catastrophic Coverage Act of 1988* (University Park: Pennsylvania State University Press, 1995).

57. Julie Rovner, "Catastrophic-Insurance Law: Costs vs. Benefits," *Congressional Quarterly Weekly Report* 46 (3 December 1988): 3450–52.

58. One of the biggest foes of the Medicare act was the National Committee to Preserve Social Security and Medicare, a lobbying group headed by James Roo-

sevelt, son of Franklin D. Roosevelt. Founded in 1982, the group claimed 5 million members by 1988. Surrounded by controversy—by 1988 both houses of Congress had held hearings on its activities—the Roosevelt group was shunned by other aged policy interest groups. Its critics said it engaged in a misinformation campaign about the act, telling seniors that all elderly would be subject to the maximum $800 premium. AARP had backed the bill and felt as stung as the lawmakers themselves by the grassroots opposition. Both members of Congress and AARP complained that those who objected to the new law did not understand what the gaps in Medicare were or how Medicare was financed in the first place, and were unduly influenced by the misinformation campaigns.

Survey evidence shows widespread ignorance about the act among seniors; see Christine L. Day, "Older Americans' Attitudes toward the Medicare Catastrophic Coverage Act of 1988," *Journal of Politics* 55 (1993): 167–77. One member of Congress interviewed by William Bianco said of the Catastrophic Act, "[Senior citizens] were stupid, and misled endlessly. One-half of those people were yelling, 'You've got to repeal it.' I asked them whether they made thirty thousand a year, and they said, 'Of course not.' So I told them about the surtax, and how they probably wouldn't pay any tax at their income levels. And then they yelled, 'You've got to repeal it.' There was no way to talk with them, the misinformation was complete." William T. Bianco, *Trust: Representatives and Constituents* (Ann Arbor: University of Michigan Press, 1994), p. 129.

59. Quoted in Martin Tolchin, "New Health Insurance Plan Provokes Outcry over Costs," *New York Times*, 2 November 1988, p. A1.

60. Quoted in Julie Rovner, "The Catastrophic-Costs Law: A Massive Miscalculation," *Congressional Quarterly Weekly Report* 47 (14 October 1989), p. 2715.

61. The Lowess curves are produced by a locally weighted smoothing technique that reduces the distorting effects of outliers. See William S. Cleveland, "Robust Locally Weighted Regression and Smoothing Scatterplots," *Journal of the American Statistical Association* 74 (1979): 829–36, and *The Elements of Graphing Data* (Monterey, Calif.: Wadsworth, 1985). Each Roper survey has approximately 2,000 respondents. For cell sizes among the 202 surveys for each age group, see appendix table A.15.

Although the twelve-month time frame may appear less than ideal for studying participatory change in reaction to specific events, the actual time frame for responses is probably shorter. Many studies show that memories telescope—people recall recent events more readily than distant ones, and many individuals cannot remember even important events in their lives for as long as twelve months. Rosenstone and Hansen found no significant difference in the response rates for the same Roper question worded with a six-month time frame, and argue that respondents are not able to recall their political activities for an entire year. See Rosenstone and Hansen, *Mobilization, Participation, and Democracy in America*, p. 69, note 21.

62. A series of dummy and counter variables, which are explained in appendix D, represent the policy events and intervening time periods.

63. The Lowess curves are locally weighted curves that ignore the delineations among the five time periods, while the MITS analysis calculates the linear ordinary least-squares slopes for each time period.

64. Federal Interagency Forum on Aging-Related Statistics, *Older Americans 2000: Key Indicators of Well-Being* (Washington, D.C.: U.S. Government Printing Office, 2000).

CHAPTER SIX
CONGRESSIONAL RESPONSIVENESS

1. For example, in the 1970s, Medicare paid doctors 85 percent of what private insurance companies paid. By 1994 this had dropped to 59 percent. Robert Pear, "Medicare Paying Doctors 59% of Insurers' Rate, Panel Finds," *New York Times*, 5 April 1994, p. A16.

2. For a thorough literature review of constituent opinion and congressional responsiveness, see Vincent Lamont Hutchings, "The Dynamics of Congressional Representation: How Citizens Monitor Legislators in the House and Senate," Ph.D. dissertation, University of California, Los Angeles, 1998.

3. Warren E. Miller and Donald E. Stokes, "Constituency Influence in Congress," *American Political Science Review* 57 (1963): 45–56.

4. Christopher H. Achen, "Measuring Representation," *American Journal of Political Science* 22 (1978): 475–510.

5. Robert S. Erikson, Norman Luttbeg, and William V. Holloway, "Knowing One's District: How Legislators Predict Referendum Voting," *American Journal of Political Science* 19 (1975): 231–45.

6. Gregory B. Markus, "Electoral Coalitions and Senate Roll Call Behavior," *American Journal of Political Science* 18 (1974): 595–607; Robert S. Erikson, "Constituency Opinion and Congressional Behavior: A Reexamination of the Miller-Stokes Representation Data," *American Journal of Political Science* 22 (1978): 511–35; Charles S. Bullock and David W. Brady, "Party, Constituency, and Roll-Call Voting in the U.S. Senate," *Legislative Studies Quarterly* 8 (1983): 29–43.

7. John R. Johannes and John C. McAdams, "The Congressional Incumbency Effect: Is It Casework, Policy Compatibility, or Something Else?" *American Journal of Political Science* 25 (1981): 512–42; Robert S. Erikson and Gerald F. Wright Jr., "Policy Representation of Constituency Interests," *Political Behavior* 1 (1980): 91–106.

8. Walter Stone, "Electoral Change and Policy Representation in Congress: Domestic Welfare Issues from 1956–72," *British Journal of Political Science* 12 (1982): 92–115; Gerald C. Wright, "Policy Voting in the U.S. Senate: Who Is Represented?" *Legislative Studies Quarterly* 14 (1989): 465–86.

9. Gary C. Jacobson, *The Politics of Congressional Elections*, 3d ed. (New York: Harper Collins, 1992).

10. Richard F. Fenno, Jr., *Home Style: House Members in Their Districts* (Boston: Little, Brown, 1978); John W. Kingdon, *Congressmen's Voting Decisions*, 3d ed. (Ann Arbor: University of Michigan Press, 1989).

11. Kingdon, *Congressmen's Voting Decisions*.

12. R. Douglas Arnold, *The Logic of Congressional Action* (New Haven: Yale University Press, 1990). Furthermore, Vincent Hutchings shows that legislators anticipate and attempt to vote in line with the potential preferences of important issue publics because those publics can be activated. Political challengers, interest groups, and the media provide information about members' positions and "interested voters pay attention to [that information] when it is provided." "The Dynamics of Congressional Responsiveness," p. 3.

13. Mark A. Peterson, "How Health Policy Information Is Used in Congress," in *Intensive Care: How Congress Shapes Health Policy*, ed. Thomas E. Mann and Norman J. Ornstein (Washington, D.C.: American Enterprise Institute and Brookings, 1995), pp. 84–103.

14. Allen Schick, "Informed Legislation: Policy Research versus Ordinary Knowledge," in *Knowledge, Power, and the Congress*, ed. William H. Robinson and Clay H. Wellborn (Washington, D.C.: CQ Press, 1991), p. 101.

15. Peterson, "How Health Policy Information Is Used in Congress," pp. 88–89.

16. Morris P. Fiorina, *Congress: Keystone of the Washington Establishment* (New Haven: Yale University Press, 1977).

17. Kingdon, *Congressmen's Voting Decisions*.

18. I also eliminated roll-call votes that concerned aspects of the programs that do not affect the main body of senior citizen recipients, such as bills limiting benefits for illegal aliens. And I discarded votes in which one party voted entirely aye or nay (three votes in the Senate, none in the House). Democrats on average represent districts and states with more seniors (in 1985, Democratic congressmen represented districts that were 11.5 percent senior on average compared with 11 percent for Republican congressmen; Democratic senators came from states that were 12.1 percent senior on average versus 11.4 percent for Republican senators). Including party-line votes would strengthen the correlation between proportion of senior population and legislators' votes. I threw out these votes because I wanted to show a correlation between senior population and roll call votes that went beyond these party differences. Thus I am posing a more stringent test on the data. Appendix table A.9 contains a list of included roll-call votes.

19. House districts in 1985 ranged from 3 to 28 percent senior. States ranged from 3 to 17.6 percent senior. Senior population quartile ranges for 1985 are listed at the bottom of table 6.2.

20. The likelihood that Republicans in both houses will vote in a pro-senior direction rises as the senior proportion in their constituency increases, after controlling for differences in ideology as measured by ADA scores. As in table 6.1, Democratic senators are more likely to vote pro-senior when they have more senior constituents; Democratic representatives are not. The positive ADA score coefficients mean that lawmakers are more likely to vote pro-senior if they are more liberal. See appendix table A.16.

21. The likelihood that Republicans switched their vote on the Catastrophic Act increased with the percentage of seniors in their districts, after controlling for ideology as measured by ADA scores. The likelihood that Democratic representatives switched their vote was not influenced by the size of their senior constituencies. See appendix table A.17.

22. Multivariate analysis by party suggests that senior affluence affected Republican representatives more than it did Democrats. Republicans in affluent districts were less likely to switch their votes on the Catastrophic Act (negative coefficient for home value) but were more likely to do so if there were more affluent seniors (positive coefficient for home value × % 65+ interaction term). See appendix table A.18.

23. I also tried alternative specifications, such as seniors as a proportion of all contactors from a state, with similar results.

24. I used twelve months to obtain a sufficient number of cases in each state. For each roll-call vote, the analysis includes data from thirty-one to thirty-eight states; Roper did not sample some smaller states at all, and dropped a number of states after 1986, and I eliminated states where even aggregating a year's worth of data yielded fewer than twenty cases of senior contacting per state.

25. Robert Pear, "Benefits Disparity Made Issue in Iowa," *New York Times*, 1 January 1988, sect. 1, p. 36.

26. Charles R. Morris, *The AARP: America's Most Powerful Lobby and the Clash of Generations* (New York: Times Books, 1996), pp. 105–6.

27. Ibid., p. 106.

CHAPTER SEVEN
THE RECIPROCAL PARTICIPATION-POLICY RELATIONSHIP ACROSS PROGRAMS

1. "Welfare" in these 1990 data is the Aid to Families with Dependent Children (AFDC) program; in 1996 the program was replaced with Temporary Assistance for Needy Families (TANF). The number of Citizen Participation Study respondents from households receiving each program: Social Security (552), Medicare (441), veterans' benefits (120), public assistance (110), food stamps (105), housing assistance (64), and Medicaid (127).

2. Veterans' benefits include monthly compensation for service-connected disability; pension benefits; medical care; long-term care; mental health service; auxiliary services, including nutrition, rehabilitation, and nursing care; and an information and referral service to acquaint veterans and their widows with these benefits. Medical care is supposed to be need based, but the needs test is not rigorously enforced. In 1971 Congress eliminated the needs test for veterans over age 65. See Bennett M. Rich and Martha Baum, *The Aging: A Guide to Public Policy* (Pittsburgh: University of Pittsburgh Press, 1984), chap. 8.

3. Note that the survey respondents are not necessarily the program recipients. The question asked whether *anyone* in the household receives Social Security, veterans' benefits, general assistance, and so on. But while the survey data reported here are not always for program recipients precisely, the data do approximately convey interprogram differences.

4. U.S. House Committee on Ways and Means, *1998 Green Book: Overview of Entitlement Programs* (Washington, D.C.: U.S. Government Printing Office, 1998), p. 406. The percentage of TANF recipients on Medicaid is lower now that the programs are administratively delinked.

5. Seymour Martin Lipset, *Political Man: The Social Bases of Politics* (1959; Baltimore: Johns Hopkins University Press, 1981), p. 193.

6. U.S. House Committee on Ways and Means, *1998 Green Book*, p. 402.

7. Marilyn Moon and Janemarie Mulvey, *Entitlements and the Elderly: Protecting Promises, Recognizing Reality* (Washington, D.C.: Urban Institute Press, 1996).

8. Daniel H. Weinberg, "Filling the 'Poverty Gap': Multiple Transfer Program Participation," *Journal of Human Resources* 20 (1985): 64–89; Isabel V. Sawhill, "Poverty in the U.S.: Why Is It So Persistent?" *Journal of Economic Literature* 26 (1988): 1073–1119.

9. Martin Gilens, *Why Americans Hate Welfare* (Chicago: University of Chicago Press, 1999).

10. I excluded the workplace from table 7.2 since few Social Security and AFDC recipients work.

11. This figure includes nonsenior Social Security recipients, which is why it is lower than the senior mobilization rates listed in chapter 3.

12. On the NWRO, see Gilbert Y. Steiner, *The State of Welfare* (Washington, D.C.: Brookings, 1971), chap. 8; Frances Fox Piven and Richard A. Cloward, *Poor People's Movements: Why They Succeed, How They Fail* (New York: Pantheon, 1977), chap. 5; and David Street, George T. Martin, Jr., and Laura Kramer Gordon, *The Welfare Industry: Functionaries and Recipients in Public Aid* (Beverly Hills, Calif.: Sage, 1979), chaps. 6 and 7.

13. R. Kent Weaver, "Ending Welfare as We Know It," in *The Social Divide: Political Parties and the Future of Activist Government*, ed. Margaret Weir (Washington, D.C.: Brookings, 1998). There are limits to proxy representation. Proxy representatives may not convey the plight of those they represent as compellingly or dramatically as the individuals would themselves. Proxy representatives may also become distracted by other concerns and loyalties; see Kay Lehman Schlozman and Sidney Verba, *Injury to Insult: Unemployment, Class, and Political Response* (Cambridge: Harvard University Press, 1979).

14. Joe Soss, "Lessons of Welfare: Policy Design, Political Learning, and Political Action," *American Political Science Review* 93 (1999): 363–80.

15. See appendix table A.10 for the regression results. Soss also found that AFDC recipiency has a positive effect on respondent internal efficacy (their personal feelings of effectiveness); see Soss, "Lessons of Welfare." Social Security recipiency has no statistically significant effect on internal efficacy. Negotiating the complex AFDC system fosters in recipients confidence in their ability to deal with the government; receiving Social Security is apparently so straightforward that it has no effect on recipients' perceptions of their abilities. These results are in table A.10 as well. Recipients of veterans' benefits have positive levels of both external and internal efficacy, although these are not statistically significant.

16. Samuel Barnes and Max Kaase, *Political Action: Mass Participation in Five Western Democracies* (Beverly Hills, Calif.: Sage, 1979); James C. Scott, *Weapons of the Weak: Everyday Forms of Peasant Resistance* (New Haven: Yale University Press, 1985).

17. Program-specific contacts are considered complaints because of the Citizen Participation Study question wording: "In the past five years, have you contacted a government official to complain about [program]?"

18. James Q. Wilson, *Bureaucracy: What Government Agencies Do and Why They Do It* (New York: Basic Books, 1989).

19. U.S. House Committee on Ways and Means, *1998 Green Book*, pp. 81, 402. Studies show that nearly all individuals eligible for Social Security actually receive benefits, while only 55 percent of families eligible for welfare get benefits; see Christopher Jencks, "Is the American Underclass Growing?" in *The Urban Underclass*, ed. Christopher Jencks and Paul E. Peterson (Washington, D.C.: Brookings, 1991). The latter figure was greater during the heyday of the National Welfare Rights Organization, perhaps as high as 90 percent; see R. Kent Weaver, *Ending Welfare as We Know It* (Washington, D.C.: Brookings, 2000), p. 55.

20. U.S. House Committee on Ways and Means, *1998 Green Book*, pp. 3, 402.

21. John R. Johannes, *To Serve the People: Congress and Constituency Service* (Lincoln: University of Nebraska Press, 1984), p. 19. The Obey Commission (formally known as the Commission on Administrative Review) was established by the House of Representatives in 1976 to make recommendations about administrative operations, financial accountability, and ethical procedures. Part of the disparity between the 1977 Obey Commission findings and the 1992 NES data may be that the number of veterans in the population is falling as the World War II generation dies off. Indeed, one might expect veterans' political clout to decrease as this "greatest generation" dies; Tom Brokaw, *The Greatest Generation* (New York: Random House, 1998).

22. Gilens, *Why Americans Hate Welfare*; Fay Lomax Cook and Edith J. Barrett, *Support for the American Welfare State: The Views of Congress and the Public* (New York: Columbia University Press, 1992).

23. The other issue areas were food stamps, AIDS, financial aid for students, blacks, the homeless, the USSR, science and technology, child care, crime, the environment, unemployment, the poor, public schools, and big cities.

24. William T. Bianco and Jamie Markham, "Vanishing Veterans: The Decline in Military Experience in the U.S. Congress," paper prepared for the 1999 Cantigny Conference on Bridging the Gap.

25. These respondents had the lowest incomes reported in the Roper Social and Political Trends dataset. The income categories on the original Roper surveys did not enable me to isolate a specific proportion of respondents, such as the lowest decile. The respondents in figure 7.1 were in the bottom 2.8 percent to 7.0 percent of all respondents in terms of income.

26. Peter T. Kilborn, "Veterans Expand Hospital System in Face of Cuts," *New York Times*, 14 January 1996, sect. 1, p. 1.

27. Ibid.

28. The earnings penalty was a Depression-era provision meant to relieve unemployment by penalizing Social Security recipients who worked. In 2000, Social Security recipients under age 70 would have lost one dollar for every three they earned over a $17,000 limit (U.S. House Ways and Means Committee, *1998 Green Book*, p. 84). On the Medicare prescription drug debate, see Robert Pear, "Senate Kills Plan for Drug Benefit through Medicare," *New York Times*, 1 August 2002, p. A1.

29. Paul Starr, *The Social Transformation of American Medicine* (New York: Basic Books, 1982), p. 289.

30. Edward R. Tufte, *Political Control of the Economy* (Princeton: Princeton University Press, 1978), chap. 2.

31. The number of veterans in the United States was 30.1 million in 1980, 26 million in 1996 and is projected to be 16 million in 2020 (Kilborn, "Veterans Expand Hospital System," p. 1; Robert Pear, "Audit of V.A. Health Care Finds Millions Are Wasted," *New York Times*, 1 August 1998, sect. 1, p. 1).

32. Kilborn, "Veterans Expand Hospital System," p. 1.

33. Bianco and Markham, "Vanishing Veterans."

34. Chuck Alston, "Powerful Veterans' Groups at Political Crossroads," *CQ Weekly Report*, 1 July 1989, pp. 1601–3.

35. Ibid.

36. Kilborn, "Veterans Expand Hospital System," p. 1.

37. Kilborn, "Veterans Expand Hospital System." The number of hospital beds in VA medical facilities did decrease from 80,000 in 1982 (Rich and Baum, *The Aging: A Guide to Public Policy*, p. 199)—as in the private sector, an increasing number of procedures are performed on an out-patient basis—but no hospitals other than those two were closed.

38. Quoted in Nina Siegal, "Protesters Seek More Money for Veterans' Health Care," *New York Times*, 31 May 1999, sect. B, p. 5.

39. U.S. Bureau of the Census, *Statistical Abstract of the United States 1999* (Washington, D.C.: U.S. Government Printing Office, 1999), p. 118.

40. D. Lee Bawden and John L. Palmer, "Social Policy: Challenging the Welfare State," in *The Reagan Record: An Assessment of America's Changing Domestic Priorities*, ed. John L. Palmer and Isabel V. Sawhill (Cambridge, Mass.: Ballinger, 1981), p. 185. See also Jens Alber, "Selectivity, Universalism, and the Politics of Welfare Retrenchment in Germany and the United States," paper prepared for the annual meeting of the American Political Science Association, 1996, pp. 20–21.

41. U.S. House Committee of Ways and Means, *1998 Green Book*, p. 402; *Social Security Bulletin Annual Statistical Supplement*, various editions.

42. In some states, like California, AFDC was indexed to inflation during the 1970s. Thanks to Henry Brady for this point.

43. Keech and Pak found no electoral cycle in benefits for another group that shares many characteristics of welfare recipients: the unemployed. Like welfare recipients, the unemployed vote at low rates and are not their own most vigorous advocates, according to Schlozman and Verba. Keech and Pak conclude that politicians do not therefore "regard these programs as a target for political gains." William R. Keech and Kyoungsan Pak, "Electoral Cycles and Budgetary Growth in Veterans' Benefit Programs," *American Journal of Political Science* 33 (1989): 901–11; Kay Lehman Schlozman and Sidney Verba, *Insult to Injury: Unemployment, Class, and Political Response* (Cambridge: Harvard University Press, 1979).

44. R. Kent Weaver, "Ending Welfare as We Know It," p. 395. There is some good news for low-income citizens. Between 1980 and 1998 Medicaid spending per recipient increased 58 percent for the AFDC/TANF population (in real dollars), although this was eclipsed by the 104 percent increase in Medicaid spending for elderly recipients; calculated from the *Statistical Abstract of the United States*, 1990 and 2000 editions. A program for low-income people that has grown dramatically is the Earned Income Tax Credit. Popular with moderates and even with

conservatives because it "rewards work," the program has grown in part because it is relatively "hidden," working through the tax code. Despite its growth, however, the program only helps those who are employed and therefore misses a large portion of the underclass. See Christopher Howard, *The Hidden Welfare State: Tax Expenditures and Social Policy in the United States* (Princeton: Princeton University Press, 1997).

CHAPTER EIGHT
PARTICIPATION, POLICYMAKING, AND THE POLITICAL
IMPLICATIONS OF PROGRAM DESIGN

1. Quoted in Saul Friedman, "Greedy Geezers: These Folks Say No," *Newsday*, 20 March 2001, p. B12.

2. P. H. Landis, "Emerging Problems of the Aged," *Social Forces*, May 1942, reprinted in *Readings in Social Security*, ed. William Haber and Wilbur J. Cohen (New York: Prentice Hall, 1948), pp. 228–38.

3. For an overview of the generational equity debate, see Jill Quadagno, "Generational Equity and the Politics of the Welfare State," *Politics and Society* 17 (1989): 253–76.

4. James M. Poterba, "Demographic Structure and the Political Economy of Public Education," *Journal of Policy Analysis and Management* 16 (1997): 48–66. See also James W. Button, "A Sign of Generational Conflict: The Impact of Florida's Aging Voters on Local School and Tax Referenda," *Social Science Quarterly* 73 (1992): 786–97.

5. Dora L. Costa, *The Evolution of Retirement: An American Economic History, 1880–1990* (Chicago: University of Chicago Press, 1998).

6. Samuel Preston, "Children and the Elderly: Divergent Paths for America's Dependents," *Demography* 21 (1984): 435–57.

7. Costa, *The Evolution of Retirement*, p. 160.

8. Preston, "Children and the Elderly."

9. The political scientist Paul E. Peterson has suggested one remedy: give children the vote. "An Immodest Proposal," *Daedalus* 121 (1992): 151–74.

10. Robert Dahl, *A Preface to Democratic Theory* (Chicago: University of Chicago Press, 1956), p. 138.

11. Sidney Verba and Gary Orren, *Equality in America: The View from the Top* (Cambridge: Harvard University Press, 1985), chap. 2

12. William Julius Wilson, *The Truly Disadvantaged: The Inner City, the Underclass, and Public Policy* (Chicago: University of Chicago Press, 1987); Theda Skocpol, "Targeting within Universalism: Politically Viable Policies to Combat Poverty in the United States," in *The Urban Underclass*, ed. Christopher Jencks and Paul E. Peterson (Washington, D.C.: Brookings, 1991).

13. Wilson, *The Truly Disadvantaged*. See also Martin Gilens, *Why Americans Hate Welfare* (Chicago: University of Chicago Press, 1999).

14. Robert D. Putnam, "Bowling Alone: America's Declining Social Capital," *Journal of Democracy* 6 (1995): 65–78; "Tuning In, Tuning Out: The Strange Disappearance of Social Capital in America," *PS: Political Science and Politics*

28 (1995): 664–83; and *Bowling Alone: The Collapse and Revival of American Community* (New York: Simon & Schuster, 2000).

15. On the use of counterfactuals in social science, see James D. Fearon, "Counterfactuals and Hypothesis Testing in Political Science," *World Politics* 43 (1991): 169–95; and Philip E. Tetlock and Aaron Belkin, *Counterfactual Thought Experiments in World Politics* (Princeton: Princeton University Press, 1996).

16. In defined-contribution pension plans, workers put aside a set amount each pay period (the defined contribution), and the ultimate size of their pension benefit is unknown and depends on market outcomes. In defined-benefit plans, the size of the pension benefit is predetermined, and in the case of Social Security, is guaranteed by the government.

17. Work by economists on privatization—both pro and con—includes Martin Feldstein, "Toward a Reform of Social Security," *Public Interest* 40 (1975): 75–95; "The Missing Piece in Policy Analysis" *American Economic Review Papers and Proceedings* 86 (1996): 1–14; and "A New Era of Social Security," *Public Interest* 130 (1998): 102–25; Henry Aaron, "Privatizing Social Security: A Bad Idea Whose Time Will Never Come," *Brookings Review* 15 (1997): 17–23; Joseph F. Quinn and Olivia S. Mitchell, "Social Security on the Table," *American Prospect* (May/June 1996): 76–81; Peter A. Diamond, "Proposals to Restructure Social Security," *Journal of Economic Perspectives* 10 (1996): 67–88; Laurence S. Seidman, *Funding Social Security: A Strategic Alternative* (Cambridge: Cambridge University Press, 1999); Dean Baker and Mark Weisbrot, *Social Security: The Phony Crisis* (Chicago: University of Chicago Press, 2000).

18. The arguments of supporters and opponents of individual accounts that follow are taken from Peter A. Diamond, ed., *Issues in Privatizing Social Security: Report of an Expert Panel of the National Academy of Social Insurance* (Cambridge: MIT Press, 1999).

19. For an excellent account of the public policy consequences of abandoning the collective safety net for privatized retirement, see Hugh Heclo, "A Political Science Perspective on Social Security Reform," in *Framing the Social Security Debate*, ed. R. Douglas Arnold, Michael J. Graetz, and Alicia H. Munnell (Washington, D.C.: National Academy of Social Insurance, 1998).

20. James M. Poterba, Steven F. Venti and David A. Wise, "Targeted Retirement Saving and the Net Worth of Elderly Americans," *American Economic Review* 84 (1994): 180–85.

21. AARP, "Beyond 50: A Report to the Nation on Economic Security" (Washington, D.C.: AARP, 2001).

22. For an analysis of four reform proposals—plans by Representatives Bill Archer and Clay Shaw, Senator Patrick Moynihan, and Senators Judd Gregg, John Breaux, Bob Kerrey, and others that establish individual accounts, plus a hypothetical plan investing a portion of the trust fund in equities and supplementing the trust fund with general revenues—see Andrew B. Lyon and John L. Stell, "Analysis of Current Social Security Reform Proposals," *National Tax Journal* 53 (2000): 473–514. In each scenario, benefits are less than under current law.

23. Robert Pear, "Study Says Disabled Would Lose Benefits under Plan to Revamp Social Security," *New York Times*, 7 February 2001, p. A12.

24. Louis Uchitelle, "Lacking Pensions, Older Divorced Women Remain at Work," *New York Times*, 26 June 2001, p. A1. On the risks of individual accounts for women, the disabled and low earners, also see Alice H. Munnell, "Reforming Social Security: The Case against Individual Accounts," *National Tax Journal* 52 (1999): 803–17. For a discussion of the ways social security systems around the world can reinforce or exacerbate gender inequalities—and the implications for U.S. reform—see Martha MacDonald, "Gender and Social Security Policy: Pitfalls and Possibilities," *Feminist Economics* 4 (1998): 1–25.

25. Danny Hakim, "401(k) Accounts Are Losing Money for the First Time," *New York Times*, 9 July 2001, p. A1.

26. David M. Cutler, "Reexamining the Three-Legged Stool," in *Social Security: What Role for the Future*, ed. Peter A. Diamond, David C. Lindeman, and Howard Young (Washington, D.C.: National Academy of Social Insurance, 1996), p. 131.

27. I am indebted to Paul Way of Zogby International for providing these data.

28. Costa, *The Evolution of Retirement*, p. 183.

29. Ibid., p. 195; Congressional Budget Office, "Baby Boomers in Retirement: An Early Perspective" (Washington, D.C.: U.S. Government Printing Office, 1993). See also Richard A. Easterlin, Christine M. Schaeffer and Diane J. Macunovich, "Will the Baby Boomers Be Less Well Off than Their Parents? Income, Wealth, and Family Circumstances over the Life Cycle in the United States," *Population and Development Review* 19 (1993): 497–522. These authors conclude that boomers are doing better than their parents at the same age in terms of both income and wealth. However, the boomers' advantage is much smaller among low-income groups. Also, boomers of all income classes will be more likely to live alone in retirement. A greater proportion have no spouse (because more remained single or divorced), and there are fewer children per woman. Thus there will be fewer family members to help with care during retirement, so that "family circumstances in retirement may mitigate the economic advantage of the boomers over their parents" (p. 519).

30. Harold D. Lasswell, *Politics: Who Gets What, When, How* (New York: McGraw-Hill, 1936).

31. Janet A. Weiss, "Policy Design for Democracy: A Look at Public Information Campaigns," in *Public Policy for Democracy*, ed. Helen Ingram and Steven Rathgeb Smith (Washington, D.C.: Brookings, 1993), p. 99.

REFERENCES

Aaron, Henry. 1997. "Privatizing Social Security: A Bad Idea Whose Time Will Never Come." *Brookings Review* 15: 17–23.

AARP. 2001. "Beyond 50: A Report to the Nation on Economic Security." Washington, D.C.: AARP.

ABC News/*Washington Post* Poll, 11–16 January 1985. In *Public Opinion*, April/May 1985, p. 22.

Abramson, Paul R. 1979. "Developing Party Identification: A Further Examination of Life-Cycle, Generational, and Period Effects." *American Journal of Political Science* 23: 78–96.

Achen, Christopher H. 1978. "Measuring Representation." *American Journal of Political Science* 22: 475–510.

Achenbaum, W. Andrew. 1978. *Old Age in the New Land: The American Experience since 1790.* Baltimore: Johns Hopkins University Press.

———. 1986. *Social Security: Visions and Revisions.* Cambridge: Cambridge University Press.

Aday, LuAnn, Ronald Andersen, and Gretchen V. Fleming. 1980. *Health Care in the U.S.: Equitable for Whom?* Beverly Hills, Calif.: Sage.

Administration on Aging, U.S. Administration of Health and Human Services. 2000. "A Profile of Older Americans: 2000." Washington, D.C.: U.S. Government Printing Office.

Alber, Jens. 1996. "Selectivity, Universalism, and the Politics of Welfare Retrenchment in Germany and the United States." Paper prepared for the annual meeting of the American Political Science Association.

Almond, Gabriel A., and Sidney Verba. 1963. *The Civic Culture: Political Attitudes and Democracy in Five Nations.* Princeton: Princeton University Press.

Alston, Chuck. 1989. "Powerful Veterans' Groups at Political Crossroads." *CQ Weekly Report* (1 July): 1601–3.

Amenta, Edwin, Bruce G. Carruthers, and Yvonne Zylan. 1992. "A Hero for the Aged? The Townsend Movement, the Political Mediation Model, and U.S. Old-Age Policy, 1934–1950." *American Journal of Sociology* 98: 308–39.

"America through the Ages: Studying the Elderly." 1985. *Public Opinion* (February/March): 30–42.

Anderson, Odin W., and Jacob J. Feldman. 1956. *Family Medical Costs and Voluntary Health Insurance: A Nationwide Survey.* New York: McGraw-Hill.

Arnold, R. Douglas. 1990. *The Logic of Congressional Action.* New Haven: Yale University Press.

Baggette, Jennifer, Robert Y. Shapiro, and Lawrence R. Jacobs. 1995. "Social Security—An Update." *Public Opinion Quarterly* 59: 420–42.

Baker, Dean, and Mark Weisbrot. 2000. *Social Security: The Phony Crisis.* Chicago: University of Chicago Press.

Ball, Robert M. 1988. "The Original Understanding on Social Security: Implications for Later Developments." In *Social Security: Beyond the Rhetoric of Crisis*, ed. Theodore R. Marmor and Jerry L. Mashaw. Princeton: Princeton University Press.

———. 1998. *Straight Talk about Social Security*. New York: Century Foundation Press.

Barnes, Samuel, and Max Kaase. 1979. *Political Action: Mass Participation in Five Western Democracies*. Beverly Hills, Calif.: Sage.

Barone, Michael, and Grant Ujifusa. 1999. *The Almanac of American Politics 2000*. Washington, D.C.: National Journal.

Barusch, Amanda S. 1994. *Older Women in Poverty: Private Lives and Public Policies*. New York: Springer.

Baumgartner, Frank, and Bryan Jones. N.d. U.S. Congressional Hearings Dataset. Policy Agendas Project, Center for American Politics and Public Policy, University of Washington. http://depts.washington.edu/ampol/hearings.html.

Bawden, D. Lee, and John L. Palmer. 1981. "Social Policy: Challenging the Welfare State." In *The Reagan Record: An Assessment of America's Changing Domestic Priorities*, ed. John L. Palmer and Isabel V. Sawhill. Cambridge, Mass.: Ballinger.

Bazargan, Mohsen, Tai S. Kang, and Shahrzad Bazargan. 1991. "A Multivariate Comparison of Elderly African Americans' and Caucasians' Voting Behavior: How Do Social, Health, Psychological, and Political Variables Effect Their Voting?" *International Journal of Aging and Human Development* 32: 181–98.

Bennett, Stephen Earl, and David Resnick. 1990. "The Implications of Nonvoting for Democracy in the United States." *American Journal of Political Science* 34: 771–802.

Berkowitz, Edward D. 1997. "The Historical Development of Social Security in the United States." In *Social Security in the 21st Century*, ed. Eric H. Kingson and James H. Schulz. New York: Oxford University Press.

Berry, Jeffrey M. 1984. *The Interest Group Society*. Boston: Little, Brown.

Bianco, William T. 1994. *Trust: Representatives and Constituents*. Ann Arbor: University of Michigan Press.

Bianco, William T., and Jamie Markham. 1999. "Vanishing Veterans: The Decline in Military Experience in the U.S. Congress." Paper prepared for the 1999 Cantigny Conference on Bridging the Gap.

Binstock, Robert H. 1972. "Interest Group Liberalism and the Politics of Aging." *The Gerontologist* 12: 265–80.

———. 1978. "Federal Policy toward the Aging—Its Inadequacies and Its Politics." *National Journal* (11 November): 1838–45.

———. 1979. "A Policy Agenda on Aging for the 1980s." *National Journal* 41 (13 October): 1711–17.

———. 1992. "Older Voters and the 1992 Presidential Election." *The Gerontologist* 32: 601–6.

———. 1997. "The 1996 Election: Older Voters and Implications for Policies on Aging." *The Gerontologist* 37: 15–19.

Bowen, William G., and T. Aldrich Finegan. 1969. *The Economics of Labor Force Participation*. Princeton: Princeton University Press.

Bowman, Karlyn. 1999. "Social Security: A Report on Current Polls." Washington, D.C.: American Enterprise Institute for Public Policy Research, April.

Brady, Henry E. 1999. "Conceptualizing and Measuring Political Participation." In *Measures of Political Attitudes*, ed. John P. Robinson, Phillip R. Shaver, and Lawrence S. Wrightsman. San Diego: Academic Press.

Brody, Richard. 1978. "The Puzzle of Political Participation in America." In *The New American Political System*, ed. Anthony King. Washington, D.C.: American Enterprise Institute.

Brokaw, Tom. 1998. *The Greatest Generation*. New York: Random House.

Bullock, Charles S., and David W. Brady. 1983. "Party, Constituency, and Roll-Call Voting in the U.S. Senate." *Legislative Studies Quarterly* 8: 29–43.

Burnham, Walter Dean. 1987. "The Turnout Problem." In *Elections American Style*, ed. A. James Reichley. Washington, D.C.: Brookings.

Button, James W. 1992. "A Sign of Generational Conflict: The Impact of Florida's Aging Voters on Local School and Tax Referenda." *Social Science Quarterly* 73: 786–97.

Campbell, Angus. 1971. "Politics through the Life Cycle." *The Gerontologist* 11: 112–17.

Campbell, John Creighton, and John Strate. 1981. "Are Old People Conservative?" *The Gerontologist* 21: 580–91.

Cannon, Lou. 1991. *President Reagan: The Role of a Lifetime*. New York: Simon & Schuster.

Chong, Dennis. 1991. *Collective Action and the Civil Rights Movement*. Chicago: University of Chicago Press.

Citrin, Jack, and Donald Philip Green. 1990. "The Self-Interest Motive in American Public Opinion." *Research in Micropolitics* 3: 1–28.

Clark, Timothy B. 1981. "Saving Social Security—Reagan and Congress Face Some Unpleasant Choices." *National Journal* 13 (13 June): 1052–57.

Cleveland, William S. 1979. "Robust Locally Weighted Regression and Smoothing Scatterplots." *Journal of the American Statistical Association* 74: 829–36.

———. 1985. *The Elements of Graphing Data*. Monterey, Calif.: Wadsworth.

Congressional Budget Office. 1993. "Baby Boomers in Retirement: An Early Perspective." Washington, D.C.: U.S. Government Printing Office.

Converse, Philip E. 1964. "The Nature of Belief Systems in Mass Publics." In *Ideology and Discontent*, ed. David Apter. New York: Free Press.

Conway, M. Margaret. 1991. *Political Participation in the United States*. 2d ed. Washington, D.C.: CQ Press.

Cook, Fay Lomax, and Edith J. Barrett. 1992. *Support for the American Welfare State: The Views of Congress and the Public*. New York: Columbia University Press.

Costa, Dora L. 1998. *The Evolution of Retirement: An American Economic History, 1880–1990*. Chicago: University of Chicago Press.

Cutler, David M. 1996. "Reexamining the Three-Legged Stool." In *Social Security: What Role for the Future*, ed. Peter A. Diamond, David C. Lindeman, and Howard Young. Washington, D.C.: National Academy of Social Insurance.

Cutler, Neal E. 1977. "Demographic, Social-Psychological, and Political Factors in the Politics of Aging: A Foundation for Research in 'Political Gerontology.'" *American Political Science Review* 71: 1011–25.

Dahl, Robert. 1956. *A Preface to Democratic Theory.* Chicago: University of Chicago Press.

———. 1998. *On Democracy.* New Haven: Yale University Press.

Dalton, Russell. 1988. *Citizen Politics: Public Opinion and Political Parties in Advanced Western Democracies.* Chatham, N.J.: Chatham House.

Davis, Karen. 1984. "Medicare Reconsidered." In *Health Care for the Poor and Elderly: Meeting the Challenge*, ed. Duncan Yaggy. Durham, N.C.: Duke University Press.

Day, Christine L. 1990. *What Older Americans Think: Interest Groups and Aging Policy.* Princeton: Princeton University Press.

———. 1993. "Older Americans' Attitudes toward the Medicare Catastrophic Coverage Act of 1988." *Journal of Politics* 55: 167–77.

Derthick, Martha. 1979a. *Policymaking for Social Security.* Washington, D.C.: Brookings.

———. 1979b. "How Easy Votes on Social Security Came to an End." *Public Interest* 54: 94–105.

Diamond, Peter. 1996. "Proposals to Restructure Social Security." *Journal of Economic Perspectives* 10: 67–88.

———. 1999. *Issues in Privatizing Social Security: Report of an Expert Panel of the National Academy of Social Insurance.* Cambridge: MIT Press.

Downey, Sheridan. 1939. *Pension or Penury.* New York: Harper and Brothers.

Downs, Anthony. 1957. *An Economic Theory of Democracy.* New York: Harper and Row.

———. 1960. "Why the Government Budget Is Too Small in a Democracy." *World Politics* 12: 541–63.

Duensing, Edward E. 1988. *America's Elderly: A Sourcebook.* New Brunswick, N.J.: Center for Urban Policy Research.

Easterlin, Richard A., Christine M. Schaeffer, and Diane J. Macunovich. 1993. "Will the Baby Boomers Be Less Well Off than Their Parents? Income, Wealth, and Family Circumstances over the Life Cycle in the United States." *Population and Development Review* 19: 497–522.

Eisner, Robert. 1997. *The Great Deficit Scares: The Federal Budget, Trade, and Social Security.* New York: Century Foundation Press.

———. 1998. *Social Security: More, Not Less.* New York: Century Foundation Press.

Elder, Janet. 1987. "Portrait of the Elderly: Still Independent despite Limitations." *New York Times*, 15 January, C1.

Epstein, Abraham. 1943. *Insecurity: A Challenge to America.* New York: Random House.

Erikson, Robert S. 1978. "Constituency Opinion and Congressional Behavior: A Reexamination of the Miller-Stokes Representation Data." *American Journal of Political Science* 22: 511–35.

Erikson, Robert S., Norman Luttbeg, and William V. Holloway. 1975. "Knowing One's District: How Legislators Predict Referendum Voting." *American Journal of Political Science* 19: 231–45.

Erikson, Robert S., and Gerald F. Wright, Jr. 1980. "Policy Representation of Constituency Interests." *Political Behavior* 1: 91–106.

Esping-Andersen, Gøsta. 1990. *The Three Worlds of Welfare Capitalism.* Princeton: Princeton University Press.

Estes, Carroll. 1979. *The Aging Enterprise.* San Francisco: Jossey-Bass.

Fairlie, Henry. 1988. "Talkin' 'bout My Generation." *The New Republic* (28 March): 19–22.

Fearon, James D. 1991. "Counterfactuals and Hypothesis Testing in Political Science." *World Politics* 43: 169–95.

Federal Interagency Forum on Aging-Related Statistics. 2000. *Older Americans 2000: Key Indicators of Well-Being.* Washington, D.C.: U.S. Government Printing Office.

Feldstein, Martin. 1975. "Toward a Reform of Social Security." *Public Interest* 40: 75–95.

———. 1996. "The Missing Piece in Policy Analysis." *American Economic Review Papers and Proceedings* 86: 1–14.

———. 1998. "A New Era of Social Security." *Public Interest* 130: 102–25.

Fenno, Richard F., Jr. 1978. *Home Style: House Members in Their Districts.* Boston: Little, Brown.

Fessler, Pamela, and Harrison Donnelly. 1981. "Congress Seeking to Assure Retirement Income Security." *Congressional Quarterly Weekly Report* 39 (28 November): 2333–36.

Fields, Gary S., and Olivia S. Mitchell. 1984. *Retirement, Pensions, and Social Security.* Cambridge: MIT Press.

Finkel, Steven E., Edward N. Muller, and Karl-Dieter Opp. 1989. "Personal Influence, Collective Rationality, and Mass Political Action." *American Political Science Review* 83: 885–903.

Fiorina, Morris P. 1977. *Congress: Keystone of the Washington Establishment.* New Haven: Yale University Press.

Fischer, David Hackett. 1978. *Growing Old in America.* Oxford: Oxford University Press.

FitzGerald, Frances. 1986. *Cities on a Hill: A Journey through Contemporary American Cultures.* New York: Simon & Schuster.

Friedman, Saul. 2001a. "Are Golden Years Much Too Golden?" *Newsday,* 6 February, B16.

———. 2001b. "Greedy Geezers: These Folks Say No." *Newsday,* 20 March, B12.

Gallup Poll. October 8–9, 1999, at www.gallup.com/poll/indicators/indsocial security.asp, viewed 3 June 2001.

Gamson, William A. 1975. *The Strategy of Protest.* Homewood, Ill.: Dorsey Press.

Gilens, Martin. 1999. *Why Americans Hate Welfare.* Chicago: University of Chicago Press.

Glenn, Norval D. 1974. "Aging and Conservatism." *Annals of the American Academy of Political and Social Science* 415: 176–86.

Godwin, R. Kenneth. 1988. *One Billion Dollars of Influence: The Direct Marketing of Politics*. Chatham, N.J.: Chatham House.

Goldin, Claudia, and Lawrence Katz. 1997. "Why the United States Led in Education: Lessons from Secondary School Expansion, 1910—1940." National Bureau of Economic Research Working Paper no. 6144.

Graber, Doris A. 1997. *Mass Media and American Politics*. Washington, D.C.: CQ Press.

Green, Donald P., and Jonathan A. Cowden. 1992. "Who Protests—Self-Interest and White Opposition to Busing." *Journal of Politics* 54: 71–96.

Gurr, Theodore R. 1970. *Why Men Rebel*. Princeton: Princeton University Press.

Hakim, Danny. 2001. "401(k) Accounts Are Losing Money for the First Time." *New York Times*, 9 July, A1.

Hall, Peter A. 1986. *Governing the Economy: The Politics of State Intervention in Britain and France*. Oxford: Oxford University Press.

Hansen, John Mark. 1985. "The Political Economy of Group Membership." *American Political Science Review* 79: 79–96.

Hansen, Orval. 1987. *Congressional Operations: The Role of Mail in Decision Making in Congress*. Washington, D.C.: Center for Responsive Politics.

Heclo, Hugh. 1998. "A Political Science Perspective on Social Security Reform." In *Framing the Social Security Debate*, ed. R. Douglas Arnold, Michael J. Graetz, and Alicia H. Munnell. Washington, D.C.: National Academy of Social Insurance.

Hill, Kim Quaile, and Jan E. Leighley. 1992. "The Policy Consequences of Class Bias in State Electorates." *American Journal of Political Science* 36: 351–65.

Hill, Kim Quaile, Jan E. Leighley, and Angela Hinton-Anderson. 1995. "Lower-Class Mobilization and Policy Linkages in the U.S. States." *American Journal of Political Science* 39: 75–86.

Himelfarb, Richard. 1995. *Catastrophic Politics: The Rise and Fall of the Medicare Catastrophic Coverage Act of 1988*. University Park: Pennsylvania State University Press.

Holtzman, Abraham. 1963. *The Townsend Movement: A Political Study*. New York: Bookman Associates.

Howard, Christopher. 1997. *The Hidden Welfare State: Tax Expenditures and Social Policy in the United States*. Princeton: Princeton University Press.

Hoxby, Caroline M. 1997. "How Much Does School Spending Depend on Family Income? The Historical Origins of the Current School Finance Dilemma." Unpublished paper, Department of Economics, Harvard University.

Huddy, Leonie. 1989. "Generational Agreement on Old-Age Policies." Ph.D. dissertation, University of California, Los Angeles.

Hutchings, Vincent Lamont. 1998. "The Dynamics of Congressional Representation: How Citizens Monitor Legislators in the House and Senate." Ph.D. dissertation, University of California, Los Angeles.

Ifill, Gwen. 1993. "Social Security Won't Be Subject to Freeze, White House Decides." *New York Times*, 9 February, A1.

Ingram, Helen, and Anne Schneider. 1993. "Constructing Citizenship: The Subtle Messages of Policy Design." In *Public Policy for Democracy*, ed. Helen Ingram and Steven Rathgeb Smith. Washington, D.C.: Brookings.

Jacobs, Lawrence R., and Robert Y. Shapiro. 1998. "Myths and Misunderstandings about Public Opinion toward Social Security." In *Framing the Social Security Debate*, ed. R. Douglas Arnold, Michael J. Graetz, and Alicia H. Munnell. Washington, D.C.: National Academy of Social Insurance.

Jacobson, Gary C. 1992. *The Politics of Congressional Elections*. 3d ed. New York: Harper Collins.

Janda, Kenneth, Jeffrey M. Berry, and Jerry Goldman. 1995. *The Challenge of Democracy: U.S. Government in America*. Boston: Houghton Mifflin.

Jankowski, Thomas B., and John M. Strate. 1995. "Modes of Participation over the Adult Life Span." *Political Behavior* 17: 89–106.

Jencks, Christopher. 1991. "Is the American Underclass Growing?" In *The Urban Underclass*, ed. Christopher Jencks and Paul E. Peterson. Washington, D.C.: Brookings.

Jennings, M. Kent. 1979. "Another Look at the Life Cycle and Political Participation." *American Journal of Political Science* 23: 753–71.

Jennings, M. Kent, and Gregory B. Markus. 1988. "Political Involvement in the Later Years: A Longitudinal Survey." *American Journal of Political Science* 32: 302–16.

Jennings, M. Kent, and Richard G. Niemi. 1981. *Generations and Politics*. Princeton: Princeton University Press.

Johannes, John R. 1984. *To Serve the People: Congress and Constituency Service*. Lincoln: University of Nebraska Press.

Johannes, John R., and John C. McAdams. 1981. "The Congressional Incumbency Effect: Is It Casework, Policy Compatibility, or Something Else?" *American Journal of Political Science* 25: 512–42.

Johnson, Donald Bruce. 1978. *National Party Platforms*. Urbana: University of Illinois Press.

Kaiser Family Foundation. 1999. National Survey of Americans on Social Security. 20 May. www.kff.org/content/archive/24. Viewed 3 June 2001.

Keech, William R., and Kyoungsan Pak. 1989. "Electoral Cycles and Budgetary Growth in Veterans' Benefit Programs." *American Journal of Political Science* 33: 901–11.

Keith, Bruce E., David B. Magleby, Candice J. Nelson, Elizabeth Orr, Mark C. Westlye, and Raymond E. Wolfinger. 1992. *The Myth of the Independent Voter*. Berkeley: University of California Press.

Kilborn, Peter T. 1996. "Veterans Expand Hospital System in Face of Cuts." *New York Times*, 14 January, section 1, 1.

Kingdon, John W. 1989. *Congressmen's Voting Decisions*. 3d ed. Ann Arbor: University of Michigan Press.

———. 1995. *Agendas, Alternatives, and Public Policies*. 2d ed. New York: Harper Collins.

Knoke, David. 1990. *Organizing for Collective Action: The Political Economies of Associations*. New York: Aldine de Gruyter.

Kollman, Ken. 1998. *Outside Lobbying: Public Opinion and Interest Group Strategies*. Princeton: Princeton University Press.

Ladd, Helen F., and Julie Boatright Wilson. 1983. "Who Supports Tax Limitations: Evidence from Massachusetts' Proposition 2½." *Journal of Policy Analysis and Management* 2: 256–79.

Lammers, William W. 1983. *Public Policy and the Aging*. Washington, D.C.: CQ Press.

Landis, P. H. 1948. "Emerging Problems of the Aged." In *Readings in Social Security*, ed. William Haber and Wilbur J. Cohen. New York: Prentice Hall.

Lassey, Marie L., William R. Lassey, and Martin J. Jinks. 1997. *Health Care Systems around the World: Characteristics, Issues, Reforms*. Upper Saddle River, N.J.: Prentice-Hall.

Lasswell, Harold D. 1936. *Politics: Who Gets What, When, How*. New York: McGraw-Hill.

Leighley, Jan E. 1995. "Attitudes, Opportunities, and Incentives: A Field Essay on Political Participation." *Political Research Quarterly* 48: 181–209.

Levy, Frank. 1998. *The New Dollars and Dreams: American Incomes and Economic Change*. New York: Russell Sage Foundation.

Lewis-Beck, Michael S., and John R. Alford. 1980. "Can Government Regulate Safety? The Coal Mine Example." *American Political Science Review* 74: 745–56.

Light, Paul. 1985. *Artful Work: The Politics of Social Security Reform*. New York: Random House.

Lijphart, Arend. 1997. "Unequal Participation: Democracy's Unresolved Dilemma." *American Political Science Review* 91: 1–14.

Lipset, Seymour Martin. 1964. "Introduction." In T. H. Marshall, *Class, Citizenship, and Social Development*. Chicago: University of Chicago Press.

———. 1981 [1959]. *Political Man: The Social Bases of Politics*. Baltimore: Johns Hopkins University Press.

Loomis, Burdett A., and Allan J. Cigler. 1995. "Introduction: The Changing Nature of Interest Group Politics." In *Interest Group Politics*, ed. Allan J. Cigler and Burdett A. Loomis. Washington, D.C.: CQ Press.

Lyon, Andrew B., and John L. Stell. 2000. "Analysis of Current Social Security Reform Proposals." *National Tax Journal* 53: 473–514.

MacDonald, Martha. 1998. "Gender and Social Security Policy: Pitfalls and Possibilities." *Feminist Economics* 4: 1–25.

MacManus, Susan A. 1996. *Young v. Old: Generational Combat in the 21st Century*. Boulder, Colo.: Westview Press.

Markus, Gregory B. 1974. "Electoral Coalitions and Senate Roll Call Behavior." *American Journal of Political Science* 18: 595–607.

Marmor, Theodore R. 1973. *The Politics of Medicare*. Chicago: Aldine.

Marshall, T. H. 1964. *Class, Citizenship, and Social Development*. Chicago: University of Chicago Press.

Maxwell, Nan L. 1990. *Income Inequality in the United States, 1947–1985*. New York: Greenwood Press.

Mayhew, David R. 1974. *Congress: The Electoral Connection*. New Haven: Yale University Press.

Mebane, Walter R., Jr. 1994. "Fiscal Constraints and Electoral Manipulation in American Social Welfare." *American Political Science Review* 88: 77–94.

Mettler, Suzanne. 1998. *Dividing Citizens: Gender and Federalism in New Deal Public Policy.* Ithaca, N.Y.: Cornell University Press.

———. 2001. "Bringing the State Back In to Civic Engagement: Policy Feedback Effects of the G.I. Bill for World War II Veterans." Unpublished paper, Syracuse University.

Mettler, Suzanne, and Eric Welch. 2001. "Policy Feedback and Political Participation: Effects of the G.I. Bill for World War II Veterans over the Life Course." Paper presented at the annual meeting of the American Political Science Association, San Francisco.

Milbrath, Lester W., and M. L. Goel. 1977. *Political Participation: How and Why Do People Get Involved in Politics?* 2d ed. Chicago: Rand McNally.

Mill, John Stuart. 1975 [1861]. *Considerations on Representative Government.* In *John Stuart Mill: Three Essays,* ed. Richard Wollheim. Oxford: Oxford University Press.

Miller, Joanne M., Jon A. Krosnick, and Laura Lowe. 1999. "The Impact of Policy Change Threat on Grassroots Activism." Unpublished paper, Ohio State University.

Miller, Warren E., and J. Merrill Shanks. 1996. *The New American Voter.* Cambridge: Harvard University Press.

Miller, Warren E., and Donald E. Stokes. 1963. "Constituency Influence in Congress." *American Political Science Review* 57: 45–56.

Moon, Marilyn, and Janemarie Mulvey. 1996. *Entitlements and the Elderly: Protecting Promises, Recognizing Reality.* Washington, D.C.: Urban Institute Press.

Morris, Charles R. 1996. *The AARP: America's Most Powerful Lobby and the Clash of Generations.* New York: Times Books.

Munnell, Alice H. 1999. "Reforming Social Security: The Case against Individual Accounts." *National Tax Journal* 52: 803–17.

Nash, Gerald D., Noel H. Pugach, and Richard F. Tomasson. 1988. *Social Security: The First Half-Century.* Albuquerque: University of New Mexico Press.

Nie, Norman H., Jane Junn, and Kenneth Stehlik-Barry. 1996. *Education and Democratic Citizenship in America.* Chicago: University of Chicago Press.

Nie, Norman H., Sidney Verba, and Jae-on Kim. 1974. "Political Participation and the Life Cycle." *Comparative Politics* 6: 319–40.

Olson, Mancur. 1965. *The Logic of Collective Action.* Cambridge: Harvard University Press.

Ornstein, Norman J., and Shirley Elder. 1978. *Interest Groups, Lobbying, and Policymaking.* Washington, D.C.: CQ Press.

Patashnik, Eric M. 2000. *Putting Trust in the U.S. Budget: Federal Trust Funds and the Politics of Commitment.* Cambridge: Cambridge University Press.

Pateman, Carole. 1970. *Participation and Democratic Theory.* Cambridge: Cambridge University Press.

Patterson, James T. 1994. *America's Struggle against Poverty, 1900–1994.* Cambridge: Harvard University Press.

Pear, Robert. 1988. "Benefits Disparity Made Issue in Iowa." *New York Times,* 1 January, section 1, 36.

———. 1994. "Medicare Paying Doctors 59% of Insurers' Rate, Panel Finds." *New York Times,* 5 April, A16.

Pear, Robert. 1999. "Audit of V.A. Health Care Finds Millions Are Wasted." *New York Times*, 1 August, section 1, 1.

———. 2001. "Study Says Disabled Would Lose Benefits under Plan to Revamp Social Security." *New York Times*, 7 February, A12.

———. 2002. "Senate Kills Plan for Drug Benefits through Medicare." *New York Times*, 1 August, A1.

Peirce, Neal R., and Peter C. Choharis. 1982. "The Elderly as a Political Force: 26 Million Strong and Well Organized." *National Journal* 14 (11 September): 1559–62.

Peterson, Mark A. 1995. "How Health Policy Information Is Used in Congress." In *Intensive Care: How Congress Shapes Health Policy*, ed. Thomas E. Mann and Norman J. Ornstein. Washington, D.C.: American Enterprise Institute and Brookings.

Peterson, Paul E. 1992. "An Immodest Proposal." *Daedalus* 121: 151–74.

Peterson, Steven A., and Albert Somit. 1994. *The Political Behavior of Older Americans*. New York: Garland.

Pierson, Paul. 1993. "When Effect Becomes Cause: Policy Feedback and Political Change." *World Politics* 45: 595–628.

———. 1994. *Dismantling the Welfare State? Reagan, Thatcher, and the Politics of Retrenchment*. Cambridge: Cambridge University Press.

———. 1996. "The New Politics of the Welfare State." *World Politics* 48 (January): 143–79.

Piven, Frances Fox, and Richard A. Cloward. 1977. *Poor People's Movements: Why They Succeed, How They Fail*. New York: Pantheon.

———. 1989. *Why Americans Don't Vote*. New York: Pantheon.

Poterba, James M. 1997. "Demographic Structure and the Political Economy of Public Education." *Journal of Policy Analysis and Management* 16: 48–66.

Poterba, James M., Steven F. Venti, and David A. Wise. 1994. "Targeted Retirement Saving and the Net Worth of Elderly Americans." *American Economic Review* 84: 180–85.

"Poverty in America." 1985. *Public Opinion*. June/July, 25.

Powell, G. Bingham. 1986. "American Voting in Comparative Perspective." *American Political Science Review* 80: 23–37.

Powell, Lawrence A., John B. Williamson, and Kenneth J. Branco. 1996. *The Senior Rights Movement: Framing the Policy Debate in America*. New York: Twayne.

Pratt, Henry J. 1976. *The Gray Lobby*. Chicago: University of Chicago Press.

———. 1993. *Gray Agendas: Interest Groups and Public Pensions in Canada, Britain, and the United States*. Ann Arbor: University of Michigan Press.

Preston, Samuel. 1984. "Children and the Elderly: Divergent Paths for America's Dependents." *Demography* 21: 435–57.

Price, Matthew C. 1997. *Justice between Generations: The Growing Power of the Elderly in America*. Westport, Conn.: Greenwood.

Putnam, Jackson K. 1970. *Old-Age Politics in California*. Stanford: Stanford University Press.

Putnam, Robert. 1995a. "Bowling Alone: America's Declining Social Capital." *Journal of Democracy* 6: 65–78.

———. 1995b. "Tuning In, Tuning Out: The Strange Disappearance of Social Capital in America." *PS: Political Science and Politics* 28: 664–83.

———. 2000. *Bowling Alone: The Collapse and Revival of American Community.* New York: Simon & Schuster.

Quadagno, Jill. 1989. "Generational Equity and the Politics of the Welfare State." *Politics and Society* 17: 253–76.

Quinn, Joseph F., and Olivia S. Mitchell. 1996. "Social Security on the Table." *American Prospect* (May/June): 76–81.

Radner, Daniel B. 1987. "Money Incomes of Aged and Nonaged Family Units, 1967–84." *Social Security Bulletin* 50: 8–28.

Reiter, Howard L. 1979. "Why Is Turnout Down?" *Public Opinion Quarterly* 43: 297–311.

Reno, Virginia P., and Susan Grad. 1985. "Economic Security, 1935–85." *Social Security Bulletin* 48: 5–20.

Rhodebeck, Laurie A. 1993. "The Politics of Greed? Political Preferences among the Elderly." *Journal of Politics* 55: 342–64.

Rich, Bennett M., and Martha Baum. 1984. *The Aging: A Guide to Public Policy.* Pittsburgh: University of Pittsburgh Press.

Risen, James. 1993. "White House Backs off Social Security Freeze." *Los Angeles Times,* 9 February, A1.

Rose, Arnold M. 1965. "Group Consciousness among the Aging." In *Older People and Their Social World: The Subculture of the Aging,* ed. Arnold M. Rose and Warren A. Peterson. Philadelphia: F. A. Davis Company.

Rosenstone, Steven J. 1982. "Economic Adversity and Voter Turnout." *American Journal of Political Science* 26: 25–46.

Rosenstone, Steven J., and John Mark Hansen. 1993. *Mobilization, Participation, and Democracy in America.* New York: Macmillan.

Rothenberg, Lawrence S. 1992. *Linking Citizens to Government: Interest Group Politics at Common Cause.* Cambridge: Cambridge University Press.

Rovner, Julie. 1988a. "Conferees Set to Begin Work on Catastrophic-Costs Bill." *Congressional Quarterly Weekly Report* 46 (13 February): 313–15.

———. 1988b. "Catastrophic-Costs Conferees Irked by Lobbying Assaults." *Congressional Quarterly Weekly Report* 46 (26 March): 777–80.

———. 1988c. "Catastrophic-Insurance Law: Costs vs. Benefits." *Congressional Quarterly Weekly Report* 46 (3 December): 3450–52.

———. 1989. "The Catastrophic-Costs Law: A Massive Miscalculation." *Congressional Quarterly Weekly Report* 47 (14 October): 2712–15.

Rubin, Rose M., and Michael L. Nieswiadomy. 1997. *Expenditures of Older Americans.* Westport, Conn.: Praeger.

Samuelson, Robert J. 1990. "Pampering the Elderly." *Washington Post,* 21 November, A19.

Sawhill, Isabel V. 1988. "Poverty in the US: Why Is It So Persistent?" *Journal of Economic Literature* 26: 1073–1119.

Schattschneider, E. E. 1960. *The Semisovereign People: A Realist's View of Democracy in America.* New York: Holt, Rinehart and Winston.

Schick, Allen. 1991. "Informed Legislation: Policy Research versus Ordinary Knowledge." In *Knowledge, Power, and the Congress*, ed. William H. Robinson and Clay H. Wellborn. Washington, D.C.: CQ Press.

Schiltz, Michael E. 1970. *Public Attitudes toward Social Security, 1935–1965*. Social Security Administration. Office of Research and Statistics. Research Report no. 33. Washington, D.C.: U.S. Government Printing Office.

Schlesinger, Arthur M., Jr. 1958. *The Coming of the New Deal*. Boston: Houghton Mifflin.

Schlozman, Kay Lehman, and Sidney Verba. 1979. *Injury to Insult: Unemployment, Class, and Political Response*. Cambridge: Harvard University Press.

Scott, James C. 1985. *Weapons of the Weak: Everyday Forms of Peasant Resistance*. New Haven: Yale University Press.

Sears, David O., and Jack Citrin. 1982. *Tax Revolt: Something for Nothing in California*. Cambridge: Harvard University Press.

Seidman, Laurence S. 1999. *Funding Social Security: A Strategic Alternative*. Cambridge: Cambridge University Press.

Sen, Amartya K. 1977. "Rational Fools: A Critique of the Behavioral Foundations of Economic Theory." *Philosophy and Public Affairs* 6: 314–44.

Shapiro, Robert Y., and Tom W. Smith. 1985. "The Polls: Social Security." *Public Opinion Quarterly* 49: 561–72.

Siegal, Nina. 1999. "Protesters Seek More Money for Veterans' Health Care." *New York Times*, 31 May, section B, 5.

Simon, Herbert A. 1983. *Reason in Human Affairs*. Stanford: Stanford University Press.

Skocpol, Theda. 1991. "Targeting within Universalism: Politically Viable Policies to Combat Poverty in the United States." In *The Urban Underclass*, ed. Christopher Jencks and Paul E. Peterson. Washington, D.C.: Brookings.

———. 1992. *Protecting Soldiers and Mothers: The Political Origins of Social Policy in the United States*. Cambridge: Harvard University Press.

———. 1995. *Social Policy in the United States: Future Possibilities in Historical Perspective*. Princeton: Princeton University Press.

Sniderman, Paul M. 1975. *Personality and Democratic Politics*. Berkeley: University of California Press.

Social Security Administration Office of Research, Evaluation and Statistics. 1998. *Income of the Aged Chartbook, 1996*. Washington, D.C.: U.S. Government Printing Office.

"The Social Security Flap." 1981. *Congressional Quarterly Weekly Report* 39 (23 May): 896.

Soss, Joe. 1999. "Lessons of Welfare: Policy Design, Political Learning, and Political Action." *American Political Science Review* 93: 363–80.

Starr, Paul. 1982. *The Social Transformation of American Medicine*. New York: Basic Books.

Steiner, Gilbert Y. 1971. *The State of Welfare*. Washington, D.C.: Brookings.

Steinmo, Sven, Kathleen Thelen, and Frank Longstreth, eds. 1992. *Structuring Politics: Historical Institutionalism in Comparative Analysis*. Cambridge: Cambridge University Press.

Stoker, Laura. 1992. "Interests and Ethics in Politics." *American Political Science Review* 86: 369–80.

Stone, Walter. 1982. "Electoral Change and Policy Representation in Congress: Domestic Welfare Issues from 1956–72." *British Journal of Political Science* 12: 92–115.

Strate, John M., Charles J. Parrish, Charles D. Elder, and Coit Ford III. 1989. "Life Span Civic Development and Voting Participation." *American Political Science Review* 83: 443–64.

Street, David, George T. Martin, Jr., and Laura Kramer Gordon. 1979. *The Welfare Industry: Functionaries and Recipients in Public Aid.* Beverly Hills, Calif.: Sage.

Sullivan, Andrew. 2000. "Golden Oldies? Pandering to Well-Off Senior Citizens Is the New Political Pastime." *Pittsburgh Post-Gazette*, 8 October, E1.

Taylor-Gooby, Peter. 1985. *Public Opinion, Ideology, and State Welfare.* London: Routledge & Kegan Paul.

Tedin, K. L., D. W. Brady, M. E. Buxton, B. M. Gorman, and J. L. Thompson. 1977. "Social Background and Political Differences between Pro- and Anti-ERA Activists." *American Politics Quarterly* 5: 395–408.

Teixeira, Ruy. 1987. *Why Americans Don't Vote: Turnout Decline in the United States, 1960–1984.* Westport, Conn.: Greenwood Press.

———. 1992. *The Disappearing American Voter.* Washington, D.C.: Brookings.

Tetlock, Philip E., and Aaron Belkin. 1996. *Counterfactual Thought Experiments in World Politics.* Princeton: Princeton University Press.

Tolchin, Martin. 1988. "New Health Insurance Plan Provokes Outcry over Costs." *New York Times*, 2 November, A1.

Toner, Robin. 1999a. "Older Voters' Shift to G.O.P. Is Democrats' 2000 Challenge." *New York Times*, 31 May, A1.

———. 1999b. "Long-Term Care Merges Political with Personal." *New York Times*, 26 July, A1.

Truman, David. 1951. *The Governmental Process.* New York: Alfred A. Knopf.

Tufte, Edward R. 1978. *Political Control of the Economy.* Princeton: Princeton University Press.

Tyack, David B. 1974. *The One Best System: A History of American Urban Education.* Cambridge: Harvard University Press.

Uchitelle, Louis. 2001. "Lacking Pensions, Older Divorced Women Remain at Work." *New York Times*, 26 June, A1.

U.S. Bureau of the Census. 1975. *Historical Statistics of the United States: Colonial Times to 1970.* Washington, D.C.: U.S. Government Printing Office.

———. 1993a. "Money Income of Households, Families, and Persons in the United States: 1992." Current Population Reports, Series P60, no. 184. Washington, D.C.: U.S. Government Printing Office.

———. 1993b. "Measuring the Effect of Benefits and Taxes on Income and Poverty: 1992." Current Population Reports, Series P60–186RD. Washington, D.C.: U.S. Government Printing Office.

———. 1998. *Statistical Abstract of the United States 1998.* Washington, D.C.: U.S. Government Printing Office.

U.S. Bureau of the Census. 1999. *Statistical Abstract of the United States 1999*. Washington, D.C.: U.S. Government Printing Office.

———. 2000. *Statistical Abstract of the United States 2000*. Washington, D.C.: U.S. Government Printing Office.

U.S. House Committee on Ways and Means. 1998. *1998 Green Book: Overview of Entitlement Programs*. Washington, D.C.: U.S. Government Printing Office.

Uslaner, Eric M. 1997. "Discount Drugs and Volunteering: Does the AARP Produce Social Capital?" Paper presented at the annual meeting of the Midwest Political Science Association, Chicago.

Van Tassel, David D., and Jimmy Elaine Wilkinson Meyer. 1992. *U.S. Aging Policy Interest Groups: Institutional Profiles*. New York: Greenwood Press.

Verba, Sidney. 2001. "Thoughts about Political Equality: What Is It? Why Do We Want It?" Paper prepared for the Inequality Summer Institute, Harvard University, 13–14 June.

Verba, Sidney, and Norman H. Nie. 1972. *Participation in America: Political Democracy and Social Equality*. New York: Harper & Row.

Verba, Sidney, Norman H. Nie, and Jae-on Kim. 1978. *Participation and Political Equality: A Seven-Nation Comparison*. New York: Cambridge University Press.

Verba, Sidney, and Gary Orren. 1985. *Equality in America: The View from the Top*. Cambridge: Harvard University Press.

Verba, Sidney, Kay Lehman Schlozman, and Henry E. Brady. 1995. *Voice and Equality: Civic Voluntarism in American Politics*. Cambridge: Harvard University Press.

Verba, Sidney, Kay Lehman Schlozman, Henry E. Brady, and Norman Nie. 1995. American Citizen Participation Study, 1990 [computer file]. ICPSR version. Chicago: University of Chicago, National Opinion Research Center (NORC) [producer]. Ann Arbor, Mich.: Interuniversity Consortium for Political and Social Research [distributor].

———. 1993. "Citizen Activity: Who Participates? What Do They Say?" *American Political Science Review* 87: 303–18.

Walker, Jack L. 1991. *Mobilizing Interest Groups in America*. Ann Arbor: University of Michigan Press.

Weaver, R. Kent. 1988. *Automatic Government: The Politics of Indexation*. Washington, D.C.: Brookings.

———. 1998. "Ending Welfare as We Know It." In *The Social Divide: Political Parties and the Future of Activist Government*, ed. Margaret Weir. Washington, D.C.: Brookings.

———. 2000. *Ending Welfare as We Know It*. Washington, D.C.: Brookings.

Weinberg, Daniel H. 1985. "Filling the 'Poverty Gap': Multiple Transfer Program Participation." *Journal of Human Resources* 20 (Winter): 64–89.

Weisberg, Herbert F., and Bernard Grofman. 1981. "Candidate Evaluations and Turnout." *American Politics Quarterly* 9: 197–219.

Weiss, Janet A. 1993. "Policy Design for Democracy: A Look at Public Information Campaigns." In *Public Policy for Democracy*, ed. Helen Ingram and Steven Rathgeb Smith. Washington, D.C.: Brookings.

Wielhouwer, Peter W., and Brad Lockerbie. 1994. "Party Contacting and Political Participation, 1952–90." *American Journal of Political Science* 38: 211–29.

Wildavsky, Aaron. 1987. "Choosing Preferences by Constructing Institutions: A Cultural Theory of Preference Formation." *American Political Science Review* 81: 3–21.

Wilensky, Harold. 1976. *The New Corporatism, Centralization, and the Welfare State*. Beverly Hills, Calif.: Sage.

Wilson, James Q. 1989. *Bureaucracy: What Government Agencies Do and Why They Do It*. New York: Basic Books.

Wilson, William Julius. 1987. *The Truly Disadvantaged: The Inner City, the Underclass, and Public Policy*. Chicago: University of Chicago Press.

Wolfinger, Raymond E. 1985. "Dealignment, Realignment, and Mandates in the 1984 Election." In *The American Elections of 1984*, ed. Austin Ranney. Durham, N.C.: Duke University Press.

Wolfinger, Raymond E., and Steven J. Rosenstone. 1980. *Who Votes?* New Haven: Yale University Press.

Wolpe, Bruce C., and Bertram J. Levine. 1996. *Lobbying Congress: How the System Works*. 2d ed. Washington, D.C.: CQ Press.

Woodward, Bob. 1994. *The Agenda: Inside the Clinton White House*. New York: Simon & Schuster.

Wright, Gerald C. 1989. "Policy Voting in the U.S. Senate: Who Is Represented?" *Legislative Studies Quarterly* 14: 465–86.

Zedlewski, Sheila, Robert Barnes, Martha Burt, Timothy McBride, and Jack Meyer. 1990. *The Needs of the Elderly in the 21st Century*. Washington, D.C.: Urban Institute Press.

Zelizer, Julian E. 1998. *Taxing America: Wilbur D. Mills, Congress, and the State, 1945–1975*. Cambridge: Cambridge University Press.

Zinni, Frank P., Jr., Laurie A. Rhodebeck, and Franco Mattei. 1997. "The Structure and Dynamics of Group Politics, 1964–1992." *Political Behavior* 19: 247–82.

INDEX

Page references followed by f *indicate figured illustrations, and* t *indicates tables.*

AARP, 75, 77, 89; effect of membership on senior participation, 78, 153t; government as patron of, 77–78; increasing Washington role of, 87; lobbying efforts of, 79; membership, over time, 76f, 88, 90, 91t; mobilization efforts of, 78–79; *Modern Maturity* magazine, 82; as nonpartisan organization, 82; and opposition to proposed Social Security cuts, 104; revenue sources of, 77–78
abortion: difficulty of studying, versus Social Security, 103
Administration on Aging, 79–80, 89
AFDC (Aid to Families with Dependent Children). *See* welfare
AFL-CIO, 76
age-related policy bureaucracy, 79–81
aged. *See* senior citizens
American Association for Labor Legislation (AALL), 77
American Association for Old Age Security (AAOAS), 77
American Association of Retired Persons. *See* AARP
Andrus, Dr. Ethel Percy, 75
Area Agencies on Aging: participatory effects of, 80
Arnold, R. Douglas, 81

baby boomers: class differences among, 144–45; retirement prospects of, 203n.29
Ball, Robert, 84
Barrett, Edith, 95
Bianco, William, 135
Bipartisan Commission on Social Security (1981–83), 104
Brady, Henry, 5, 60
busing, 98

campaign work: and age, 26; effect of AARP membership on senior, 78, 153t; and income, 51–54, 52f; increasing se-

nior/nonsenior ratio of, as retirement rate increases, 34, 35f; means-tested versus non-means-tested program recipients rates of, 130–32, 130t, 131t; mobilization for, by age, 56t; predictors of, 147t, 149t-153t; rates of, by age over time, 30, 32f; senior versus nonsenior levels of, 26, 87
Carter, Jimmy, 104
Church, Frank, 82
churches. *See* religious institutions
Citizen Participation Study: characteristics of, 9, 13
citizenship. *See* democratic citizenship
civic duty, 41, 142
civic generation, 141–42
civic skills: and education, 41; of means-tested versus non-means-tested program recipients, 127–28, 127t; as a political resource, 61–62t; senior levels of, versus nonseniors, 44, 45t; senior sources of, 44, 45t
Civic Voluntarism Model, 5, 60–61; seniors versus nonseniors, 149t-151t
Clinton, Bill, 93, 135
Cloward, Richard, 3
cohort effects, 141–42, 171n.24
collective action problem: role of political efficacy in overcoming, 99; senior ability to overcome, 99–101
Committee on Economic Security, 77
Congress: casework, 81, 117, 132; constituency preferences and legislator behavior, 115–17; denouncement of proposed Social Security cuts, 104; and government program recipients, 132; hearings on senior issues, 88f, 91t; House Select Committee on Aging, 82, 90; information gathering efforts of, 116; predictors of Medicare Catastrophic Coverage Act vote switching, 160t, 196n.21; predictors of Social Security and Medicare roll-call votes, 159t, 196n.20; respon-

PRINCETON STUDIES IN AMERICAN POLITICS:
HISTORICAL, INTERNATIONAL, AND COMPARATIVE PERSPECTIVES

How Policies Make Citizens: Senior Political Activism and the American Welfare State by Andrea Louise Campbell

Managing the President's Program: Presidential Leadership and Legislative Policy Formulation by Andrew Rudalevige

Shaped by War and Trade: International Influences on American Political Development edited by Ira Katznelson and Martin Shefter

Dry Bones Rattling: Community Building to Revitalize American Democracy by Mark R. Warren

The Forging of Bureaucratic Autonomy: Reputations, Networks, and Policy Innovation in Executive Agencies, 1862-1928 by Daniel P. Carpenter

Disjointed Pluralism: Institutional Innovation and the Development of the U.S. Congress by Eric Schickler

The Rise of the Agricultural Welfare State: Institutions and Interest Group Power in the United States, France, and Japan by Adam D. Sheingate

In the Shadow of the Garrison State: America's Anti-Statism and Its Cold War Grand Strategy by Aaron L. Friedberg

Stuck in Neutral: Business and the Politics of Human Capital Investment Policy by Cathie Jo Martin

Uneasy Alliances: Race and Party Competition in America by Paul Frymer

Faithful and Fearless: Moving Feminist Protest inside the Church and Military by Mary Fainsod Katzenstein

Forged Consensus: Science, Technology, and Economic Policy in the United States, 1921-1953 by David M. Hart

Parting at the Crossroads: The Emergence of Health Insurance in the United States and Canada by Antonia Maioni

Bold Relief: Institutional Politics and the Origins of Modern American Social Policy by Edwin Amenta

The Hidden Welfare State: Tax Expenditures and Social Policy in the United States by Christopher Howard

Morning Glories: Municipal Reform in the Southwest by Amy Bridges

Imperiled Innocents: Anthony Comstock and Family Reproduction in Victorian America by Nicola Beisel

The Road to Nowhere: The Genesis of President Clinton's Plan for Health Security by Jacob Hacker

The Origins of the Urban Crisis: Race and Inequality in Postwar Detroit by Thomas J. Sugrue

Party Decline in America: Policy, Politics, and the Fiscal State by John J. Coleman

The Power of Separation: American Constitutionalism and the Myth of the Legislative Veto by Jessica Korn

Why Movements Succeed or Fail: Opportunity, Culture, and the Struggle for Woman Suffrage by Lee Ann Banaszak

Kindred Strangers: The Uneasy Relationship between Politics and Business in America by David Vogel

From the Outside In: World War II and the American State by Bartholomew H. Sparrow

Classifying by Race edited by Paul E. Peterson

Facing Up to the American Dream: Race, Class, and the Soul of the Nation by Jennifer L. Hochschild